ENTREPRENEURSHIP IN COOPERATIVES

ENTREPRENEURSHIP IN COOPERATIVES

By

Dr. M. Karthikeyan

Assistant Professor

Department of Cooperatives

Faculty of Business & Economics

Hawassa University

Hawassa

Email: mkeya2003@gmail.com

mkeya2003@yahoo.com

DPH

DISCOVERY PUBLISHING HOUSE PVT. LTD.

NEW DELHI-110 002

Published by:
Tilak Wasan
DISCOVERY PUBLISHING HOUSE PVT. LTD.
4383/4A, Ansari Road, Darya Ganj
New Delhi-110 002 (India)
Phone : +91-11-23279245, 43596064-65
Fax : +91-11-23253475
E-mail : parul.wasan@gmail.com
discoverypublishinghouse@gmail.com
web : www.discoverypublishinggroup.com

***First Edition:* 2012**
ISBN: 978-93-5056-053-2

Entrepreneurship in Cooperatives

Printed at:
Shree Balaji Art Press
Delhi

Preface

Dear Readers! It is my pleasure to introduce the textbook on **Entrepreneurship in Cooperatives** to you. It has been designed in a detailed manner so as to help you understand the basic concepts of Entrepreneurship and Entrepreneurship in Cooperatives. This textbook is unique and I have tried to dovetail inline with entrepreneurship in cooperatives.

This work is based on my experience as teacher, trainer and researcher in the field of cooperatives for more than 15 years. The present work is the outcome of my experience and many articles published in reputed journals. This book is very unique in the field of cooperative entrepreneurship. Few attempts have been made in cooperative entrepreneurship and in a book form this is the pioneering effort. This book will be very much useful to the entrepreneurs and cooperative stakeholders, the trainers who are working in various training establishments and the students of management and cooperatives at undergraduate level. I have drawn the inputs from various sources: papers, journals, books and I have consulted several of my friends, colleagues and field experts. I am ever grateful and thankful to them for their immense support and healthy criticism. I hope that the readers of this book will get knowledge on entrepreneurship in cooperatives. Any useful comments, suggestions to improve the present version are welcome and solicited from the readers. I am thankful to Mr. Parul Wasan of Discovery Publishing House Pvt. Ltd., New Delhi for publishing this textbook neatly under his renowned label for the cooperative knowledge community.

M. Karthikeyan

Contents

1

Entrepreneur

Evolution of the term "Entrepreneur"

Before having the present definition the term of entrepreneur was related to a lot of assertions. The following are among the significant developments that gave the present form to entrepreneur:

- The word entrepreneur first appeared in the French language as 'entreprendre', which means, 'to undertake'.
- From the 14th up to the end of the 17th century, the term entrepreneur was applied to persons like leaders of military expedition, tax collectors, adventurers and architects who were responsible for construction of roads, bridges, and buildings.
- Writers of 17th and 18th century stressed on the two essential characteristics of entrepreneur was taking of risks and creating innovation.
- Richard Calliton became the first person to relate entrepreneur to economic activities, because he defined entrepreneur as a person who buys service factors at certain prices and sell products at uncertain price in the future. By this definition, we can observe that entrepreneur surely face risk as there is possibility of bankruptcy and inconsistent demand.
- J.B. Say defined entrepreneur as 'Economic agent who unites all means of production— the labor, the capital or the land of the other and who finds in the value of products which results from their employment, reconstitution of the entire capital that he utilizes and the value of the wages, the interest and the rent which he pays as well as profit belonging to himself'.

- FH Knight (1921), in his book referred entrepreneurs as specialized group of people who bear risks and deal with uncertainty.
- Leon Walras (1945) considered entrepreneur as a coordinator of the factors of production. He treated entrepreneur as the fourth factor of production, as one who hires factors of land, labour and capital.
- Schumpeter (1960s) defined entrepreneur for developed and developing nation.

For developed countries: Entrepreneur is the one who innovates; raises money, assembles inputs, chose manager and sets the organization with his ability to identify them.

For developing countries: Entrepreneur is the one who start an industry (old or new) undertake risk, bears uncertainty and also perform managerial function of decision-making and coordination.

In general Schumpeter regarded entrepreneur basically as an innovator who carries out new combination to initiate and accelerate economic development. This is the intersection point of his two definitions.

As we can see from the selected evolutions, the aspects given to the entrepreneur has expanded as the evolution continues to get modernized. Anciently, entrepreneur was referred to people that are not considered as entrepreneurs today. Also, the importance given to entrepreneur in terms of economic enhancement and development has significantly upgraded by the trend of the evolution. To sum up in the light of the developments, there are four key elements of entrepreneurs. These are:

1. Vision (identifying emerging opportunities)
2. Innovation (creating new business or new ways of doing something)
3. Risk bearing (taking risk and facing uncertainty)
4. Organizing (collection and coordination of the necessary resources)

The Entrepreneur

Entrepreneurs have many of the same character traits as leaders. Similarly to the early great man theories of leadership, however, trait-based theories of entrepreneurship are increasingly being called into question. Entrepreneurs are often contrasted with managers and administrators who are said to be more methodical and less prone to risk-taking. Although such person-centric models of entrepreneurship have shown to be of questionable validity, a vast but clearly dated literature studying the entrepreneurial personality found that certain traits seem to be associated with entrepreneurs:

- For example, in 1961, David McClelland described the entrepreneur as primarily motivated by an overwhelming need for achievement and strong urge to build.

- Collins and Moore (1970) studied 150 entrepreneurs and concluded that they are tough, pragmatic people driven by needs of independence and achievement. They seldom are willing to submit to authority.
- Bird (1992) sees entrepreneurs as mercurial, that is, prone to insights, brainstorms, deceptions, ingeniousness and resourcefulness. They are cunning, opportunistic, creative, and unsentimental.
- Busenitz and Barney (1997) claim, entrepreneurs are prone to overconfidence and over generalisations.
- According to Cole (1959), there are four types of entrepreneur: the innovator, the calculating inventor, the over-optimistic promoter, and the organisation builder. These types are not related to the personality but to the type of opportunity the entrepreneur faces.
- Burton W. Folsom, Jr. distinguishes between what he calls a 'political entrepreneur' and a 'market entrepreneur'. The political entrepreneur uses political influences to gain income through subsidies, protectionism, government-granted monopoly, government contracts, or other such favorable arrangements with government(s) (see *Crony Capitalism* and *Corporate Welfare*). The market entrepreneur operates without special favors from government.

Definition of Entrepreneur

(*a*) An entrepreneur is a person who organizes and manages any enterprise, esp. a business, usually with considerable initiative and risk.

(*b*) An employer of productive labor; contractor.

(*c*) He is the one to deal with or initiate as an entrepreneur.

Entrepreneur, just like management, has no single definition. It can be defined from different perspectives. The most important perspectives from which entrepreneur can be defined include the following:

For an Economist: Entrepreneur is one who brings resources and assets into combination that makes their value greater than before and is also one who introduces change and new order while contributing to economic development of a nation.

For a Psychologist: Entrepreneur is a person that is typically driven by certain internal forces— need to obtain something, experiment and escape authority of others.

For a Businessman: Entrepreneur is either a threat (aggressive competitor) or an ally (source of supply, customer, etc.)

To a Capitalist Philosopher: Entrepreneur is one who creates wealth for others, who produces jobs others are glad to get.

Definitions by some Authors

Schumpeter—'Entrepreneurship essentially consists in doing things that are not generally done in the ordinary course of business routine'.

Ronstadt—'Entrepreneurship is the dynamic process of creating incremental wealth. This wealth is created by individuals who assume the major risks in terms of equity, time, and career commitment of providing value for some product or service'.

Peter Drucker—'An entrepreneur is one who always searches for change, response to it and exploit it as an opportunity'.

Robert Hisrich—'An entrepreneur is the person who will establish a successful new business venture. Besides, he must also be a visionary, leader — a person who has great dreams'.

From the above definitions, we can explain the meaning of entrepreneurship as follows:

1. An entrepreneurship function is undertaken in extraordinary course of business.
2. It is a process of creating wealth.
3. An entrepreneur is one who searches for change and convert it as an opportunity.
4. Innovation is the tool of entrepreneurs.
5. An entrepreneur will search for success.
6. He/she is also a visionary and leader who has great dreams.

Characteristics of an Entrepreneur

The characteristics, nature, feature or qualities of entrepreneur as an individual are essential to contribute to the success of an enterprise. Mc Clelland stated the characteristic of successful entrepreneur as an individual with technical competence, risk taking, high initiative, good judgment, intelligence to analyze and solve problem areas, leadership qualities, confidence, positive attitude, high level of energy, creativeness, honesty, integrity, emotional stability and fairness.

An entrepreneur should have the first hand knowledge of the product, process and end uses to bring inventive ability and sound judgment of the planned project. Flexibility, good social behaviour, open mind and the desire to take personal responsibilities will fit in the qualities of a true entrepreneur. There is no one universally accepted approach that best describes the traits and characteristics of entrepreneurs. But every approach has their own significance.

Some Authors' point of view the following are characteristics of an Entrepreneur:

- The entrepreneur has an enthusiastic vision, the driving force of an enterprise.
- The entrepreneur's vision is usually supported by an interlocked collection of specific ideas not available to the marketplace.
- The overall blueprint to realize the vision is clear, however details may be incomplete, flexible, and evolving.
- The entrepreneur promotes the vision with enthusiastic passion.
- With persistence and determination, the entrepreneur develops strategies to change the vision into reality.
- The entrepreneur takes the initial responsibility to cause a vision to become a success.
- Entrepreneurs take prudent risks. They assess costs, market/customer needs and persuade others to join and help.
- An entrepreneur is usually a positive thinker and a decision-maker.

Characteristics denote qualities, features, attributes, and traits. The characteristics of an entrepreneur are developed on the basis of:

1. the history of thought on the term entrepreneur;
2. studying the characteristics of the successful entrepreneurs;
3. differentiating the term entrepreneur from related terms such as manager; and
4. myths on entrepreneur.

Some of the characteristics of the entrepreneur are as follows:

Self confident and optimist: An entrepreneur is having more confidence on himself and thinks positively.

Taking risk: An entrepreneur is willing to take risk so that he can achieve things.

Respond positively to changes: An entrepreneur is also ready to face challenges in his business.

Flexible and adapt: An entrepreneur is flexible to changing needs and times.

Knowledgeable of markets: He knows better about the market and the changes that are taking place in the market.

Able to get along well with others: He moves closely with others and creates friendship and business relationship with others.

Independent minded: In taking decisions, he is quite independent.

Knowledge: He is very particular to know the latest knowledge on all aspects of his business.

Energetic and diligent: He works hard using all his intelligence.

Creative: He introduces creativity in planning, execution, and management of his business and venture.

Dynamic leader: He is a leader, who gives leadership to people around him.

Responsive to suggestions: Any useful suggestion is welcomed by him.

Take initiatives: For new programmes he himself takes initiatives.

Resourceful and persevering: He is ready to work hard.

Perceptive with foresight: Future is always his concern.

Responsive to criticism: He is ready to face criticisms positively to improve his business.

Traits of a True Entrepreneur

Several research studies have been carried out to identify the traits of a true entrepreneur. A distillation from fifty research studies reveals the following entrepreneurial traits.

- Capacity to take risk
- Capacity to work hard
- Above average intelligence and wide knowledge
- Self (inner) motivation
- Vision and foresight
- Willingness to defer consumption
- Imagination, initiative and emulation
- Inventive ability and sound judgment
- Flexibility and sociability
- Desire to take personal responsibility
- Desire to seek and use feedback
- Persistence in the face of adversity
- Innovativeness and future-orientation
- Mobility and drive
- Creative thinking
- Storing need for achievement
- Ability to marshal resources

- High degree of ambition
- Will to conquer and impulse to fight
- Will to prove superior to others.

Why do people want to become entrepreneurs?

Today, people are becoming entrepreneurs at an alarming rate. The fact that the number of today's entrepreneurs when compared to the figure before ten years,.is almost quadruple tells too much about the increasing number of entrepreneurs. These days, many people share a dream of becoming entrepreneurs. This shows, there are a lot of factors that push ordinary people to become entrepreneurs. This ranges from the tangible and psychological benefit of putting themselves in the world of entrepreneurship. In brief these factors are:

Opportunity

Chance to be part of a new environment or to be exposed to a new environment.

Chance to share the dream of many people.

Profit

Fast road to richness.

Independence

Not working for others. Some people have a phobia of being a servant of others.

Challenge

To take risk. People like to take risks to test themselves and to get the happiness after surpassing those risks.

Who are Entrepreneurs?

Let us have a look at some of the approaches that tried to give answer to our big question: who are entrepreneurs?

Approach 1

Entrepreneurs are:

Self-directed (Self-disciplined): Entrepreneurs have independent mind, i.e. mind that is not drive and manipulated by others. Their mind is not pushed by anyone's.

Self-nurturing: Entrepreneurs believe in their ideas even if no one else does.

Action oriented: Entrepreneurs have a burning desire of building their dreams in to reality.

They understand that business ideas are not enough by themselves unless they are implemented

Highly energetic: Entrepreneurs are emotionally, mentally and physically able to work long and hard.

Tolerant of Uncertainty: Entrepreneurs have the ability of taking risk and facing uncertainty.

Approach 2

Entrepreneurs have the following qualities:

Strong mental ability, intelligent, creative and analytical.

Clear objectives: Entrepreneurs chase clear purposes.

Business Secrecy: Ability to guard trade secrets.

Human relation ability: Entrepreneurs display polished behaviour while dealing with customers, employees, suppliers, government etc.

Communication skill: Entrepreneurs are excellent communicators.

Technical knowledge: Entrepreneurs have sound knowledge about production process and techniques.

Approach 3

Entrepreneurs have the following psychological qualities:

High need for achievement: Every human being possess three basic needs. These are need for power, need for affiliation and need for achievement and only one is dominant. For entrepreneurs need for achievement is dominant.

Entrepreneurs need to be successful in all assignments.

High self determination (Internal locus of control): Entrepreneurs are quite confident in their ability to perform and succeed which gives rise to external locus of control, i.e. blaming others for failure and take credit for success.

Desire for self independence: Entrepreneurs act according to their personal vision, analysis and decision making. They don't want to work under other's influence.

Innovative and action-oriented: Entrepreneurs are always ready (impulsive) to implement their ideas.

High tolerance for ambiguity: Entrepreneurs can work under dynamic and uncertain environment.

Moderate risk takers: Entrepreneurs are not gamblers (not high risk takers).

Myths of an Entrepreneur

Myth denotes the beliefs of an entrepreneur. Certain myths may be right or wrong; certain myths may become true or become a dream.

1. *Entrepreneurs are driven by money:* Money is the main motivation for an entrepreneur. Some people are driven for money but some may not go after money.
2. *Entrepreneurs are high risk takers:* By nature, an entrepreneur has to take risk to achieve things and earn money. Sometimes, even without taking risks entrepreneurs may succeed.
3. *All entrepreneurs are wealthy and successful:* It may be true in a country like America, but in developing countries this may not be true. Many new entrepreneurs are self-made people.
4. *Entrepreneurs are born not made:* Here also comes the difference between developed countries and developing countries, between the rich families and poor ones.
5. *Anyone can start a business:* Anyone can start a business, but to survive in the business and make it a success is a great thing.
6. *Entrepreneurs are gamblers:* Successful entrepreneurs take calculated risks. Gamble may lead to success or total failure.
7. *Entrepreneurs want the whole show to themselves:* Some entrepreneurs may think that they have done everything by themselves for their success. But many think their success was made by others also.
8. *Entrepreneurs are their own bosses and completely independent:* An entrepreneur has to serve many masters like partners, investors, customers, suppliers, employees, etc.
9. *Entrepreneurs work longer and harder than managers:* Many entrepreneurs work more than their managers but some may not.
10. *They face great deal of stress and pay a high price:* An entrepreneurship is stressful, painful, and demanding. But many entrepreneurs work hard and they take no rest.
11. *Starting a business is risky and ends up in failure:* Those who failed in their ventures say like this.
12. *Money is most important to start a business:* More than money, courage, faith, risk-taking, etc are important for entrepreneurship.
13. *Entrepreneurs should be young and energetic:* This may not be true in all cases.
14. *Entrepreneurs seek power and control over others:* Some may like power and some entrepreneurs may want to share it.

15. *Any entrepreneur can raise money:* Through confidence and leadership, an entrepreneur can raise money.

Background of Entrepreneurs

Background means origin. Under this title, we will try to look at the common origins that holds true on the majority of entrepreneurs, as justified by various researches.

Childhood background

Most entrepreneurs are either the first child or the only child for their family.

Parental background

The parents of most entrepreneurs are self-employed running their own business.

Age background

Most male entrepreneurs became entrepreneurs in their early 30s.

Most female entrepreneurs become entrepreneurs in their late 30s.

Educational background

Most entrepreneurs at least hold 1st degree (more usually BA degree). In other words, people with first degree become entrepreneurs than any other qualification.

Marriage background

Most entrepreneurs are married.

Parental relationship background

The relation of most entrepreneurs with their parents is proved to be strong.

Work history

Most entrepreneurs have some previous work experience especially the type of work that resembles to their present business.

Work environment eackground

The work environment under which most entrepreneurs had been working under was more presumably unsatisfying. That is one of the push factors for becoming an entrepreneur.

Role of Entrepreneur in an Organisation

An entrepreneur is someone who organizes a system. He is the person who creates a product or service in order to gain profit. However, there is a general sense that entrepreneurship involves the establishment of a new venture while adopting some of the risk and being ready for failure. There is no general definition for the word, as it has been used in a large variety of ways. Some scholars of entrepreneurship, such as Prof. W. Long have tried to develop a specific definition by studying the evolution of the word's usage 'Encyclopedia'.

As a risk bearer

An entrepreneur is an agent who buys factors of production at certain prices in order to combine them into a product with a view to selling it at uncertain prices in future. Uncertainty is defined as a risk, which cannot be insured against and is incalculable. There is a distinction between ordinary risk and uncertainty. A risk can be reduced through the insurance principle, where the distribution of the outcome in a group of instances is known. On the contrary, uncertainty is a risk, which cannot be calculated. The entrepreneur, according to *Knight*, is the economic functionary who undertakes such responsibility of uncertainty, which by its very nature cannot be insured, or capitalized or salaried to. *Mark Casson* has extended this notion to characterize entrepreneurs as decision-makers who improvise solutions to problems which cannot be solved by routine alone.

As an organizer

An entrepreneur is one who combines the land of one; labor of another and the capital of yet another, and, thus, produces a product.

By selling the product in the market, he pays interest on capital, rent on land and wages to laborers and what remains is his or her profit.

As a leader

Scholar R.B. Reich considers leadership, management ability, and team-building as essential qualities of an entrepreneur.

Entrepreneur is sometimes mistakenly equated with "opportunist". An entrepreneur may be considered one who creates an opportunity rather than merely exploits it, though that distinction is difficult to make precise.

Types of Entrepreneurs

There are so many ways of classifying entrepreneurs. The most important bases are discussed below.

Classification by Danhof

Danhof classified entrepreneurs as follows:

(*a*) *Innovative entrepreneurs:* An innovative entrepreneur is the one who introduces new goods, inaugurate new method of production, discovers new market and recognizes the enterprise. It is important to note that such entrepreneur can work only certain level of development is already achieved, and people look forward to change and improvement.

(*b*) *Imitative entrepreneurs:* Imitative entrepreneurs do not innovate the change themselves, they only imitate techniques and technology innovated by others. Such type of entrepreneurs are particularly important for underdeveloped region for bringing mushroom drive of imitation of new combination of factors of production already available in developed regions.

(*c*) *Fabian entrepreneurs:* Fabian entrepreneurs are characterized by very great caution and skepticism in experimenting any change in their enterprises. They imitate only when it becomes perfectly clear that failure to do so would result in a loss of the relative position in the enterprise.

(*d*) *Drone entrepreneurs:* These are characterized by a refusal to adopt opportunity to make change in production formulae even at the cost of severely reduced returns relative to other producers.

Classification according to Type of Business

When we divide entrepreneurs by type of business they engage in, we have the following:

Business entrepreneur: These entrepreneurs are individuals who conceive an idea for a new product or service and then create a business to materialize their ideas in to reality. They have both production and marketing resources in their search to develop a new business opportunity.

Trading entrepreneur: This type of entrepreneur is the one who undertakes trading activities and is not concerned with the manufacturing work he or she identifies.

Industrial entrepreneur: Essentially a manufacturer who identifies the potential needs of customer and sells a product or service to meet the market need. The entrepreneur is a product-oriented person who starts an industry unit because of the possibility of making some new product.

Corporate entrepreneur: Corporate entrepreneur is an individual who plan and develop, and manages a corporate.

Agricultural entrepreneurs: These are those entrepreneurs who undertake agricultural activity such as raising and marketing of crop and agricultural input.

Classification According to Motivation

Motivation is the force that influences the effect of the entrepreneur to achieve his or her objective.

Pure entrepreneur: He is an individual who is motivated psychological and economic reward. The entrepreneur undertakes the enterprise for his personal satisfaction.

Induced entrepreneur: He is the one who is induced to take up entrepreneurial task due to the policy measures of the government that provides assistance, incentive and necessary overhead facilities to start a venture.

Motivated entrepreneur: Motivation is the desire for self-fulfillment. They come into being because of the possibility of making and marketing some new product.

Spontaneous entrepreneur: He is the one who is motivated by his/her natural talent to begin a business. This kind of entrepreneurs is very confident in their natural blessings from God and wants to undertake business because they believe their natural gifts will enable them to do so.

Classification according to Use of Technology

Technical Entrepreneurs: This type of entrepreneur have technical knowledge regarding innovation of new products. They concentrate on manufacturing (technical aspect) rather than marketing.

Non technical Entrepreneurs: Are not concerned with technical aspect of a product. They concentrate on developing alternative marketing, distribution and promotion aspects of their product rather than manufacturing aspect.

Professional Entrepreneurs: They are interested neither in the technical aspect nor in the non-technical aspects of a product. They are interested in establishing a business but doesn't have the interest to manage or operate once a business is established. Professional entrepreneurs sell their business ideas and look on to creating another business.

Classification according to Stage of Development

First Generation Entrepreneur: They start an industrial unit by innovative skill i.e., combines different technology to produce marketable product.

Modern Entrepreneur: They undertake those ventures which go well along with changing demand in the market i.e., he or she chooses those ventures that suit to current marketing needs.

Classical Entrepreneur: This type of entrepreneur is stereotyped business who is only motivated by economic gain i.e., they run businesses that give them the maximum economic benefit? He or she tries to increase their profit by developing self supporting ventures

Classification according to Growth

- Growth Entrepreneurs

- Super growth Entrepreneurs

Classification according to Area

- Urban Entrepreneurs
- Rural Entrepreneurs

Classification according to Gender and Age

- Men Entrepreneurs = Young, middle-aged and old entrepreneurs
- Women Entrepreneurs

Classification according to Scale of Operation

- Small scale Entrepreneurs
- Large scale Entrepreneurs

Some more categories

1. *Individual and institutional entrepreneurs:* In the small scale sector individual entrepreneurs are dominant. Small enterprises outnumber the large ones in every country. Such entrepreneurs have the advantages of flexibility, quick decision-making and state patronage. But a single individual can establish, operate and control an organization up to a limit. Thereafter, it becomes necessary to institutionalize entrepreneurship. A group of entrepreneurs has to be developed to handle the increasingly complex network of decision-making. The central function of the entrepreneur remains the same but the basic decisions like the line of business, the amount of capital employed, etc. are taken collective by the group of promoters at the helm of affairs. Thus, individual entrepreneur and institutional entrepreneur coexist and support each other. Corporate sector is the symbol of institutional entrepreneurship.

2. *Entrepreneurs by inheritance:* At times, people become entrepreneurs when they inherit the family business. In France and India, there are a large number of family-controlled business houses. Firms in these houses are passed from one generation to another.

3. *Technologist entrepreneurs:* With the decline of joint family business and the rise of scientific and technical institutions, technically qualified persons have entered the field of business. These entrepreneurs may enter business to commercially exploit their inventions and discoveries. Their main asset is technical expertise. They raise the necessary capital and employ experts in financial, legal, marketing and other areas of business. Their success depends upon how fast they start production and on the acceptance of their products in the market.

4. *Forced entrepreneurs:* Many persons become entrepreneurs on account of the circumstances. The moneylenders of yesteryears enter into business due to decline of moneylending business with the growth of Banking and Government regulations. Neorich Ethiopians returning from abroad (NREs) and educated unemployed seeking self-employment may also be described as forced entrepreneurs. This class of entrepreneurs accounts for the maximum number of failures because there is no proper screening of misfits.

Behavioural Pattern of Entrepreneurs

This title focuses on the socio-economic factors that affect the type activities of entrepreneurs. People with diverse backgrounds enter into different types of industry depending on their experiences. The following are among the behavioural patterns of entrepreneurs:

- People from agricultural background usually gravitate towards industries, where technology is elementary and capital requirement is the modest.
- Off springs (sons and daughters) of professional and skilled craftsmen are usually attracted towards undertakings that have complex production methods because they have specialized knowledge.
- People from commerce are likely to set up large sized firms with the help of their accumulated wealth.
- Professionals and craftsmen have little opportunity for accumulation of wealth and are likely to begin small scale firms.

Entrepreneur *vs*. Enterprise

According to the classical economists, entrepreneur is one who provides the fourth factor of production, namely 'enterprise'. As the fourth factor, it assembles, coordinates and manages the other factors namely land, labour and capital.

But in a true sense, an enterprise consists of a group of dedicated people who work together in the organizational structure primarily for the purpose of making and/or selling a product or service by pooling their recourses (skills). Entrepreneurs create an enterprise as one part of organizing function.

Entrepreneurs *vs*. Managers

An entrepreneur is different from a manger. But it doesn't mean that they are entirely different from each other. That means they also have their own intersection points.

Similarities

- Both make decisions

- Both are visionary
- Both are accountable for their actions
- Both work under constraints
- Both are organizers
- Both perform management functions

Differences

The main points of difference between the two may be described as follows:

1. *Primary Motive:* The entrepreneur is primarily driven by innovation, profit and need for independence. On the other hand, the manager is driven by power and compensation.
2. *Focus:* Entrepreneurs focus more on exploiting new opportunities. But managers focus is more on optimizing the existing resources.
3. *Risk taking:* An entrepreneur takes calculated risks of a business venture. He may jeopardize his own financial security for losses that may occur. By contrast, the manager does not face the uncertainty of a new venture with its potential for failure and financial loss. He does not share any business risks.
4. *Reward:* An entrepreneur is motivated by profits while the manager is motivated by externally imposed goals and rewards. The gains of an entrepreneur are uncertain and irregular and can at times be negative. The salary of a manager is on the contrary, fixed and regular and can never be negative.
5. *Skills:* An entrepreneur needs intuition, creative thinking and innovative ability among other skills. On the other hand, a manager depends more on human relations and conceptual abilities.
6. *Status:* An entrepreneur is self employed and he is his own boss. On the contrary, a manager is a salaried person and he is not independent of his employer, the entrepreneur.

Functions of Entrepreneurs

General Functions

Broadly speaking, there are three most important general functions performed by entrepreneurs. These are:

1. *Innovation:* Innovation implies doing new things or doing of things that are being done in a new way. It includes introduction of new products, creation of new markets, application of new process of production,

discovery of new and better sources of raw materials and developing a new and better form of industrial organization.

2. *Risk taking:* Risk taking or uncertainty bearing implies assuming the responsibility for loss that may occur due to unforeseen contingencies of the future. An entrepreneur provides or invests capital in order to establish and run the enterprise. He guarantees interest to lenders, wages to employees, rent to the landlord. After making payment to these persons little or nothing may be left for him. Thus business is a game of skill wherein risks and rewards both are great.

3. *Organizing:* Organization and management of the enterprise is the main function of an entrepreneur. It implies bringing together the various factors of production. The purpose is to allocate the productive resources in order to minimize losses and reduce costs in production. While organizing, human resource and physical resources are among the two types of resources that are coordinated. Entrepreneurs coordinate human resources to create enterprise or a group of committed people.

Specific Functions

Kilby identified thirteen functions of an entrepreneur, which included some of the managerial functions also. These functions are as follows:

1. Perceiving market opportunities
2. Gaining command over scarce resources
3. Purchasing inputs
4. Marketing of the products and responding to competition
5. Dealing with the public bureaucracy (concessions, licenses and taxes)
6. Managing human relations within the firm
7. Managing customer and supplier relation
8. Managing finance
9. Managing production (control by written records, supervision, coordinating input flows with orders, maintenance.
10. Acquiring and overseeing assembly of the factory
11. Industrial engineering
12. Upgrading process and product quality; and
13. Introducing new production techniques and products

Kilby has classified the above functions into four groups viz., Exchanges relationship (1-4), political administration (5-7), management control (8-9), and technology (10-13). He has suggested that in the strict sense entrepreneur will perform only first two functions listed above and for the other eleven functions, he will employ experts in the related lines.

Arthur H. Cole has described the following functions of an entrepreneur:

1. The determination of those objectives of the enterprise and the change of those objectives as conditions required or made advantageous.
2. The development of an organization including efficient relation with subordinates and all employees.
3. Securing adequate financial resource, the relations with existing and potential investors.
4. The requisition of efficient technological equipment and the revision of it as new machinery appeared.
5. The development of a market for the products and the devising of new products to meet or anticipate consumers demand.
6. The maintenance of good relations with public authorities and with society at large.

Based on the above discussion, each specific functions of an entrepreneur can be grouped in one of the general functions. In other words the above list is of no exception to the general functions list.

Responsibility of Entrepreneurs

To the Nation	To the Enterprise
Tax timely	Survival and growth
Follow rules and regulation	Profit
Adding to the national wealth	Company image
	Fair compensation
To the Society	**To their Business Associates**
Using resources properly	Profit or dividend fairly
Employment	Future certainty
Minimizing toxic levels	Fair knowledge of company performance

Summary

- The word entrepreneur first appeared in the French language as 'entreprendre', which means, 'to undertake'.
- The characteristics of successful entrepreneur are: as an individual with technical competence, risk taking, high initiative, good judgment, intelligence to analyze and solve problem areas, leadership qualities, confidence, positive attitude, high level of energy, creativeness, honesty, integrity, emotional stability and fairness.
- Entrepreneurs as risk bearers, organizers and as leaders perform general and specific functions. There are similarities and differences between entrepreneurs and managers.

Self-learning Activity

Try to answer the following questions on your own:

1. Define Entrepreneur?
2. What are the traits of an entrepreneur?
3. Give an account of myths of an entrepreneur?

2

Entrepreneurship

Evolution and Development of Entrepreneurship

Just like a human being gets born, gets young and flourish, entrepreneurship as a discipline and as a practice have grown. The earliest practice of entrepreneurship was observed 4000 years ago witnessed by a piece of writing on small business describing how banker's loaned money on interest. In fact, the Arabs, Babylonian, Egyptians, Greeks, Romanians, Indians and Jews were among pioneers as entrepreneurs some 2500 BC. But the true development of entrepreneurship is best signified and initiated by small businesses. Small businesses flourished in all civilization. Industrial revolution kicked up entrepreneurship in a big way and due to liberalization policy by most countries, small businesses has got special emphasis and now contributes majority in employment and economic activities. During 1980's and 1990's small business began to enjoy more esteem and prestiges than ever, due to its ability to invent new products, create new jobs, customize products and respond quickly to changes. Even today, fortune 500 companies depend heavily on small business for parts and equipment for creating their own products. Previously, entrepreneurship was the last option and people used it if there is no job opportunity. But today, undertaking entrepreneurship is the dream of many people.

Definition of Entrepreneurship

Entrepreneurship, like an entrepreneur, has no single definition. The main difference between entrepreneur and entrepreneurship is their attachment. Entrepreneur is a person while entrepreneurship is a process. When it is put in other way, entrepreneurship is a process undertaken by entrepreneur to augment his/her business interest. Broadly defined:

- Entrepreneurship is a dynamic process undertaken by an entrepreneur to create incremental value and wealth by discovering investment opportunities, organizing an enterprise, undertaking risk and economic uncertainty and thereby contributing to economic growth.
- Entrepreneurship is the process of creating something different with value by devoting the necessary time and effort, assuming the accompanying financial, psychic and social risks, and receiving the resulting rewards of monetary and personal satisfaction and independence.

When the first definition is explained in other words, entrepreneurship is a function of seeing investment and production opportunity, organizing an enterprise to undertake a new production process, raising capital, hiring labour, arranging for the supply of raw materials and selecting managers for the day to day operation of an enterprise (Higgins), that is, through the process of entrepreneurship, entrepreneur organizes an enterprise that is committed to undertake the basic activities essential in making and selling entrepreneur's product.

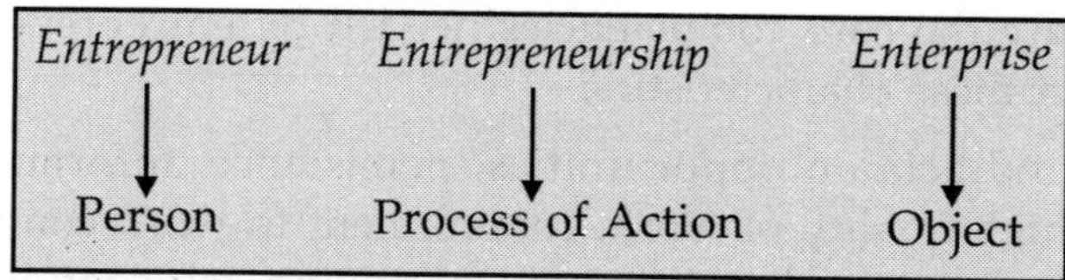

So, entrepreneurship

- is both a science and an art;
- involves vision and passion of innovation and creation;
- requires willingness to undertake calculated risk;
- involves building a committed and dedicated team;
- more over involves accepting challenges, managing skills and organization of resources.

In general the four key elements in entrepreneurship are:

1. Vision (identifying emerging opportunities)
2. Innovation (doing some thing new)
3. Risk taking (assuming different types of risks: financial, psychological, social)
4. Organizing (coordinating resources and creating enterprise)

What is Entrepreneurship?

In a narrow sense, the term 'entrepreneur' refers to the individual 'who undertakes an enterprise, especially a commercial one, often at personal risk'. This definition is clearly inappropriate for cooperatives. A more comprehensive definition has been offered by Robert E. Nelson:

"An entrepreneur may be defined as a person who is able to look at the environment, identify opportunities to improve the environment, marshall resources, and implement action to maximise those opportunities. The term is used in its broadest sense and includes persons who work in large, medium and small enterprises, as well as those who work in cooperatives and government".

Increasingly therefore, 'entrepreneurship' is being used to describe a set of skills employed by persons working in large, medium and small enterprises, cooperatives, public institutions, non-commercial undertakings such as community associations, charitable foundations and others. These skills usually include the ability to search for new opportunities and to respond effectively to these opportunities in an innovative and purposeful manner.

What, therefore, are the core competencies needed by entrepreneurs? Nelson and Nguiru list these characteristics:

"Initiative, sees and acts on opportunities, persistence, information seeking, concern for high quality of work, commitment to work contract, efficiency orientation, systematic planning, problem solving, self-confidence, expertise, recognizing own limitations, persuasion, use of influence strategies, assertiveness, monitoring, credibility, integrity, sincerity, concern for employee welfare, recognizing the importance of business relationships, building capital, concern for the image of products and services".

Therefore we can see that psychological factors are considered to be the central entrepreneurial characteristics without which the would-be entrepreneur is unlikely to be successful. These factors are many but perhaps the most important are: personal motivation, a positive self-concept, initiative, innovation, problem-solving tendencies and risk-taking. David McClelland has emphasized the importance of 'achievement motivation', or a subconscious 'need to achieve'.

The abilities needed to perform these functions effectively may in some cases be 'inborn', but a more reasonable and modern approach recognizes that training can play an important role in developing the necessary competencies for successful entrepreneurship.

Elements of Entrepreneurship

Entrepreneurship has certain elements, which are noted below:

1. *Innovation:* Innovation refers to the new ideas or solutions found by an individual entrepreneur for his industry or for the whole industries in a locality. Innovation refers to new product developments, finding new markets, finding new processing technologies, finding new markets abroad, etc.
2. *Risk taking:* This element of entrepreneurship is related to the particular individual. That individual should have courage to face problems, confidence in himself to meet challenges like labour problems, government regulations, threat from competitors, etc.
3. *Vision:* Vision denotes the forecasting of future. An entrepreneur should forecast a positive vision to expand his business and find out ways and means to achieve them. Sometimes, a vision may become a dream.
4. *Ethics:* Ethics denotes the good qualities of an entrepreneur, which includes character and values in life. They are inherent qualities and inner strength of an individual. They are influenced by family atmosphere, culture, and beliefs of an entrepreneur.
5. *Organizing skills:* These are certain abilities, which may be found within an individual or can be learned through experience. Organizing skills are managerial skills required for the success in terms of coordination, control, direction, and communication.

Benefits and Drawbacks of Entrepreneurship

Truly speaking, when most entrepreneurs start operating entrepreneurship, they more presumably start from a scratch. That means at the first glance of living in the world of entrepreneurship, they will only be the owners of small business. Of course, this may be an exception when businesses are inherited from rich parents. But the true adventure of entrepreneurship is observed when businesses start from a scratch or small businesses. That is why we will discuss the general benefits and drawbacks of entrepreneurship from the stand point of small entrepreneurs.

Benefit and Opportunity of Small Business Entrepreneurship

Pull Factor

- *Opportunity to gain control over your own destiny:* Owning a business gives the entrepreneur the independence and the opportunity to achieve what is personally important.
- *Opportunity to reach your full potential:* Small business is an instrument for self-expression and self-actualization. Many entrepreneurs don't enjoy working for some one else. No body limits you because you are independent and there is likely that you have challenging job.

- *Opportunity to reap unlimited profit:* Although money is not the primary force driving most entrepreneurs, their ability to keep their business earns the money certainly is a critical factor in their decision to create companies.
- *Opportunity to contribute to the society:* Small business owner enjoy the recognition they received from customers whom they have served faithfully over the years.
- Opportunity to turn previous work experience into business for self and family.

Push Factor

- Redundancy (unable to recycle a job)
- Job insecurity or unemployment
- Disagreement with previous employer

Potential Drawbacks of Small Business Entrepreneurship

- *Uncertainty of income:* The entrepreneur of small business cannot be 100 per cent sure about the level of revenue that he will earn because there could be more powerful competitors.
- *Risk of losing entire capital:* Small businesses fail more than any other business type. If they completely fail, their owner looses hi entire capital.
- *Psychological and Social Tensions:* When you run a small business, you question yourself whether it will be successful or not i.e., torturing your psychology. On the other hand, there could be some social outcastings. Others may neglect you and even laugh at you when you start your own business because they may feel that you want to be special from them and this results in some social tensions.
- *Long hours and hard work:* Opening small business needs a devotion of your entire time. You may work for more than 60 hours per a week.
- *Lower quality of life until the business get established:* Your frequent food and drink can be 'shiro' and 'water' till your financial power gets more enhanced.
- Complete responsibility on those issues which you don't have a complete knowledge.
- *Tremendous competition:* Stiff competition from established businesses can be faced by small business entrepreneurs.

What is Small Business?

Small business is a business which is independently owned and operated, not dominated in its field of operation and meets certain standard of number of employee and capital. In Ethiopian case, small businesses have the following criteria. There are two approaches to the criteria.

Size Criteria

Less than 50 employees.

Less than 50,000 birr of sales volume

Economic/Control Criteria

Market share: Low, not dominant

Personalized management: Not professionals

Independence: Independent

Reasons for Failure of Small Business

Many small businesses fail due to various reasons. Presumably, most of the reasons are artificial i.e., the majority of the reasons are created by faults and mistakes of human beings. Some of the reasons include the following:

- Management incompetence,
- Poor financial control,
- Lack of adequate capital,
- Over investment in fixed asset,
- Failure to plan current as well as future operation,
- Failure to adopt proper inventory control system,
- Improper attitude (The entrepreneur may not respect time, employees and may have lazy lifestyle and dictatorial style of work),
- Inadequate marketing plan,
- Incorrect market identification,
- Poor distribution channel,
- Weak marketing communication or promotion.

How to Avoid the Pitfalls

Know your business in depth: Knowing your industry well can be one of the ways of minimizing the failures of small businesses. Also knowing your business well by preparing documented business mission, objective, strategies and policies is another method.

Have a good relation with stakeholders: Personal contact with suppliers, customers, trade association and even competitors is one of the ways to get knowledge.

Prepare business plan: A well-written plan is a crucial ingredient for the success of small business. Answering, "What business I am in?" leads to the establishment of goals and objectives. In turn these serve as aids in creating strategies, policies and procedures.

Managing financial resources: The first step in managing financial resource is to have adequate start up capital. The most valuable financial resource to small business is cash. You cannot maintain control over a business unless you are not able to judge its financial health.

Understanding financial statement: To understand what is truly going on in the business you must have at least basic understanding of accounting and finance that would help to recognize the financial position of your business from time to time.

Learn to manage people effectively: Every business depends on a foundation of well-trained, motivated employees. You would only do this if you learn how to manage people more effectively.

Keep in tune with yourself: The success of your business will depend on your constant presence and attention and so it is critical. As an entrepreneur you must always physically and mentally fit through adjusting yourself with time.

Take up short professional courses in management (entrepreneurship): Improve your managerial skills.

Be sensitive to your customers: Your best opportunity lies within your customers. If you loose them, you will be hurt. So as an entrepreneur, don't ever give yourself a chance to disappoint them. The other is being wise in identifying the present and future needs of your customers through the analysis of the changes in their interests.

Importance of Entrepreneurship

One of the important inputs in any economic development of a country is entrepreneurship. More the entrepreneur activity betters the development. Entrepreneurship is the life blood of any economy and it applies more to a developing economy like Ethiopia. The areas of development are:

- Taking to higher rate of economic growth by creation of value.
- Speed up the process of industrial use of the factors of production.
- Creation of employment opportunity.
- Dispersal of economic activities to different sectors of the economy and identifying a new venues of growth.
- Development of backword and tribal areas.
- Better social changes.
- Improvement of the standard of living of different weaker sections in the society.

- Bringing social and political change in the society.
- Develop technological know how.
- Improve culture of business and expand commercial activities.
- Entrepreneurship acts as a change agent to meet the requirement of the change in markets and customer preferences.

The Process of Entrepreneurship

The decision about weather to start a new business is best considered in light of an understanding of the entrepreneurial process. The entrepreneurial process has four steps:

1. Identifying and evaluating business opportunity;
2. Developing business plan;
3. Determining the resources required for business; and
4. Managing the enterprise.

Identifying and Evaluating business opportunity

Although most entrepreneurs do not have formal mechanism for identifying business opportunities. Some sources are: consumers and business associates, member of distribution system and technical people. New business opportunity may be the result of technological change, market shift, government regulation, or computation. It is important to understand the cause of the opportunity. Since these factors and the resulting opportunity have a different market size and time dimension.

Whether the opportunity is identified with the input from customers, business associates, channel member or technical people; each opportunity must be carefully screened and evaluated. This evaluation of the opportunity is perhaps the most critical element of the entrepreneurial process as it allows the entrepreneur to assess whether the specific product or service has the return needed for the resource required. This evaluation process involve looking at the creation and length of the opportunity, its real and perceived value, its risk and returns, its fit with the personal skills and goals of the entrepreneur, and its differential advantage in competitive environment.

Develop a business plan

A business plan is a document the entrepreneur prepares before going to the implementation stage. It details every aspect of the business the entrepreneur aspires to establish: description of the business and the marketing, financial, organizational and operational plans necessary for the foundation of the venture. A good business plan is important in developing opportunity and also important in determining the resource required, obtaining those resources and successfully managing the resulting venture.

Determining the resources required

The resource needed for the opportunity must also be assessed. The process started with an appraisal of the entrepreneur's present resources. Care must be taken not to underestimate the amount and variety of resources needed. An entrepreneur should strive to maintain as large an ownership position as possible, particularly in the start up financing stage. As the business develops, more funds will probably be needed to finance the growth of the venture, requiring more ownership to relinquish.

Managing the enterprise

After resources are acquired the entrepreneur must employ them trough implementation of business plan. The operational problem of the growing enterprise must also be dealt with. These involve implementing a management style and structure, as well as determining the key variable for success. A control system must be identified so that any problem areas can be carefully monitored.

Entrepreneurship as a 'Principal Equation'

Entrepreneurship suffers greatly from the lack of common understanding as to what, exactly, it is. Before describing a model for entrepreneurship, it may therefore be useful to say briefly what it is not:

- It is not innovativeness or creativity. Innovation and creativity are one of the hallmarks of entrepreneurship, but they are a response to the entrepreneurial equation, rather than an input. For entrepreneurship to exist and to function, it needs a context that includes a specific project with measurable outcomes, inadequate resources and clear ownership. There are countless examples of creative people doing innovative things that are worthy or essential, but have nothing to do with entrepreneurship, because they lack one or more of these contextual imperatives.
- Entrepreneurship is not about an organization, nor is it about an individual. It is about the development of an organization under the leadership of an entrepreneur. The entrepreneur is inseparable from the organization — the organization is defined by the entrepreneur's individual vision, which cannot be realized without the organization.
- Entrepreneurship does not have to exist in the context of an entire organization—it can function in a discrete part of a larger organization, as long as that part meets the criteria of a specific project, inadequate resources and clear ownership. This means that numerous independent entrepreneurs can exist in the context of a firm led by someone who may or may not be an entrepreneur — so that each entrepreneurial part is lead by an entrepreneur, without there having to be an entrepreneur at the top (although it helps if there is one at top).

- Entrepreneurship is not a personality stereotype. Despite thousands of hours of research, no-one has found a personality template that fits all entrepreneurs — they come in every size, shape, gender, race, IQ, EQ, background, training, personality and character. They may be born entrepreneurs (many show signs of it at a very early age), but there are also countless examples of people who have become entrepreneurs through their life experiences. Entrepreneurship is a behavioural phenomenon, not a personality type.

In proceeding to describe what entrepreneurship is, it is helpful to think of it as a "principal equation" that can be activated only with certain necessary inputs. The principal equation is the specific project, which starts with an idea, is made possible by attracting the necessary resources and is brought to fruition through concerted, competent effort at combining the resources and the idea to produce a measurable outcome. The project can be of short duration or it can last a lifetime. Or it can be a series of short-term projects that goes on for a lifetime.

Before this chain reaction can occur, however, there have to be two necessary catalysts — an entrepreneur with an appropriate set of core characteristics and motivations and an environment that allows entrepreneurship to breathe and survive.

For the organization to succeed, the entrepreneur must have a strong need to achieve (which alone provides the resilience and stamina to overcome all the hurdles), must be a leader in order to attract resources and must be an owner in whatever sense ownership may apply to the project (more about that shortly). Equally, entrepreneurship can be sparked only in a market characterized by instability. There are two aspects to an unstable market - first it is a free market, where people have the right to choose or not choose whatever suits them best, and second, it must be unstable, because stable markets are always dominated by large organizations that do not have to be entrepreneurial to survive.

This combination of the principal equation and its two catalysts are illustrated in figure 2.1.

There is a high degree of interaction between all the elements of entrepreneurship. However, the core is the principal equation of entrepreneurship, which is a sequence of three elements running through the centre of the model — opportunity orientation without regard to resources, risk and competence. Before embarking on a more detailed discussion of the principal equation, we will review the role of the market, since the assumptions inherent in a market environment inform much of the model's functioning.

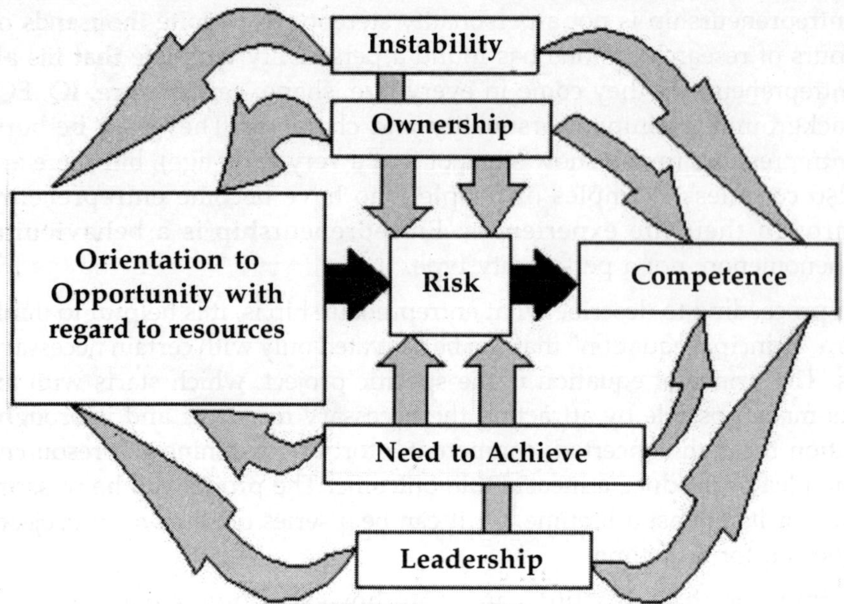

Fig. 2.1: **Combination of the Principal Equation and its Two Catalysts**

Summary

- 'Entrepreneurship' is being used to describe a set of skills employed by persons working in large, medium and small enterprises, cooperatives, public institutions, non-commercial undertakings such as community associations, charitable foundations and others. These skills usually include the ability to search for new opportunities and to respond effectively to these opportunities in an innovative and purposeful manner.
- One of the important inputs in any economic development of a country is entrepreneurship. More the entrepreneur activity betters the development.
- The principal equation is the specific project, which starts with an idea, is made possible by attracting the necessary resources and is brought to fruition through concerted, competent effort at combining the resources and the idea to produce a measurable outcome.

Self-learning Activity

Try to answer the following questions on your own:

1. What is entrepreneurship?
2. Discuss the elements of entrepreneurship?
3. Explain the process of entrepreneurship?

3

Entrepreneurship, Economic Development and Business Environment

Factors for Economic Development

In manufacturing a commodity or service, the following factors are needed. They are called as factors of production.

1. *Land:* Land is the basic factor for organizing a concern or undertaking activities like agriculture.
2. *Labour:* Ideologists like Karl Marx insisted that, among all the factors of production labor is the supreme one. All other factors of production must be subordinated to labour.
3. *Capital:* In free enterprises or capitalistic order of the society, capital is given more importance. Capital may be in the form of cash, finances and natural resources.
4. *Organization:* Organization denotes the managerial ability of an enterprise.

In a country all factors of production may not be available. So entrepreneurs apply the resources that are available abundantly to the maximum extent. The scarce resources are used to the minimum. The following are the factors for economic development.

1. *Natural resources:* Natural resources make a country rich. By means of using the natural resources industries and business concerns can be organized. The important natural resources are agricultural resources, metal and mineral resources, oil resources and sea/water resources.
2. *Human resources:* In developed countries human resources form the major part of economic development. Human resources are expressed in educated manpower, skilled manpower and the development of science and technology. The factor that decide the human resources in a country is population. Within the population the size of age group is important.

If a country has young people with good education, it is a great assets to the country. The second aspect of human resource is level of education. Education can be classified as formal education, higher education and technical education.

3. *Industrialization:* For the fast growth of an economy and to have higher income for the population, a country should have industries. The following factors decide the industrialization of the country:
   (*a*) Availability of raw materials
   (*b*) Infrastructure facilities (road, transport, communication, sea port, airport etc.)
   (*c*) Skilled manpower
   (*d*) Labor intensity
   (*e*) Technology (traditional, intermediate, latest)
   (*f*) Market (local and foreign)
4. *Poverty and unemployment:* For the economic development of the country poverty must be abolished and the rate of unemployment must be kept low. Poverty is contributed by factors like illiteracy, low development of agriculture, lack of industrialization, political instability etc. Unemployment is caused by heavy dependents on agriculture, low level of industrialization, lack of technical education etc.
5. *Cultural factors:* Cultural factors are decided by the hereditary of the country, religion, family etc. In advanced countries, culture allows equal opportunity for all types of population. Gender equality, giving equal freedom to human, is one of the factors for economic development. Women must be given equal rights and opportunities in the fields of education, employment, administration and politics.
6. *Foreign private investment:* These are the days of economic liberalization. Developing countries have the freedom to invite foreign private investment and start industries and business in their own countries. Developed countries extend their investments in poor and developing countries. This opportunity must be used by the developing countries for their industrialization, employment, export trade and general economic development.
7. *Globalization:* Globalization implies the movement of goods and services, industries and businesses to move from one country to another. By means of globalization consumers can get all types of goods from various countries at a lower price. But globalization led to the disappearing of local industries. Because local industries with their low technology, low investment and limited market could not compete with foreign goods.

Role of Entrepreneurs in Economic Development

Entrepreneurs are the pioneering people who take the initiative to organize the new industries and business.

(*a*) *Increasing per capita income:* Entrepreneurs through their hard work increase their income and the income of the workers they employ. Through this process per capita income in a country increases.

(*b*) *Wealth creation and distributions:* When new entrepreneurs enter the new fields, income and wealth of the country increases. Entrepreneurs are small-scale industrialists who distribute the wealth equitably. Through them industries are started throughout a country which avoids regional imbalances.

(*c*) *New products and services:* Entrepreneurs go for innovations and they produce new goods and services, which helps the economic development.

(*d*) *Employment generation:* Small-scale industries organized by new entrepreneurs create a lot of employment opportunities. They also use the locally available raw materials.

(*e*) *Better production methods:* New entrepreneurs are innovators and they introduce better production methods through which the cost of production is reduced.

(*f*) *Conversion of natural resources:* Natural resources available from agricultural and related areas are converted into finished forms, which provide employment, income generation, marketing etc.

(*g*) *Abolition of monopoly:* Entrepreneurship is encouraged in small and medium industries. Large industries create monopoly and concentration of industries in few places. But small-scale industries can be located in all parts of the country and can abolish monopoly.

(*h*) *Export:* When new products are manufactured such products will have export market also.

(*i*) *Development of complimentary goods:* When one industry is coming up, based on it so many other industries will also be developed. For example, when a sugar factory is organized, based on it liquor factories, paper factories etc. can be organized.

(*j*) *Business opportunities:* When new industries are coming up, business opportunities increase. A network of suppliers, wholesalers and retailers are appointed and they provide employment opportunity and regulate the flow of goods.

(*k*) *Revenue to government:* Entrepreneurs provides income to government by paying various types of taxes like income tax, excise duties, VAT etc.

Employment

Employment has three parts namely unemployment, under-employment and full employment. Unemployment denotes jobless nature. Under-employment denotes a qualified individual getting a low salary for a low level of job. Full employment denotes work for all people. The causes for unemployment are as follows:

1. *Low level of education:* If a country has low level of education, it will lead to unemployment.
2. *Natural resources:* Non availability of natural resources may lead to poor industrialization and unemployment.
3. *Lack of industries:* Only industries can provide more employment opportunities compared to agriculture.
4. *Low income and low purchasing power:* Lower income of the population leads to lower purchasing power and further employment opportunities cannot develop.
5. *Population:* Huge population and high density of population may also lead to unemployment.
6. *Lack of competition:* If competition is not there, industries and business cannot grow fast which may lead to stagnation in employment.
7. *Hard working:* Hard working nature of people can provide good employment. Otherwise it may lead to unemployment.
8. *Lack of EDP:* Lack of entrepreneurial development and new entrepreneurs may lead to unemployment.

Entrepreneurship and Society

Entrepreneurship helps the society as well as the entrepreneur itself. The benefits of an entrepreneurship may be divided into three distinct categories that include the benefits to the nation, benefit to the society and the benefit to the individual.

As already discussed, an effective entrepreneurship venture fosters the production of wealth for a nation. When many of the entrepreneurship produce an output greater than the input, the economy of the nation is directly bolstered. Another advantage to the nation is the creation of jobs for its people. Such a job creation utilizes the human resources of that particular country and helps the natural talent materialize. With the new inventions and development in the new technology a nation can use its resources more effectively. Since, a majority of the entrepreneurship projects are private; it provides an environment of competitiveness which further increases the quality of the products in the national markets. By privatizing the local economy, entrepreneurship ventures help attract eager foreign firms who are otherwise reluctant to do business with the government subsidized economy.

The income level of the average person and the standard of living of a society increase with every successful entrepreneurship project that is undertaken. There is an increase in the employment level on the regional scale. It is also noticeable that an entrepreneurship helps develop other entrepreneur businesses because of the extra incentives that it can provide to a new entrepreneur in the shape of capital, knowledge and technology. Entrepreneurship helps the societies to fulfill its basic needs in the world that calls for the 'survival of the fittest'. Entrepreneurs lead by example in assisting the society and therefore boost the moral of the public.

An entrepreneur helps himself while creating opportunities for others. It is a fact that by doing so an entrepreneur fulfills his creative urge. Each successful project carried out by the entrepreneur leads to self satisfaction. The greatest satisfaction is derived from the fact that the individual is his own boss and therefore can use its creativity without any fear of repercussion. The quality of every good entrepreneur project is the profit and the fame that such a career provides. In fact, entrepreneurs always enjoy respect and high status in their communities.

Entrepreneurship and Business Environment

The status of the society and the government are interdependent on the many entrepreneur projects being undertaken around the world. The role of each entrepreneurship projects differs widely on a global scale due to the disparities in the local business environment. In developing countries, the process of privatization has helped to eliminate restrictions on the kind of opportunities that exist in the market. Whereas, socialist countries have historically helped entrepreneurs who have shown keen interest in optimizing the plans of the government. On the other side, less developed countries have rarely provided the entrepreneur a thriving atmosphere.

The major hurdles that the new entrepreneurs face are the availability of resources to carry out such a business. The most important is the allocation of funds that comes in the form of money to research and development. Another largely ignored factor is the availability of knowledgeable partners who can run a successful entrepreneurship after its initial stage. This is so because there is a great tendency for the entrepreneur to move from one project to another. The lack of knowledge on part of the management can halt the development process, if adequate training is not provided. Historically, women-owned businesses have not been successful even in the developing countries due to the lack of government support. It remains the most significant problem in mainly the theoretical and male dominated societies.

Governments can help improvise the entrepreneurial spirit by not only removing the hurdles described above but by creating an industrial atmosphere that is favorable to the structural change. If the resources are allocated from the losers to gainers by purchasing the sales of assets, the entry and exist of the firms and rise and fall of the industries, the governments can effectively allocate resources to the successful entrepreneurs.

Experts agree that the most effective method of managing the entrepreneurship industry is to foster the start-ups. Among other techniques, this can be achieved by minimizing the paper work and formalities for the new starter. A single identification number should be issued to every new entrepreneurial project to track down each case. The authorization process should not take long and the case decisions should be made by a fixed date. Tax treatment of the new subsidiaries and the policies on induction of new employees should be simplified.

Rural Entrepreneurship

These days rural entrepreneurship is seen as the largest force in the development of the rural areas. In fact, many of the developing countries in the world have used the concept of rural entrepreneurship as a very successful method of deterring rural unrest. The greatest asset that the rural areas have is not the natural resources but it is the vast uncultivated land. Due to the ever-growing population of the world and the expansion of the metropolitan areas, government's reliance on the rural land has significantly increased. These lands are used in the development of industry and establishing manufacturing base. Many countries have used these lands to establish recreational and educational facilities. This is one of the primary reasons that most new institutions of higher education are opening in suburbs and small towns.

Another great advantage in the rural entrepreneurial projects is the availability of cheap labor that can reduce the cost of production. It is also well known that the less technical projects have a chance of success in rural communities because of the closely knit together communities that can carry out the communication much better than the workforce in the cities. The production plants of many large entrepreneur projects are always located in these rural communities because not only does these projects provide employment opportunities but also prosper on behalf of the hard working labor force.

Governments and companies are promoting rural entrepreneurship by providing extra incentives to women who have been allocated to the traditional feminine jobs. Many companies have established training centers in order to educate the rural workforce on technical matters. Historically, governments have eliminated many of the requirements for the rural entrepreneurs who want to set up an industry in their regional areas. Similarly, many of the entrepreneurs, who want to set up rural industries, are exempt from strict laws that govern the urban development.

Problems of Rural Entrepreneurship

Rural entrepreneurship has its own drawbacks. Policies such as keeping of land in protection when there is already an over-production and pricing subsidy policies that helps to retain the minimum income are two of the greatest threats to rural development. Due to the remote access and unavailability of knowledgeable labour, it is difficult to advise the local entrepreneurs who are willing to take risk. Access to capital labor, commercial markets and the managerial staff are hindered due to the remote locations.

In order to alleviate the problems of rural agriculture, a competitive agriculture entrepreneurship, under the government supported resources, is needed. The government should set aside a quota for the rural entrepreneurship projects and select only the very best ideas that directly benefits not only the community but can compete on a global scale. It is also vital for the success of the rural communities that the development of each rural project remains in the hand of the local agencies which in return cooperate with the government to oversee the entire project. Entrepreneurship education is the leading factor that can help develop the rural areas. Governments should encourage the foundation of a local network that can communicate with the rural population and try to abridge the gap between the extended and remote communities.

Summary

- In a country all factors of production may not be available. So entrepreneurs apply the resources that are available abundantly to the maximum extent. The scarce resources are used to the minimum.
- Entrepreneurship helps the society as well as the entrepreneur, itself. The benefits of an entrepreneurship may be divided into three distinct categories that include the benefits to the nation, benefit to the society and the benefit to the individual.
- The status of the society and the government are interdependent on the many entrepreneur projects being undertaken around the world. The role of each entrepreneurship projects differs widely on a global scale due to the disparities in the local business environment.

Self-learning Activity

Try to answer the following questions on your own:

1. What is role of entrepreneurs in economic development?
2. Describe the relationship of entrepreneurship with society?
3. Give an account of rural entrepreneurship?

Theories of Entrepreneurship

Entrepreneurship Theories

Business academics have two classes of theories of how people become entrepreneurs, called *supply* and *demand* theories, after Economics. In the *supply* theory, entrepreneurs arise as they are born, with personality traits which drive them to become entrepreneurs. In the *demand* theory, anyone could be recruited by circumstance or opportunity to become an entrepreneur.

Several research studies have shown that entrepreneurs are convinced that they can command their own destinies. *Behavioural scientists* express this by saying that entrepreneurs perceive the *'locus of control'* to be within themselves. It is this self-belief which stimulates the entrepreneur, according to supply-side theorists.

A more generally held theory is that entrepreneurs emerge from the population on demand, from the combination of opportunities and people well-positioned to take advantage of them. The entrepreneur may perceive that they are among the few to recognize or be able to solve a problem. In this view, one studies on one side the distribution of information available to would-be entrepreneurs (see *Austrian School economics*) and on the other, how environmental factors (access to capital, competition, etc.) change the rate of a society's production of entrepreneurs.

Some authorities have given the following theories:

Economic Theory

Economists view entrepreneurship as a process where entrepreneurs are driven by profit motive and maximization of wealth by combining different factors of production.

Socio-cultural Theory

Sociologists view entrepreneurship as a process where an entrepreneur acts as a role model, senses expectations of society and tries to bring about products/services as per culture, norms and tradition of society.

Psychological Theory

Psychologists view it as a process where an entrepreneur acts as a change agent with tremendous psychological drive (need) for innovation, experimentation and seize unusual opportunities of environment.

Managerial Theory

Professional managers view entrepreneurship as a process where an entrepreneur performs managerial functions (planning, organizing, staffing, leading and controlling) to make new products for business to compete (a rival) and an ally (business associate).

There are many theories of entrepreneurship; in some authors' view the important ones are as below:

Schumpeter's Theory of Innovation

According to his theory, economic development of an entrepreneur takes place through innovation. Innovation takes place under the following five categories:

(*a*) Introduction of new products
(*b*) Introduction of new technology
(*c*) Opening a new market
(*d*) New source of raw material
(*e*) Creating new forms of organization — mergers, acquisitions, etc.

McClelland's Theory of Achievement

According to his theory, an individual has a desire to achieve, i.e., achievement motive. For an entrepreneur, the achievement motive comes through the following sources:

(*a*) Taught by parents
(*b*) Profit is not the main motive
(*c*) Takes calculated risk
(*d*) Have high inner spirit

According to him, aimless life is a goalless game.

Peter Druckers' Theory of Innovation

Drucker also insists innovation as the basis for entrepreneurship. He puts the following conditions for innovation:

(*a*) It requires knowledge and ingenuity

(*b*) It must be built on one's own strength

(*c*) It should be closer to market

Harbinson's Theory of Organization Building Function

According to him, an entrepreneur must have the organizing skill. His theory is opposite to Schumpeter's theory and Drucker's theory of innovation. An entrepreneur must be an organizer and he must be a leader. Through organizing abilities, an entrepreneur can come up. So, for Harbinson, managerial skill is important.

Moreover, there are contributions in the form of schools by different authorities on entrepreneurship. The following are some of the entrepreneurship theories emerged out of different schools:

NEOCLASSICAL SCHOOL

The literature on innovation and technical change is discussed from our perspective in 'Devine' (forthcoming); see also Metcalfe (1995). The standard theory views the firm in purely technological terms, with the management knowing the firm's cost and revenue functions and performing a mathematical calculation in order to achieve optimal values for all its decision variables. Management is nothing in this setting but 'a passive calculator that reacts mechanically to changes imposed on it by fortuitous external developments over which it does not exert, and may not even attempt to exert, any influence' (Baumol, 1993, p. 13). Thus, there is no need, indeed no room, for entrepreneurial action. It is evident that this fundamental characteristic remains intact even if the model assigns to the objective function a task other than profit maximisation.

The neoclassical approach also recognises that there may be government failure, a consequence of which is that profits might be maximised not from the rules of economic rationality applied to production but from a patron-client network. In this regard, Baumol's argument that how a firm acts will depend heavily on the reward structure in the economy is telling. He concludes that, although entrepreneurial activity *per se* cannot be analysed within a neoclassical framework, the allocation of entrepreneurial ability between productive and unproductive activities will be profoundly influenced by the rules of the game. However, although this approach, and more generally the literature on rent-seeking and bribery, offers an understanding of the optimal behaviour of firms under different settings, at an epistemological level it is no different from the standard neoclassical theory of the firm.

All decisions are construed as constrained maximisation problems, with the constraints known beforehand, at least in probabilistic terms. The outcome, therefore, is that 'automaton maximizers the business people are and automaton maximizers they remain' (Baumol, 1993, p. 14). There have also been attempts within a game theoretic framework to analyse innovative activities undertaken in an imperfectly competitive environment. These may be classified under three headings. *First*, given that the less successful rivals of successful innovators may use their capabilities to launch counter-measures to neutralise or even destroy the innovators' competitive advantage, innovative effort and 'enterprising' sabotage have been analysed as an interactive game (Baumol, 1993, Chapter 5). *Second*, in other game theoretic models of innovator-imitator interactions (Dasgupta and Maskin, 1987; Dasgupta, 1988), firms either race for a patent on a winner-take-all basis or firms wait for someone else to incur the bulk of the risk. *Finally*, technology-sharing consortium situations have been analysed in which firms will benefit by sharing complementary information but will be even better off if they retain their information while others share, with the outcome depending on whether the game is finite or infinite (Baumol, 1993). While neoclassical models such as these may offer some insights into various aspects of the innovative process, they contribute nothing to an understanding of the dynamics of entrepreneurship, since in all such models the outcome is predetermined, the rules of the game having been set in advance. Returning to Kirzner's quotation, mistakes in a neoclassical setting occur if and only if there are 'mistakes in arithmetic'.

The neoclassical models discussed so far remain essentially production functions and assume away the existence of firms and the relationships between individuals within them. However, building on the work of Coase (1937), neoclassical models have been developed that explain the existence and boundaries of the firm as the outcome of maximising individuals' decisions in conditions of opportunistic behaviour, asymmetric information, bounded rationality or incomplete contracts, and asset specificity. Two strands have emerged in this literature. *First*, the 'nexus of contracts' or 'property rights' approach (associated with Alchian & Demsetz, 1972, and Jensen & Meckling, 1976), emphasises the residual rights of control over the firm's physical assets or the property rights of the 'indispensable agent'. *Second*, the 'transactions costs approach' (associated with Williamson, 1985, 1989), focuses on the relative efficiency of different governance structures. The relevance of these developments within neoclassical theory for the purpose of this paper is whether they provide scope for introducing an analysis of entrepreneurship.

Both perspectives rest on the concept of a 'contract' between various input owners to create an optimal governance structure, under the assumption that inputs, outputs and production technology are well-known (Aoki, Gustaffson & Williamson, 1990; Milgrom & Roberts, 1992). The contractual approach, according to Witt (1998, p. 161), 'has been increasingly attracted to one theme: how is opportunism kept under control so that it cannot eat up the gains on transaction costs that can be achieved by setting up a firm as a special way of coordinating individual economic activities [and so that it cannot] discourage asset-specific investments by the firm members where these create potentially sizeable quasi-rents?' These attempts certainly lead to a richer and more realistic portrayal of firms than the production function versions of neoclassical theory, but they again fail to create room for entrepreneurial activity since the outcome of the interactions between the various actors is nothing but the result of a contract assumed to be optimally designed. As Foss (1996, pp. 8-9) emphasises, 'It is outside the prerogative of standard contractual analysis to examine how new resource uses are discovered, how resources are accumulated, how firms learn, which governance structures best promote learning under which circumstances, etc.

To sum up, the neoclassical approach is incapable of usefully addressing the issue of entrepreneurship due to its epistemological standpoint. We now turn to the ways in which the Austrian approach deals with entrepreneurship.

AUSTRIAN SCHOOL

According to the Austrian school the economic problem consists of the social mobilisation of tacit knowledge, by definition fragmented and dispersed, through the interaction of rival entrepreneurial activities. Thus, the two core concepts in the Austrian approach are the tacitness of knowledge, as elaborated by Hayek, and entrepreneurship, as emphasised by Mises. The social mobilisation of tacit knowledge occurs via entrepreneurial actions, with entrepreneurs directing their efforts toward the achievement of potential profits and thereby discovering what is and what is not possible. The discovery of tacit knowledge in a world that is inherently in a process of continuous change (Hayek, 1937, 1945) is therefore the starting point of the Austrian approach. Since the world is characterised by uncertainty, the discovery process necessarily involves failure as well as success. Entrepreneurs act on their perceptions, or their hunches, and discover whether they were well-founded or in error, in which case they are revised. Thus, the Austrian view of entrepreneurship also has built into it a process for the correction of error. The epistemological standpoint underlying this approach is quite distinct from that underlying the neoclassical school. As Kirzner (1997, p. 64) has recently put it: 'In the neoclassical world, decision makers know what they are ignorant about. One is never surprised. For Austrians, however, to abstract from these qualities of imagination, boldness, and surprise is to denature human choice entirely'. In this regard, it was Knight (1921) who elaborated the concept of unmeasurable uncertainty, separating it from risk which is defined as measurable uncertainty. He stressed that change in line with known laws does not cause uncertainty and that predictable events present no problem of action. Problems of action arise out of departures from routine, from the possibility or occurrence of unpredictable events. Entrepreneurship, therefore, is human action 'seen from the aspect of the uncertainty inherent in every action' (Mises, 1949, p. 254).

In this setting, the Schumpeterian entrepreneur, who plays a disequilibrating role by innovating, and the Misesian-Kirznerian entrepreneur, who plays an equilibrating role by detecting and exploiting? It has been suggested that while the property rights approach remains within an orthodox neoclassical framework, Williamson's transactions costs approach is less neoclassical in that it embraces Simon's concept of bounded rationality (Foss, 1993). It has also been suggested that the transactions costs approach 'by viewing optimal contractual design as a reality that will only be revealed *ex post*, can arguably accommodate a concept of entrepreneurship'. This is an interesting idea which, to be developed, would involve the transactions costs approach moving away from the neoclassical optimising framework within which it is at present firmly located. There is clearly a tension between Williamson's adoption of bounded rationality, which Simon (1979) associates with 'satisficing', and his insistence that opportunistic behaviour is maximising behaviour (Williamson, 1989). We are grateful to Martin Currie for this latter point (see Currie & Messori, 1998). Opportunities that others failed to notice, emerge as the two different types of entrepreneur.

EARLY SCHUMPETERIAN ENTREPRENEUR

In the *Theory of Economic Development* (1911), Schumpeter outlines a theory of endogenous change in which the entrepreneur, the underlying force in economic development, breaks away from the path of routine. According to Schumpeter, under constant conditions consumers' and producers' goods of the same kind and quantity would be produced and consumed in each successive period, with people abiding by their previous experience and following established methods in familiar ways. Schumpeter then questions what would happen if change occurs, disturbing the smooth flow of economic life. Thus, 'It is the spontaneous and discontinuous change in the channels of the flow, disturbance of equilibrium, which forever alters and displaces the equilibrium state previously existing' (1911, p. 64). Economic development is defined by the implementation of new combinations and it is in this context that Schumpeter emphasises the importance of the entrepreneurial function. Entrepreneurial profit is a surplus over costs, as new combinations will persist only if they turn out to be more advantageous. Then, as new businesses arise, entrepreneurial profit disappears as a new equilibrium position is reached. Schumpeter distinguishes the entrepreneur from the capitalist, while acknowledging that entrepreneurs may need to borrow initial capital in order to be able to carry out their new combinations. The Schumpeterian entrepreneur receives profit, but is not the risk bearer in terms of financial responsibility. Schumpeter also distinguishes his entrepreneur from the 'inventor' by claiming that 'As long as they are not carried into practice, inventions are economically irrelevant. And to carry any improvement into effect is a task entirely different from the inventing of it, and a task, moreover, requiring entirely different kinds of aptitudes' (1911, p. 88). Thus, for the early Schumpeter, entrepreneurial talents make themselves felt by introducing new ideas, new combinations, with the consequence that established firms are challenged and the pre-existing ways of economic life are disrupted. Schumpeter identifies five types of new combination:

- the introduction of a new good;
- the introduction of a new method of production, not yet tested by experience;
- the opening up of a new market;
- the conquest of a new source of supply of raw materials or semi-manufactured goods; and
- the implementation of a new organisation of industry, such as the creation or breaking up of a monopoly position.

These points should not be interpreted to mean that the Schumpeterian entrepreneur does not take any responsibility. Schumpeter is careful to point out that the entrepreneur 'may risk his reputation' (1911, p. 137).

KIRZNERIAN ENTREPRENEUR

Kirzner uses the Misesian notion of 'human action' to analyse the entrepreneurial role: 'the humanaction concept, unlike that of allocation and economizing, does not confine the decision-maker (or the economic analysis of his decisions) to a framework of given ends and means' (Kirzner, 1973, p. 33). Thus, the entrepreneurial element in human decision-making is defined by Kirzner (1973, p. 35) as 'the element of alertness to possibly newly available resources and to possibly newly worthwhile goals which is absent from economizing behaviour but present in human action'. The Kirznerian entrepreneur notices 'profit opportunities that exist because of the initial ignorance of the original market participants and that have persisted because of their inability to learn from experience' (Kirzner, 1973, p. 14). In this setting, the knowledge required for entrepreneurship is alertness, defined as 'knowing where to look for knowledge' (Kirzner, 1973, p. 35), and it is assumed that by using this superior knowledge the entrepreneur will capture profits. In answering criticisms that the entrepreneur in many instances creates rather than merely sees a given opportunity, Kirzner replies that the more fundamental function is that of discovery: 'This insight is simply that for any entrepreneurial discovery creativity is never enough: it is necessary to recognize one's own creativity' (Kirzner, 1994, p. 109). Although defined in this way the scope for entrepreneurial decision-making may be in danger of disappearing, since the services of individuals with knowledge can be hired, like those of any factor of production, Kirzner argues that the person who hires 'alertness' in fact displays alertness of a still higher order. Kirzner is clear that in an equilibrium state, where there is no lack of coordination and no ignorance, the entrepreneur cannot contribute to the reallocation of resources or products to remove inefficiencies. However, he argues that 'The entrepreneurial market process may indeed reflect a systematically equilibrative *tendency*, but this by no means constitutes a *guaranteed* unidirectional, flawlessly converging trajectory' (Kirzner, 1997, p. 72). Kirzner (1992) emphasises that ownership and entrepreneurship are completely separate functions. The pure entrepreneur starts out with no means and must acquire from the capitalist the capital with which to initiate entrepreneurial activity. However, the capitalist's decision to lend also contains an entrepreneurial element, since in conditions of uncertainty it involves being alert to whether or not an investment offers a real possibility of gain. Kirzner also accepts that entrepreneurship involves an element of risk but argues that this does not mean rejecting the view that the essence of entrepreneurship is perceiving opportunities: 'To recognize that alertness in a world of uncertainty may call for good judgement and lively imagination does not, surely, affect the centrality of the insight that entrepreneurship refers, not to the deliberate exploitation of perceived opportunities, but to the alert perception of opportunities available for exploitation. While the entrepreneur operates under uncertainty, and therefore displays imagination, judgement and creativity, his role is not so much the *shouldering* of uncertainty as it is his ability to *shoulder uncertainty aside* through recognizing opportunities in which imagination, judgement and creativity can successfully manifest themselves' (Kirzner, 1994, pp. 108-109).

A Fusion of Schumpeterian and Kirznerian Concepts of Entrepreneurship

For Schumpeter entrepreneurial activity involves innovation through the introduction of new goods or methods of production, the opening up of new markets, the conquest of a new supply of materials, the reorganisation of an industry. Kirzner, however, sees entrepreneurial activity as the discovery of opportunities rather than the creation of them: 'the function of the entrepreneur consists not of shifting the curves of cost or of revenues which face him, but of noticing that they have in fact shifted' (1973, p. 81). Thus, arbitrage, in the sense of taking advantage of price differences, would be an entrepreneurial activity for Kirzner, but not for Schumpeter. In Schumpeter's analysis, imitators, who move the economy towards a new equilibrium following a disruption as a result of an innovation, are not engaging in entrepreneurial activity. In Kirzner's analysis, by noticing opportunities and acting to take advantage of them, they certainly are. However, in his more recent work, Kirzner is in the end unwilling to draw a definite line between his concept of entrepreneurship and Schumpeter's concept of creative innovation: 'Discovery would include not only one of hitherto unknown natural resources (as in oil discovery) but also of new kinds of output (as through entrepreneurial product-innovation), or of new additional productivity (of known outputs) available from known inputs (as when an entrepreneur innovates a new productive technique)' (Kirzner, 1997, p. 75).

With regard to the identity of entrepreneurs in the two conceptions, as Witt (1994, p. 541) indicates, 'Being an entrepreneur is, according to Schumpeter, not an occupation or a profession, but rather a unique, and rarely found, capacity to carry out new combinations of resources; that is innovations. The basis of this capacity is held to be a peculiar personality and motivation, an interpretation with obvious elitist connotations. In this respect, Schumpeter clearly contrasts with Mises and Kirzner who interpret the entrepreneurial element as a basic human capacity, an lertness that everyone possesses more or less'. Finally, although for Schumpeter the entrepreneur is the disruptive, disequilibrating force, for Kirzner (1973, p. 127) the entrepreneur remains 'the equilibrating force whose activity responds to the existing tensions and provides those corrections for which the unexploited opportunities have been crying out' (see also Kirzner, 1999). To what extent is a fusion of these two concepts possible? According to Casson (1987, p. 151), once the entrepreneur is defined as 'someone who specialises in taking judgmental decisions about the allocation of scarce resources', then the Kirznerian *arbitrageur* and the Schumpeterian innovator can be thought of as 'special cases of the general concept of entrepreneurial speculation based upon self-confident judgement'. We agree with Casson that, while it is necessary to recognize the two distinct functions of entrepreneurship, the umbrella concept of the judgmental decision-maker is a helpful further insight.

Absence of Firms in the Austrian Approach

Firm behaviour is not theorised in Austrian economics. As Foss & Christensen (1996, p. 11) comment, the Austrians' focus on the study of spontaneous order seems to have 'taken precedence over the study of designed order, such as organisations'. Questions concerning the existence, boundaries and internal organisation of firms have not been addressed; nor, a *fortiori*, have the entrepreneurial activities of firms. The Austrian school's epistemological position concerning the tacit nature of knowledge and the uncertainty inherent in economic life is much more realistic than the over-formalised and over-simplified world of the neoclassical paradigm and this *ipso facto* applies to the Austrian approach to entrepreneurial activities.

However, by confining themselves to the analysis of individual action in a market process, the Austrian school finds it difficult, if not impossible, to address entrepreneurial activities within different micro organisational settings. See also McNulty (1987), who suggests that the two concepts are complementary in the sense that disequilibrating and equilibrating activities are part of a single process. For further discussion, see Foss (1994), Loasby (1989) and Minkler (1993). For recent contributions seeking to construct a theory of the firm in the spirit of the Austrian approach, see Foss (1994, 1997), Ioannides (1998) and Sautet (2000). However, such attempts necessarily depart from the Austrian school's basic principle of subjectivism.

Although in his later work Schumpeter focused on the activities of the large corporation, by undermining the individualistic nature of economic dynamism he also distanced himself from the Austrian tradition. In *Capitalism, Socialism and Democracy* (1942) Schumpeter discarded his earlier individualistic conception of the entrepreneur and argued instead that entrepreneurship was increasingly being undertaken by the research and development departments of corporations rather than by individuals. While he recognised that innovating firms might be large or small, he believed that small firms were more and more being pushed to the margin owing to the superior access of large firms to financial resources. Furthermore, although uncertainty provides entrepreneurial opportunities, it may easily become so great as to paralyse action. Hence, increasingly only large-scale enterprises would be ready to undertake entrepreneurial risk. However, once conceived in this way, the Schumpeterian entrepreneur loses his or her defining function, which is to revolutionise the pattern of production and consumption: 'For, on the one hand, it is much easier now than it has been in the past to do things that lie outside the familiar routine—innovation itself is being reduced to routine. Technological progress is increasingly becoming the business of teams of trained specialists who turn out what is required and make it work in predictable ways' (Schumpeter, 1942, p. 132). In fact, Schumpeter and the Austrians from the beginning had little in common apart from a general distancing of themselves from the neoclassical school and, in the early Schumpeter, the issue of entrepreneurship. For discussion of the innovativeness of small *versus* large firms and of concentrated industries *versus* atomistic industries, see Loasby (1982), Malerba & Orsenigo (1995), Scherer (1984), Sylos-Labini (1992) and Teece (1996).

COMPETENCE THEORY OF THE FIRM

The competence, or capabilities, or knowledge-based theory of the firm emphasises the importance of specific stocks of knowledge that are tacit, socially produced and reproduced, and path-dependent. It seeks to explain on the one hand the sources of competitive advantage and on the other hand the existence and boundaries of firms. The tacit nature of knowledge refers to the non-codifiable, person-specific and context-specific dimension of knowledge. The social dimension stems from the interaction between members of economic organisations which creates an accumulation of knowledge that is more than the sum of each individual's personal knowledge and is typically embedded in routines. Path dependency, finally, arises from the role that each economic organisation plays in providing a unique framework for the generation, mobilisation and articulation of knowledge. The three elements are interwoven, with the possibilities that the firm faces in efficiently using its knowledge base being shaped and reshaped within an interactive process. Thus, the competence perspective provides much greater scope for explaining the dynamics of economic life than the static framework of the neoclassical approach; at the same time, since it focuses on the firm as the site for individual action, it goes well beyond the Austrian approach (Hodgson, 1998a).

The Competence Theory has roots in both the Austrian and the evolutionary literature. It shares the Austrian epistemological standpoint on the tacit nature of knowledge, but not the Austrian school's subjectivism. One of the key insights of the Competence Theory is that tacit knowledge does not have to be 'individual' knowledge but may also be 'social' knowledge. It is this insight that enables the Competence Theory to go beyond the Austrian approach by focusing on the firm as a central part of the social framework within which the actions of individuals are shaped and their individual tacit knowledge is mobilised to produce social knowledge. Competence theorists develop the Austrian approach by arguing that knowledge can be held by both individuals and collectivities in either explicit or tacit form. Tsoukas argues that explicit and implicit knowledge and individual and social knowledge are mutually defined and cannot be separated from one another. He adds that 'a firm's knowledge is distributed in the sense that it is inherently indeterminate: nobody knows in advance what that knowledge is or need be. Firms are faced with *radical uncertainty:* they do not, they cannot, know what they need to know' (1996, p. 22). Since competence is a 'determinant of economic behaviour—meaning that economic competence is embodied in the very ways economic decisions are made' (Pelikan, 1989, p. 283), it must be seen as a scarce resource and hence the process by which it is allocated matters for efficiency. Furthermore, given the nature of their knowledge base, economic organisations 'are [to be] seen as being in constant flux, out of which the potential for the emergence of novel practices is never exhausted' (Tsoukas, 1996, p. 22), i.e. collective or social human action is inherently creative. In this context, the organisational form of the firm is conceptualised as 'a means of acquiring, combining, utilizing and maintaining' knowledge that is by definition not available to any one single agent (Witt, 1998, p. 162). Thus, the firm turns out to be the central entity in the competence approach as the site for generating, mobilising and allocating knowledge—a key input in production. The concept of tacit knowledge was independently developed by Hayek (1937, 1945) and by Michael Polanyi (1962, 1967), who first coined the term. For discussion of the link between them, see Lavoie (1985). In addition, Liebeskind (1996, p. 94) has argued that, in an economy based on private ownership, firms as institutions play a critical role in protecting valuable knowledge from 'expropriation and imitation', since property rights in knowledge, such as patents and copyrights, are very narrowly defined under the law and are costly to write and enforce. From the evolutionary literature, the competence theory takes explicitly the concept of economic development, in particular the development of the firm and its internal organisation. The key authors referred to in this context include Marshall (1920), Nelson & Winter (1982), Penrose (1959), Richardson (1972) and Veblen (1904).

Nelson & Winter (1982) note that the firm's explicit and tacit stocks of knowledge are articulated and mobilised in the course of interaction with the external economic environment and what is learnt is then loaded in the firm's 'routines', which makes it available for future use. Since these routines are open to improvement, the firm is conceptualised as a 'learning' body, with organisational knowledge emerging as the outcome of this learning process (Aoki, Gustafson & Williamson, 1990; Dosi & Marengo, 1994; Lazonick, 1994; Teece & Pisano, 1994).

Hodgson (1998a, p. 184) suggests the further clarification that learning should be conceptualised as 'a developmental and reconstitutive process', as opposed to the way in which the neoclassical school (as exemplified by Bray & Kreps, 1987) treats it as 'the cumulative discovery of pre-existing "blueprint" information, or Bayesian updating of subjective probability estimates in the light of incoming data'.

The general framework of the competence approach allows a natural role for entrepreneurship, although this has not yet been much elaborated. One reason for this is that the two literatures have developed separately and are based on different discourses, as is evident from the fact that discussions of tacit knowledge in the competence theory rarely make explicit reference to the central role played by tacit knowledge in the Austrian approach, perhaps due to their rejection of the Austrians' subjectivism. It is evident that a concept of entrepreneurship based on the premises of the competence theory would differ significantly from concepts of entrepreneurship based on individualistic premises. One attempt to develop such a concept has been made by Foss. Starting from the position that 'What competence really implies is a view of rationality that is very different from maximisation', he notes that 'Means and ends are not simply given to the decision-maker through some unexamined historical process', with the corollary that 'means-ends-structures have to be set up by the agents themselves' and this, according to Foss, 'is the meaning of the competence known as "*entrepreneurship*" (Foss, 1993, p. 134). This approach in a sense echoes the much earlier contribution by Penrose (1959, p. 31) on the role of entrepreneurs: 'the introduction and acceptance on behalf of the firm of new ideas.' Penrose's perspective has been confirmed and modified recently by Eliasson (1990) who identifies the competence endowment of firms as the ability to sense direction, i.e., intuition, willingness to undertake risk, efficiency in identifying mistakes, effectiveness in correcting mistakes, effectiveness in managing successful experiments and effectiveness in feeding acquired experience back into intuition.

The competence approach welcomes entrepreneurial inputs from any layer within the firm, as stated by Tsoukas (1996, p. 23): 'Given the distributed character of organisation knowledge, the key to achieving coordinated action does not so much depend on those "higher up" collecting more and more knowledge, as on those "lower down" finding more and more ways of getting connected and interrelating the knowledge each one has. A necessary condition for this to happen is to appreciate the character of a firm as a discursive practice: a form of life, a community, in which individuals come to share an unarticulated background of common understandings'. Sustaining a discursive practice is just as important as finding ways of integrating distributed knowledge. For further discussion of the origins of the Competence Theory of the firm, see Foss (1996, 1998), Hodgson (1998a) and Loasby (1998). However, this does not mean that there is no role for imagination or leadership, even if this dimension has been somewhat neglected in work on the Competence Theory (Witt, 1998). For early Schumpeter and the Austrians such qualities are theorised within a subjectivist framework, with a role for the firm, if any, only as the vehicle for the implementation of the entrepreneur's pre-existing insight or vision. By contrast, the competence theory implies that imagination draws on and is shaped by the social knowledge embedded in the firm and that leadership takes the form of nurturing the firm's discursive practice and developing consensus around the new means-ends-structures that emerge.

ENTREPRENEURSHIP IN A PARTICIPATORY CONTEXT

An Evaluation of the Literature on Entrepreneurship

What are the implications of this literature for the relationship between entrepreneurial activity and type of economic organisation? Although rarely made explicit, the assumption underlying most, if not all, of the literature is a capitalist system based on the private ownership of capital. Yet, the *raison d'être* of private ownership, the alleged necessity of private ownership for the flourishing of entrepreneurial activity, is never theorised. The Austrian school, of course, constantly claims that social ownership is incompatible with the mobilisation of tacit knowledge through entrepreneurial activity, as in the socialist calculation debate. However, the Austrian contribution to that debate consists of a critique of neoclassical central planning and neoclassical market socialism, both based on state ownership. While we agree with this critique of neoclassical socialism, in our view, as we have argued elsewhere, the Austrian claim that their critique necessarily applies to any form of socialism is mere assertion and has never been theoretically established (Adaman & Devine, 1996). A second implicit assumption in the literature is that entrepreneurial activity is in general socially productive, with the possible relationship between the existence of a capitalist system and unproductive entrepreneurial activity discussed, if at all, only in terms of rent-seeking behaviour. In none of the literature is the possibility even considered that there may be a systemic bias in a capitalist private ownership system towards unproductive entrepreneurial activity. Let us, therefore, summarise the principal themes that have been discussed in the literature on entrepreneurship reviewed in Section 2 and then relate these to different types of economic organisation. Four, possibly complementary, roles for entrepreneurship have been identified:

(i) the equilibrating activities to alert individuals in pursuit of their private gain as the essence of the way in which the market process works;

(ii) the innovative activities of heroic individuals of a special mould forcing through non-incremental change as the way in which the economy develops;

(iii) decision-making in conditions of uncertainty; and

(iv) the exercise of individual or collective competence in establishing new means-ends relationships in uncertain, open-ended conditions. In a paper titled 'Why are there no Austrian socialists?', Boettke (1995) cites five propositions offered by Rizzo (1992) as summarising Austrian political economy. The fifth proposition is that socialism is not feasible because of the difficulties of economic calculation without private property and the price system. No supporting argument is provided. In addition to the Austrian school, the other body of theory that makes claims with respect to the question of ownership is the property rights approach. However, property rights analysis is focused on the relationship between residual rights and efficiency within a neoclassical optimizing framework and therefore does not, and cannot, address

the issue of entrepreneurship. Furthermore, even within its own framework the property rights approach is unable to 'take account of the separation of ownership and control present in large, publicly held corporations' (Hart, 1989, p. 1773).

In the course of the discussion five principal and recurring themes have emerged. *First,* the tacit nature of much of the knowledge relevant for entrepreneurial activity is recognised by both the Austrian and the Competence perspectives. *Second,* it is central to the competence perspective that tacit knowledge arises in relation to both individuals and organisations and that such knowledge is not only tacit but also social and path-dependent. *Third,* it is universally agreed that tacit knowledge is generated, mobilised and articulated through a social process—individual rivalry through the market process for the Austrians; the internal processes within the firm, mediated by its routines and discursive practices, for the competence perspective. *Fourth,* in the literature on entrepreneurship a clear distinction is drawn between the entrepreneur and the capitalist, while in the literature on the competence perspective the issue is rarely explicitly addressed. Of course, it is explicitly or implicitly recognised that entrepreneurial activity requires access to capital, but why this depends on the private ownership of capital is not discussed.

Finally, there is the question of the motivation giving rise to entrepreneurial activity, which is often not made explicit. The Misesian—Kirznerian analysis starts from the premise that since the knowledge required for all effective action, however motivated, is tacit and can only be discovered by acting, through trial and error, all human action has an entrepreneurial element. Yet the Austrian school's analysis privileges a subset of entrepreneurs, who have access to capital and are assumed to be motivated to participate in the market process solely or primarily by the prospect of private financial gain. While this may be a reasonable assumption for some forms of entrepreneurial activity in the institutional context of a capitalist economic system, there is nothing necessary about it. Schumpeterian entrepreneurs, while they may end up with great riches, are motivated more by the need for achievement, while what motivates the actors in the discursive community that constitutes the firm in the competence perspective is typically left unanalysed. It is worth noting that these five themes are also present in the most recent literature on innovation and technical change, even though this literature for the most part does not discuss such change explicitly in terms of entrepreneurial activity (Devine, forthcoming; Metcalfe, 1995).

The Austrian and the Competence approaches explicitly or implicitly assume a capitalist institutional framework with privately owned economic units competing against each other. Resources are allocated and reallocated through the operation of market forces in accordance with the discovery of unexploited opportunities or the selection of preferred innovations, as judged in both cases by the criterion of expected and realised profitability. Explicitly or implicitly it is accepted that there is a control group within the firm, i.e., the owner-manager or the management on behalf of the owners, which has the responsibility and the power to make strategic decisions. Of course, discussion of different forms of more or less co-determined internal firm organisation has proliferated, as economists have come to recognise the tacit, social, path-dependent nature of knowledge and the discursive practices that generate, mobilise and articulate it. However, in all these forms the owners and their hired managers decide if, when and how the other employees of the firm take part in decision-making and, whatever the subjective motivation of the owners may be, the ultimate criterion of survival and success is profitability. Thus, the internal allocation of resources to potential entrepreneurial and innovative activities, the micro level definition of what are productive and unproductive activities, is determined by judgements of expected profitability. The findings of McCleland's (1961) study as summarised by Baumol (1993, p. 272).

> 'entrepreneurs are motivated by n-achievement (the need for achievement) and not by desire for money. ... In his tests, people with high levels of *n*-achievement do no better when offered larger amounts of money for success, whereas people with low *n*-achievement scores do much better when offered money. ... *n*-achievers choose smaller risks than the average person: they are not gamblers but calculators and planners. ... [T]he *n*-achiever is not an individualist and does not depend for success on private enterprise. ... Such persons get just as much satisfaction from the manipulation of a committee, or for working for a government, since their interest is in results rather than in considerations such as profit or status. This is perhaps one reason why huge committee-run corporations can be successful'.

See Ioannides (1998) for discussion of a possible Austrian theory of the firm with a controlling ownership interest; and Ioannides (1994) for an argument that a controlling ownership interest is also required. We conclude from this evaluation that entrepreneurial and innovative activity requires an organisational context in which:

(i) the generation, mobilisation and articulation of tacit, social, path-dependent knowledge is facilitated, which we take to involve participation in the discursive practices and decision-making processes within the firm; and

(ii) there exist (*a*) criteria embedded in the firm's evolving routines for the internal allocation of resources across potential entrepreneurial activities, (*b*) selection mechanisms that select across the output of the firms making up the economy according to socially agreed criteria of social productiveness and

unproductiveness, (*c*) processes that allocate capital for future entrepreneurial and innovative activities according to these criteria, and (*d*) feedback processes which enable the outcome of the selection mechanisms in (*b*) and the allocation processes in (*c*) to be used to modify the routines in (*a*).

While a capitalist economic system clearly constitutes such a context, the necessarily limited participation afforded by private ownership and the one dimensional criterion of profitability that animates processes (*a*) to (*d*) above suggest that a participatory economic system based on social ownership may have comparative advantages in contributing to human well-being.

A NEW PERSPECTIVE: PARTICIPATORY ENTREPRENEURSHIP

We define a participatory economic system, following Devine (1988), as an interlocking network of social relationships, mediated through a set of interlocking institutions, in which the values and interests of people in the different aspects of their lives interact and shape one another in a discursive process of decision-making through negotiation and cooperation. Given this paper's focus on entrepreneurship, participation will be discussed at the intra-firm and extra-firm levels—within the firm, where tacit knowledge is generated, mobilised and articulated; and outside the firm, where the output of the entrepreneurial activities of firms is evaluated and the allocation of, or access to, the capital needed to engage in future entrepreneurial activity is determined. Generalised participation may be thought of as the direct or indirect involvement in social practice, on an equal footing, of all those with either a relevant input to contribute or a legitimate interest in the outcome, i.e., all those who are affected by an activity. With respect to economic activity, the institutional form corresponding to generalised participation is that of social ownership, ownership by those with an interest in the use of the assets involved in the activity in question. Social ownership defined in this way has clear similarities with the concept of stakeholding, with the stakeholders being those inside or outside an organisation who have a specific interest in its activities. Both concepts require criteria for determining the principal interest or stakeholding groups or constituencies, the basis or weight of representation, and the way in which representatives should be chosen. The institutional form through which the social owners at different levels might be determined may be thought of by way of analogy with the bodies that determine the boundaries of electoral constituencies in the UK. Just as such boundaries are changed as population densities and community identities change, so the social owners would change as the activity in question and those with an interest in it changed. Neoclassical firm in both its nexus of contracts/ property rights and transactions costs versions. For extended discussion of the concept of social ownership, see Devine (1988, (esp. pp. 149-152), and 9 (esp. pp. 222-234). The concept of stakeholding associated with social ownership needs to be distinguished from (i) recent discussion of stakeholding which assumes a capitalist economic system, with the organisational form through which stakeholding is institutionalised at the micro level being some sort of trusteeship or consultative process rather than legal social ownership by the stakeholders (Kay, 1997; Parkinson, 1997; Williamson, 1997), although this would also require a method for determining who the stakeholders were; and, a *fortiori*, from (ii) the macro level concept of 'stakeholder capitalism' which seeks to analyse the conditions necessary for social inclusion, with all sections of society having their legitimate interests met to an acceptable level, within a private ownership. Since knowledge is now generally recognised to cover a spectrum from tacit to explicit, with all knowledge consisting of both, albeit in differing combinations, it can be argued that social ownership and the generalised participation that it makes possible are likely to constitute a more efficient form of economic organisation for the social mobilisation of knowledge than either private or state ownership (Adaman & Devine, 1996, 1997). Furthermore, since social ownership involves all those with an interest in the use of the assets that are concerned, the criteria and judgements used in deciding the allocation of those assets across different alternatives can be arrived at through a discursive process of cooperative interaction in which the people constituting the relevant 'community', the social owners, 'come to share an unarticulated background of common understanding' (Tsoukas, 1996, p. 23), which facilitates the more explicit process of negotiation between the different interests. In order to evaluate our claim that a participatory economic system would be more efficient at mobilising knowledge than a capitalist system and would be able to apply wider criteria than profitability for the allocation of resources, we first briefly outline the principal characteristics of such a system. It follows from our definition of social ownership that the social owners will differ according to the nature of the economic activity in question. The participatory model, we advocate, rests on the distinction between market exchange and market forces. Market exchange involves the use of existing capacity-selling and buying what can be produced using the existing assets of the firm. Market forces are the process through which changes in the structure of capacity are brought about in capitalist societies. Investment or disinvestment is undertaken atomistically by individual capitalist enterprises.

The outcome is dependent on the aggregate effect of these atomistic decisions which are then coordinated *ex post*. In a system based on social ownership, market exchange would continue but firms would be owned by those who are affected by their activities. Market forces, however, would be replaced by a process of negotiated coordination in which those who would be affected, the social owners at this level, would seek to agree on a coherent package of investments and disinvestments, coordinated *ex ante*, that would best meet their interests. Thus, the social owners with respect to investment decisions would embrace a wider set of interests than the social owners with respect to existing assets. At the level of the firm, both those who work within it and those outside it who have an interest in its activities constitute the social owners. Representation on the Board of Directors of these internal and external interests enables generalised participation in the determination of strategic objectives and the monitoring of the firm's senior managers and performance. Whether the senior management is appointed by the workforce, on the principle of worker self-management, or by the Board, may be considered a secondary issue, since the concept of generalised participation could be interpreted either way. The process of generating, mobilising and articulating the tacit, social, path-dependent knowledge that gives rise to potential entrepreneurial and innovative activities within the firm takes place in this participatory context. The output of the firm's entrepreneurial and innovative activity is then offered for sale in the market. Since the knowledge base or competence of firms is path-dependent, each firm is unique. The internal processes of each unique firm therefore generate variety in the products, both final and intermediate goods that are offered for sale. In the course of market exchange selection occurs and information is generated, in the form of the degree of capacity utilization and relative profitability, about which products users prefer capitalist society (Hutton, 1994; Kelly, Kelly & Gamble, 1997). We have elsewhere drawn an analogy with the M-firm corporate structure in which the divisions engage in market exchange and the headquarters deals with investment and disinvestment (Adaman & Devine, 2001). One of us has elsewhere argued for internal worker self-management (Devine, 1988).

What happens then? In a capitalist economic system market forces, despite imperfections, in general allocate capital to the firms that are or are expected to be the most profitable. Other firms seek to imitate them, incremental innovation takes place, diffusion occurs and from time to time new non-incremental innovations and general purpose technologies emerge. Schumpeter's gale of creative destruction proceeds, sometimes in the form of firm bankruptcies or takeovers, more generally in the form of new products, technologies and production units replacing old, frequently accompanied by a geographical redistribution of economic activity, both within countries and globally. What is evident about the operation of market forces is that it allows no scope for generalized participation, indeed for any real participation, in the determination of the overall allocation and reallocation of economic activity. Instead of the process of economic change being consciously shaped in accordance with people's explicit and tacit knowledge as to how they might be affected by it, the outcome is what no one willed.

Of course, for the Austrian's this creation of 'spontaneous order' is the real attraction of the market process. In the context of the objective of generalised participation, however, a model of democratic planning through negotiated coordination provides an alternative to the operation of market forces as a process for consciously selecting across the entrepreneurial and innovative output of firms and allocating capital for future entrepreneurial and innovative activities according to socially agreed criteria. The process of negotiated coordination is envisaged as being mediated through an interlocking set of institutions extending beyond the firm and constituted at differing levels, e.g., industry or sector, locality, national region, nation, international region, global. The composition of the social owners at each level, indeed the specification of the different levels, would depend on the nature of the economic activities involved and would be expected to change as technology or markets change, much like the constant redrawing of boundaries discussed in recent theories of the firm, and as social values and priorities change, for instance, in favour of more local and less global production. The outcome of the negotiations would be an allocation of capital constituting a coordinated programme of investments that balanced considerations of revealed productive efficiency and entrepreneurial competence, the consequences for the communities involved, and the judgments of the social owners as to their priorities for future entrepreneurial and innovative activities.

AN EVALUATION OF PARTICIPATORY ENTREPRENEURSHIP

This organisational context seems to us to incorporate both the efficiency and the criteria arguments set out at the beginning of the previous section. Our claim is, first, that the process of mobilising knowledge, tacit and explicit, is likely to be more efficient in a participatory system based on social ownership than in a system made up of privately owned capitalist firms; and, second, that the criteria used for allocating the firm's internal resources and selecting across the entrepreneurial and innovative activities of firms are able to embrace a wider set of social concerns than capitalism's single overriding criterion of expected or realised profitability.

The Austrian school claims that the market process is the most, indeed the only, efficient way to mobilise social knowledge and that this process depends on private ownership. Since we have already argued that the alleged necessity of private ownership is mere assertion and has never been theorised, we concentrate here on the case for the market process. The Austrian argument is that the tacit knowledge of individual entrepreneurs can only be drawn upon by the individuals themselves, who then discover whether their judgements are correct by engaging in market competition.

Our evaluation of the literature on entrepreneurship concluded, *inter alia*, that 'tacit knowledge arises in relation to both individuals and organisations and that such knowledge is not only tacit but also social and path-dependent'. Thus, it is the characteristics of the enterprise that are relevant when considering the efficiency with which knowledge is generated and mobilised within the firm. The socially owned firm is a more inclusive and participatory community than the capitalist firm, able to draw on the wider knowledge base of the tacit knowledge of all its social owners, rather than just that of the individual Austrian entrepreneur or the top management of the capitalist corporation or state enterprise. The essential element of trial and error, given the inherent uncertainty associated with entrepreneurial and innovative activity, is present in the competition between firms as they engage in market exchange and discover whether their judgements are well-founded. Would-be entrepreneurs and innovators, whether individuals or existing enterprises, need access to capital. The socially owned extra-firm institutions that allocate capital across firms in our model are more inclusive and participatory communities than capitalist financial institutions, with again a wider knowledge base. These institutions would have available as a basis for their decisions the two forms of knowledge that have been conceptualised in the literature on entrepreneurship and innovation—explicit and tacit. Explicit knowledge would include the relevant firm-based data on degrees of capacity utilisation and profitability, reflecting the choices made by potential users when selecting across the output of different firms in the course of engaging in market exchange. Tacit knowledge would be mobilised in the process of negotiation within the socially owned financial institution. The representatives of the social owners would seek to articulate and evaluate the reasons for the differential performance of firms, the ways in which they would be affected by alternative responses to that differential performance, the characteristics of the innovation programme proposed and the likelihood of future success. Just as the decision-making processes of firms, which incorporate tacit social knowledge, are revised in the light of experience, thus constituting the firm as a learning organisation, so the same is true of financial institutions, whether they are privately or socially owned. The difference is that socially owned financial institutions, like socially owned firms, are able to draw on a wider set of information inputs when reaching their decisions. This is the fundamental reason, in our view, why a system of negotiated coordination has clear advantages over market forces as an allocative and evolutionary selection mechanism. It would be more efficient, since firms and financial institutions are able to draw on the knowledge of all those involved in productive and innovative activities. The selection of the future activities for which capital would be made available would be on the basis of a wider set of criteria than the single criterion of expected private profitability. The criteria would be arrived at and agreed upon by those who would be affected by the outcome of these activities, rather than being imposed by the coercion of market forces, or by the authority of the state or any other agency acting on behalf of some presumed, known-from-above, general interest.

The difference can be illustrated in the context of a judgement in relation to how much of society's limited resources should be allocated to similar innovative projects. If too many parallel projects are financed, the result will be unnecessary duplication and waste; if too few, the necessarily experimental nature of innovative activity, in conditions of radical uncertainty, will be stifled. Dasgupta & Maskin (1987), working within a neoclassical game theoretic framework, conclude that capitalist rivalry results in social inefficiency, with too many resources being devoted to parallel projects; Metcalfe (1997), from within an evolutionary framework, argues that parallel projects are a necessary part of technological competition as a trial and error process of discovery and selection.

While we agree with Metcalfe that the uncertainty inherent in innovation means that parallel projects are likely to be necessary, the resources devoted to innovation in capitalist economies reflect not only uncertainty but also oligopolistic rivalry. From the standpoint of the criteria that might emerge from a participatory process of deliberative democracy, the resources allocated to innovation might well be judged excessive. Negotiated coordination based on social ownership would make it possible for competition to be combined with cooperation, with the risk associated with radical uncertainty being borne collectively, the outcome of innovative activity resulting in public rather than private knowledge, and the decision on how much resources to allocate to which inherently uncertain activities being made by the community that bears the risk and benefits from the outcome. A further advantage of negotiated coordination is that, although in the case of innovative entrepreneurial activity the irreducible element of radical uncertainty is likely to be relatively large, some forms of uncertainty present in a capitalist economic system can be reduced significantly through the conscious coordination of interrelated activities. As Demsetz (1997, p. 28) has observed, commenting on recent developments in neoclassical theory.

> 'the focus in this effort has led to the neglect of information problems that do not involve agency relationships. These are associated with planning in a world in which the future is highly uncertain, and they include problems of product choice, investment and marketing policies, and scope of operations'.

Although Demsetz's comment is in the context of planning in relation to interdependent privately owned firms, social ownership makes it all the more possible to coordinate the interrelated activities of firms through negotiation and cooperation. Indeed, the process of negotiated coordination makes it possible to combine the *ex ante* adjustment classically associated with economic planning (Dobb, 1955, 1960) and the *ex post* adjustment classically associated with market forces and the invisible hand. Extra-firm institutions allocate capital according to the criteria they have evolved, taking account of known inter-dependencies, but they are path-dependent learning organisations able to revise the criteria they use and improve their competence in applying them (Adaman & Devine, 1997).

This discussion of a new perspective on entrepreneurship, that of participatory entrepreneurship, has embraced both the firm, as the institution within which entrepreneurial activity results in innovative output, and the extra-firm processes and institutions that select across firms and allocate capital for future entrepreneurial activity. The perspective is one of an evolutionary process, based on trial and error and selection, that fully recognises the inherent uncertainty associated with entrepreneurial and innovative activity. We have sought to examine both the ways in which generalized participation might be achieved and the advantages of generalised participation in both parts of the evolutionary process. In our view, it is important to emphasise that firm and extra-firm processes are inseparably linked. Participation at the level of the firm alone, with selection and allocation left to market forces, is inevitably subject to the coercion of expected profitability as the sole criterion for decision-making. This is the fallacy of market socialism (Adaman & Devine, 1996, 1997; Devine, 1992).

The central concept of our system of participatory entrepreneurship is that of decision-making through a process of negotiated coordination between those who will be affected by the outcome, the social owners. However, innovation disrupts existing patterns, has differential effects on different groups. Is it not likely that those who will be *prima facie* adversely affected by potential innovations will seek to block them, thus imparting a conservative bias to the system? More generally, what if negotiation fails to result in agreement? Furthermore, are there not likely to be power imbalances, enabling some groups, perhaps the more forceful and articulate, to impose their interests on the rest? These are real issues, to which we have sought to respond elsewhere (e.g. Devine, 1988, Adaman & Devine, 2001).

The classic distinction is between uncertainty that is due to unpredictable events or outcomes, including innovative attempts to do something that has not been done before, and uncertainty due to a form of economic organisation based on atomistic decision-making, so that decision-makers are unaware of decisions made simultaneously but which affect the outcome of their own decision (Devine, 1988; Dobb, 1960; Koopmans, 1957). We are grateful to an anonymous referee for reminding us of these issues.

In summary, we have argued that social owners should be represented on decision-making bodies in proportion to the degree to which they are affected and we have suggested ways in which this might be determined. We believe that a process of negotiated coordination has a dynamic that makes for agreement, since it encourages people to be aware of the interests of others as well as of their own interests. However, although we favour consensual decision-making, if agreement cannot be reached decisions would be made through an agreed formal voting procedure. We are fully conscious of the fact that the personal resources available to people when participating in social life differ and are shaped by their lifetime experience. It is for this reason that we have argued for the abolition of the social (not the functional) division of labour, so that everyone has access to the different types of self-developmental experience necessary to enable real as opposed to merely formal participation. We envisage movement towards a participatory society as a slow process involving continuous struggle over the distribution of ownership, power and life experiences. However, while aware of these problems, we are equally aware of the far greater problems and injustices in capitalist societies that arise from the unequal distribution of power and the fact that conflicts of interest are resolved by the privileged position of privately owned capital and the coercion of market forces. There remains the question of motivation. Within a capitalist economic system it is perhaps not unreasonable to assume that people in their economic lives act primarily in the expectation of financial gain. However, there is a substantial body of theoretical and empirical work which suggests that even in capitalist economies human motivation cannot be reduced to the single dimension of financial gain (see e.g. Bowles, 1998; Hodgson, 1998b; Margolis, 1982; Sen, 1977; Solow, 1994). Furthermore, the motivation of financial gain is not at all obviously the prime mover in relation to entrepreneurial activity in the capitalist firm. The desire for achievement, or self-realisation, or even the concept of 'self-competition' (Khalil, 1997) may be sufficient motivation. Of course, if access to capital, to the means for engaging in entrepreneurial activity and therefore to the opportunity to seek achievement or self-realisation from such activity, is allocated according to the sole criterion of the expected profitability of the activity, then a bias is imparted to the type of entrepreneurial activity that will be undertaken. As we have seen, Baumol has argued that the allocation of entrepreneurial effort across different activities will depend on the structure of rewards attached to those activities. In an economic system based on social ownership, generalised participation and negotiated coordination, with a reward system structured accordingly, the desire for achievement and self-realisation would be directed towards those activities that were judged by the communities affected to be socially productive, based on the criteria that they had themselves established. Furthermore, the motivations not associated with personal financial gain already present in capitalist economic systems are likely to be greatly strengthened in a participatory economic system. Finally, generalised participation would create a framework and an ethos, a moral community, in which responsibility and accountability to others is part of the generally accepted underlying assumptions on the basis of which people engage in social, including economic, life.

To sum up, it is argued that entrepreneurial and innovative activity cannot only thrive in a participatory economic system based on social ownership and negotiated coordination, but can contribute more effectively to human well-being in such a system than in a capitalist economic system based on private property. The criteria for success would be defined by the pluralistic interests constituting the relevant community, and entrepreneurial activity would be embedded in the activities of those who would be affected by it. Much experience has been gained and much research has been undertaken on various. 'It is often assumed that an economy of private enterprise has an automatic bias towards innovation, but this is not so. It has a bias only towards profit' (Hobsbawm, 1969, p. 40). Participatory schemes at different levels. This has recently been primarily at the micro level (see e.g. Levine & Tyson, 1990; Winther & Marens, 1997), but earlier experience at the macro level should not be forgotten (Crouch & Dore, 1990; Schmitter & Lehmbruch, 1979). In a sense these studies represent tentative acknowledgements of the interrelationship between participatory cooperation and participation in defining the criteria of success. What has been missing in these approaches, in our view, has been a clear recognition that participation at the micro and the macro levels must be seen as part of a single participatory process if their full potential is to be realised. The further exploration of these issues constitutes a rich agenda for future research.

Categorization of Theories of the Entrepreneurship

There is a categorization, the different writers on entrepreneurship in terms of the following dimensions of the theory of entrepreneurship:

- Market discussed
- What is forecasted by the Entrepreneur
- Number of forecasts made by the Entrepreneur
- Action taken by Entrepreneur
- Entrepreneur's Perception of Risk
- Cause of Entrepreneurial Profit
- Effect of Entrepreneurship on Equilibration of Economy

Summary

- There are different theories contributed by various personalities. There are economic theory, socio-cultural theory, psychological theory, and managerial theory of entrepreneurship.

- Schumpeter, Mcclelland, Peter Drucker, Harbinson are some of the contributors on entrepreneurship theories.
- Neoclassical School, Austrian School, Early Schumpeterian Entrepreneur, The Kirznerian Entrepreneur, Competence Theory of Firm, and Participatory Entrepreneurship as a new approach are also discussed elaborately in this chapter.

Self-learning Activity

Try to answer the following questions on your own:

1. Write short notes on: (*a*) Psychological Theory of Entrepreneurship; (*b*) Managerial theory of Entrepreneurship.
2. Discuss about Neoclassical School?
3. Explain Competence Theory of Firm?

5

Forms of Business Enterprises

Legal Forms of Business Organization

Business undertakings can be organized as public or private form of ownership. From the point of view of private organization or ownership, there are four forms of organizations for a business unit. It may be organized by an individual as sole proprietorship, by mutual agreement of two or more persons as partnership or by an association of persons who form a cooperative society for specific purpose, or else it may be organized by a number of persons as Joint Stock Company or Corporation. The law prescribes a variety of forms of business ownerships the choice of which depends upon size, type and objectives of individual functions and goals critical to the success of the organization formed.

For business purpose, the chief forms of private ownership or organizations are:

1. Sole proprietorship (ownership by one individual)
2. Partnership (ownership by two or more people)
3. Corporation (ownership by the shareholders)
4. Cooperatives (by, for and of the members)

Characteristics of an Ideal Form of Organization

In choosing a particular form of organization, an entrepreneurship will try to find out how far his requirements will be met by a particular form of organization. He/she will generally consider the following factors while making this type of assessment:

1. *Ease of formation:* An ideal form of organization is one, which can be brought into existence with the least difficulty. A good form of

organization, as judged from the point of view of ease of formation, is one that involves the least expense in formation and minimum legal formalities.

2. *Ease of raising capital:* Where a large amount of capital is needed, it is desirable to ensure that investors in the business concerned are assure of safety of investment, fair return on investment and the transferability of investment.
3. *Limited liability:* From the point of view of risk, the entrepreneur will naturally prefer limited liability. This means that in case of insolvency or winding up, the owner or owners will be held responsible only up to the amount of capital agreed to be contributed by them.
4. *Direct relationship between ownership control and management:* The right of an individual or a group of individuals represents ownership of a business. As a rule, the control should lie where the ownership lies. This will ensure that the management will take active interest in the efficient running of the enterprise.
5. *Flexibility of operation:* A good form of organization offers the maximum flexibility and adaptability to situations.
6. *Continuity or stability:* An ideal form of organization enjoys uninterrupted existence over a long period of time.
7. *Retention of business secrets:* The entrepreneur will also have to be careful to ensure that the form of organization chosen by him will allow the vital business secrets to be retained without being leaked out to the competitors.
8. *Freedom from state regulation:* Various forms of organizations are exposed to varying degrees of control and regulations by the state. Where the extent of regulations by the government is considerable, the enterprise may have to spend considerable amount of time, money and energy in complying with legal formalities and instructions.
9. *Low tax burden:* Various forms of organizations are assessed to income tax on different bases. Obviously other things being equal, the ideal form of organization will be that which will attract the minimum amount of tax liability.

It will be naïve to expect all the above features in any one form of organization. No single form can be called ideal for each lacks in one criteria or the other.

SOLE PROPRIETORSHIP

It is a form of business ownership in which a single individual assumes all the risk of operating the business, owns its assets, controls and uses any profit that is made. This form is known also as individual or single proprietorship, sole ownership or individual enterprise.

The individual may run the business alone or take the help of the members of the family or may obtain the assistance of employees. The owner drives the total benefit and assumes the risk to which the business is exposed. In the eyes of the law there is no distinction between the business and individual private affair, meaning that the law recognizes the individual and the business as being one and the same. This business is very common form of ownership carried out in different areas where the capital required is small and the risk is not quite heavy.

Salient Features

The salient features of this form of business organization are as follows:

1. *Single ownership:* The business is owned by a single individual who finances, controls and manages the business and consequently enjoys the profits or suffers losses solely and exclusively.
2. *Owner-manager:* Ownership and management of the business concern rests in the hands of the sole proprietor who enjoys full control over the business.
3. *No separate legal entity:* The sole proprietorship firm has any separate legal identity of its own as distinct from its owner. Both are treated as one and the same in the eyes of the law.
4. *Undivided risk:* The question of sharing the profits or losses of the business by another person other than the sole owner does not arise and the proprietor bears the risks all by himself/herself.
5. *Unlimited liability:* In case of losses the liability of the sole owner is unlimited and his personal property may also be attached, if needed, to discharge the debts incurred in running the business.
6. *Freedom from government control:* Except for the permission required to be obtained from the legal authorities, this form of organization has virtually no government control and is free from government regulation.

Advantages

1. *Ease and low cost of formation and dissolution:* It is easy to form a sole proprietorship because the legal formalities or other complicated procedures required are less and if all debts of the business are paid and the businessman is not willing to carry on or wants to change it to other form, it is easy to dissolve as was to form it.
2. *Direct motivation and personal care:* In this form of organization, all the profits of the business belong to one person and he faces every loss. This gives greater incentive to the owner to take personal interest in his business and manage it most efficiently.

3. *Freedom and promptness in action:* In matters of business dealing, the sole proprietor can take his own decisions and there is no question to his authority. This type of freedom of action promotes initiatives and self reliance. As there is no need to consult other person, the sole proprietor can take prompt decisions.
4. *Business secrecy:* In this type of business organization, it is easy to maintain the secrecy of business. Since confidential information is the key to success for a competitive business, it is unlikely that owner will leak the information vital to the business.
5. *Social desirability:* From the social point of view, the sole proprietorship is desirable as it ensures that too much wealth does not concentrate in the hands of few. It may be one of the ways in which equitable distribution of the wealth is ensured.
6. *Absolute control:* The sole proprietor has direct and absolute control over his business affairs and he is free to act or manage the business in his own chosen way. His control on all business operations is complete which minimizes outside interference or influence.
7. *Flexibility in operations:* Since the sole proprietor does not need to consult any one or is not obliged to discuss with anybody in regard to his business operations there is greater scope for flexibility. This form of ownership allows for maximum flexibility as the sole owner can, at his will, change the business operations to suit the changing business conditions.
8. *Minimum government control:* Any central or state law, except the general laws of contract and sale of goods, does not regulate this form of business ownership. Consequently, there is little interference or control by government in day to day business affairs. The sole trader is not required to submit any profit and loss account to the government.
9. *Personal touch:* Customer satisfaction and worker's motivation are two most important factors that contribute to the success of business. By paying personal attention to the customers and by maintaining an intimate personal touch with the workers, the sole proprietor will boost the business prospect as well as his own personal image which helps to make him flourish beyond his own expectations.

Disadvantages

1. *Limited resources and size:* In this type of concerns, the resources (capital, human, material, informational) are limited. As only one person is responsible for the business these resources are limited to his capacity.
2. *Unlimited liability:* The sole proprietorship will be liable for all debts of the business. At times of loss and bankruptcy, if the business assets are

not sufficient to satisfy the obligations or debts of creditors, his personal and real property may be required to pay off. This indicates how the owner is committing his personal assets for the business failure.

3. *Limited managerial skills:* A sole proprietor may not be expected to perform every function like purchasing, selling, accounting, hiring and other necessary functions which may lead to business suffer from not being managed properly. Due to limited financial capability he may not be able to afford to employ trained and professional managers thus depriving the business specialization and expertise in the field of balanced management.
4. *Uncertain future:* This kind of business suffers from uncertain future that means there is no stability or lack of continuity. This business may come to an end if the owner cannot continue the business due to death, insanity, imprisonment or bankruptcy.

PARTNERSHIP

This form of organization represents the second in the evolution of the forms of business organization. It grew essentially to meet the requirements of expanding business which calls for more capital, increased risk, and more managerial ability that were considered as limitations of the individual proprietorship.

In Ethiopian as per the commercial code of 1960, Article 211, reads as, "A partnership agreement is defined as a contract whereby two or more persons who intend to join together, make contribution for the purpose of carrying out activities of an economic nature and of participating in the profit and loses arising out there of if any".

Characteristics of Partnership

From the above definition of partnership, which is almost similar in all countries' regulations, the following general characteristics can be indicated:

1. *Plurality of persons:* This form of business requires the existence of two or more persons entering into contract which is an agreement between parties known as Memorandum of Association or Article of Partnership deed.
2. *Contractual relationship:* Partnership comes into existence by mutual agreement which stipulates the contractual relationship between the partners. The memorandum lays down the terms and conditions of partnership and the rights, duties and obligations of partners.
3. *Capital contribution:* In this form of business, every partner shall make a contribution which may be in money, debts, other property or skills. The contribution that is to be made for the business shall be equal unless otherwise agreed.

4. *Management:* Every partner has the right to take an active part in the management of the firm's affairs. But the partnership agreement may provide the pattern of managing indicating how the management activity is shared among the different partners according to experience and knowledge.
5. *Duration:* The partnership firm legally comes to an end if any of the partners withdraws or dies or is no longer able under the law to be partner or declared bankrupt.
6. *Unlimited liability:* The liability of each partner of the firm is unlimited in respect of the firm's debts. The liability of the partner is joint, in the sense that the creditors can recover their dues from the property of any or all partners in case the firm's assets are insufficient.
7. *Agency relationship:* The partner will be liable for the faults and wrongful acts of a co-partner in the course of the firm's business while acting for the business. Since every partner has the right to take part in the management activity, when acting on his given specified areas, every partner has the authority to act on behalf of his fellow partners and the firm in the ordinary course of business. Thus, he is an agent of the firm and other partners.
8. *Utmost good faith and trust:* There must be highest standards of honesty among the partners. Partnership agreement is based on mutual confidence and trust of the partners. The partner must, therefore, be just and honest to other partners.
9. *No separate legal entity:* The partnership firm has an independent legal existence apart from the persons who constitute it. In the eyes of the law, like that of sole proprietorship, there is no distinction between the partners and the firm.
10. *Restriction on transfer of interest:* A partner cannot transfer his share or give his ownership to outsiders without the consent of other partners. In other words, no partner is entitled to bring in another person as partner without the permission of existing partners.
11. *Unanimity of consent:* No changes may be made in the nature of business and no partner can act out of the specified way or any partner cannot make any decisions without the consent or agreement of all the partners.

Types of Partnership

There are two types of partnership, namely:

1. General partnership and
2. Special partnership

The basic difference between the two is that while the former has unlimited liability and the latter type allow for a limited liability to its partners. Under each category there are other types of partnership as well, which are as under:

General Partnership

1. *Partnership-at-will:* In this form, no stipulation is made as to when and how the partnership will come to an end. In the absence of any specific provision in partnership deed about the duration of the partnership, a partner can pull out of the firm after giving certain number of days notice to the firm withdrawing from the partnership or terminating the Deed of Agreement.
2. *Particular partnership:* This type of partnership specifies a fixed period of time for completion of a particular business venture and after achieving the objective or after expiry of stipulated period, it automatically becomes dissolved.
3. *Ordinary joint venture:* This, in fact, is a temporary partnership arrangement between two or more persons to carry out a particular business venture. After accomplishing the tasks, the joint venture comes to an end. In joint venture, generally the right of management is delegated to one of the partners who are accountable to other members. While in a general partnership, all the partners are entitled to carry out the business; in a joint venture all the members do not enjoy the right of implied agency.

Special partnership

1. *Limited partnership:* In this form there is at least one partner whose liability is unlimited and one or more partners whose liability is limited to the extent of capital contributed. The duties and obligations of the limited partner are:
   - (*a*) The limited partner is not entitled to take an active part in the management of the business and as such cannot bind by his acts.
   - (*b*) He cannot withdraw any part of his capital nor can he transfer his interest to others without the consent of the general partner.
   - (*c*) The general partner who has unlimited liability need not take the consent of the limited partner to admit a new partner into the business.
   - (*d*) The death or insolvency of the limited partner does not affect the business or the limited partnership.
2. *Special joint ventures:* In this form, the partners have limited liability and they will terminate after accomplishing the task for which they are created.

Kinds of Partners

Partner of a firm may be classified into the following categories:

1. *Active Partner:* A person who takes an active part in the conduct of business and manages its affairs is called an active partner or working partner.
2. *Sleeping partner or dormant partner:* He who does not take any part or active interest in the conduct of business is called sleeping or dormant partner. He only contributes a limited capital and his liability is also limited to that extent.
3. *Nominal or ostensible partner:* A nominal partner is one who does not invest any money nor takes any share in the profits but he only lends his name to the firm. He does not take any active part in the business.

IDEAL PARTNERSHIP

A partnership survives and succeeds on the strength of its members in terms of morality, good faith and mutual trust. In order to be called an ideal partnership it must have the following essential characteristics:

1. *Mutual trust and good faith:* There must be proper understanding and mutual trust between the partners.
2. *Common approach:* The partners must have a like-minded common approach to all the business problems. There must be cooperation and coordination among the partners for smooth running of business.
3. *Adequate capital:* Both the long-term and short-term capital requirements must be met by the partners alleviating the need for borrowing from outsiders.
4. *Written agreement:* In order to avoid disputes and misunderstandings among the partners at a later stage, the partnership agreement must be reduced to writing.
5. *Registration:* Although registration is not compulsory, an ideal form of partnership must get itself registered as otherwise it cannot enforce its rights against outsiders in the courts.

Advantage of Partnership

1. *Ease of organization:* Except some formalities like that of proprietorship, the partnership is quite easily formed. All that is required is an agreement among partners. The initial expenses are less and legal formalities are simple.
2. *Large financial and managerial resources:* In this form of organization compared to sole proprietorship, the capital to be raised will be more because the financial resources of the two or more persons will be available and this will make the business to enjoy high credit standing and get more credit.

3. *Personal supervision:* Partners look after the business personally and guard against the wastage and other inefficiencies because they are initially interested in the success of the business and also known if there is any failure on their part they may put even their private property in jeopardy.
4. *Reduced risk:* The losses incurred by the firm be shared by all partners and hence the share of loss of each partner will be less than in case of sole proprietorship.
5. *Flexibility:* The partnership firm is not subjected to government interference or regulation in the day-to-day functioning. Hence, partners are free to change the line of business or the place of business at their will.
6. *Democratic functioning:* In a partnership firm every partner has a right to participate in the decision-making process or management of the firm irrespective of his status based on capital contribution.
7. *Better public relations:* The reputation of a sole proprietor rests on one person whereas all the partners of a partnership firm can pool in their resourcefulness and goodwill to boost up the image and business prospects of the firm.
8. *Tax liability:* A partnership firm is not subjected to double taxation. Either it is assessed for tax as individual or its income is taxable in the hands of the partners.

Disadvantage of Partnership

1. *Unlimited liability:* If the assets of the partnership are not sufficient to meet the obligations, the creditors may choose to sue any or all to satisfy the debts.
2. *Risk of implied agency:* A dishonest or incompetent partner may make, by his acts, misjudgments or faults, the firm in difficulties because his acts would bind the firm and the remaining partners.
3. *Lack of harmony:* As every partner has equal voice in the management, everyone would try to assert his position and try to promote his personal interest and this may lead to internal frictions and misunderstandings.
4. *Lack of continuity:* The business can come to an end due to death, retirement or withdrawal of a partner for any reasons like dissatisfaction, bankruptcy or any serious disagreements.
5. *Non-transferability of interest:* Yet, another disadvantage in a partnership firm is that no partner can transfer his interest or get back his investment in business by selling off to outsiders whenever he wants without the consent of the other partners.

6. *Lack of public confidence:* A partnership firm is not legally bound to disclose its affairs and statements of accounts to general public. Since, even registration is not compulsory the firm is virtually free from government control or regulations. In absence of public scrutiny of its affairs or auditing of its accounts, public can have little confidence in the soundness of the firm and hence hesitate to deal with the firm in any way.

JOINT STOCK COMPANY (CORPORATION)

A joint stock company is essentially a group of persons coming together voluntarily to carry on certain business by organizing themselves into a single entity with a view to function as an artificial person in the eyes of the law.

Corporation as defined by Chief Justice Marshal: 'An artificial being, invisible, intangible and existing only in contemplation of law being the mere creature of law, it possesses only those properties, which the character/certificate of incorporation of its creation confers upon it'.

Features of Corporation

1. *Separate legal entity:* The right and privileges are given to it by its character, which is granted by the state in which it is incorporated, gives privileges to it. Thus, the corporation becomes the legal entity and is granted the right to manage its own affairs, the right to sue and be sued, and the right to own and dispose of property.
2. *Limited Liability:* Since the company has a separate legal entity, its debts are its own.
3. *Transferability of shares:* The shareholder of the business can transfer to others without consulting other shareholders.
4. *Perpetual existence:* The corporation can be dissolved in only three ways: (*a*) by court order; (*b*) by the approval of majority of the shareholders or: (*c*) by expiration of the corporate charter.
5. *Common seal:* A company, not being a natural person, cannot sign document for itself. The common seal with the name of the company engraved on it is, therefore, used as a substitute for its signature.
6. *Separation of ownership from management:* Here all the owners, large in number, do not have the opportunity of managing the day-to-day working of the company.

Corporate Structure

There are three groups that comprise the corporate structure:

1. The stockholders;
2. The Board of Directors; and
3. The officers of the corporation.

The stockholders are known as the owners of the corporation. They are the individuals who bought shares of stock that show the proof of ownership.

Group Rights of Shareholders

(*i*) The right to elect directors;

(*ii*) The right to vote and amend the by-laws;

(*iii*) The right to change the charter;

(*iv*) The right to vote on the disposal of corporate assets;

(*v*) The right to dissolve the corporation.

Individual Rights of Shareholders

(*i*) The right to buy, sell and transfer his/her stock;

(*ii*) The right to receive dividends in proportion to the number of shares owned;

(*iii*) The right to inspect and review the company's records;

(*iv*) The right to vote at stockholder's meeting;

(*v*) The right to receive evidence of ownership (stock certificates);

(*vi*) The right to sue officers and director for fraud;

(*vii*) The right to share in distribution of assets in event of dissolution.

Advantage of Corporation

1. *Financial Strength:* The Company can raise a large amount of capital by issuing shares. It can also attract capital from thousands of varying incomes. It can also expand as long as investors are willing to purchase additional shares of stock.
2. *Limited Liability:* The shareholders liability is limited to the extent of the face value of the shares held by him and his personal properties are not affected. The creditors cannot look beyond the assets of the corporation to settle their debts.
3. *Scope of expansion:* As large capital is invested, it would be possible to use up-to-date equipments and expensive machinery and carryout operations at large scale which leads to economies of scales, leading to higher profits.
4. *Stability:* The Company enjoys perpetual succession, which means that bankruptcy, insanity or death of a shareholder, change in management or owners etc., cannot affect the continuity of the company.
5. *Efficient and bolder management:* There is availability of managerial talent because the most efficient persons may be chosen as directors and if found unsatisfactory they can be fired. Since the persons who manage

the company have relatively smaller financial stakes, they will have an adventurous spirit and can undertake big risks needed to infuse innovation and success in the business.

6. *Diffused Risk:* The risk is spread over several members of the company and is reduced for each member, which helps the business in attracting more investors and to venture in new opportunities.
7. *Public confidence:* No company can keep its affairs or accounts secret because its existence, activities and even dissolution are governed by statutory laws. In fact, by advertising its records and business secrets it wins the confidence of the public.

Disadvantage of Corporation

1. *Difficulty of formation:* Before a company can start functioning, though vary from country to country there are numerous requirements of the law to be complied with. This form of organization requires huge amount of money and thus a large number of people have to be approached for raising the required capital.
2. *Lack of owner's personal interest:* These forms of organizations are managed by directors and paid officials and employees who may not be expected to have such an intense interest in the success of the business. Even the owners may be having only a small percentage of the total equity so they also do not put forth their maximum efforts.
3. *Delay in decision-making:* Decisions, especially on key issues, require consent of the general meting of the shareholders which may be then delayed because of the time interval between the meetings, difficulty of getting the required numbers of the members to pass the decision.
4. *Fraudulent management:* Though democratic in nature, but actually the management is concentrated in few hands who, if consist of dishonest persons, may resort to fraudulent practices and window dressing of accounts.
5. *Taxation:* These forms of organizations attract quite a large amount of taxation nearing to 35 per cent of the total profits.
6. *Lack of secrecy:* The publication of the financial reports of a corporation becomes a matter of public record. Therefore, the large corporation is unable to keep confidentiality in certain areas that they may not wish to reveal allowing competitors to alter their plans based on data disclosed.
7. *Expensive management:* A company is huge corporate body that has to necessarily employ a team of competent and professional managers to organize and manage its affairs. This increases the cost of expenses incurred.

COOPERATIVES

Definition

'A cooperative is an autonomous association of persons united voluntarily to meet their common economic, social and cultural needs and aspirations through a jointly-owned and democratically controlled enterprise'.

Explanation

The definition emphasizes the following characteristics of a cooperative:

(*a*) The cooperative is autonomous: that is, it is as independent of government and private firms as possible.

(*b*) It is 'an association of persons' this means that cooperatives are free to define 'persons' in any legal way they choose. Many primary cooperatives around the world choose only to admit individual human beings. Many other primary cooperatives admit 'legal persons', which in many jurisdictions includes companies, extending to them the same rights as any other member. Cooperatives at other than primary level are usually cooperatives whose members are other cooperative. In all case, the membership should decide how it wishes the cooperative to deal with this issue.

(*c*) 'The persons are united voluntary'. Membership in a cooperative should not be compulsory. Members should be free, within the purpose and resources of the cooperatives, to join or to leave.

(*d*) 'Members of a cooperative meet their common economic, social and cultural needs'. This part of the definition emphasizes that cooperatives are organized by their members, for their members. Member needs may be singular and limited, they may be diverse, they may be social and cultural as well as purely economic, but whatever the needs, they are the central purpose for which the cooperative exists. The term 'aspirations' here denotes strong desire or ambition for advancement.

(*e*) 'The cooperative is a jointly owned and democratically controlled enterprise'. This phrase emphasizes that ownership is distributed among members on a democratic basis. These two characteristics of ownership are particularly important in differentiating cooperatives from other kinds of organizations, such as capital-controlled firms. Each cooperative is also an 'enterprise' in the sense that it is an organized entity, normally functioning in the market place; it must strive to serve its members efficiently and effectively.

Cooperative Values

Cooperatives are based on the values of self-help, self-responsibility, democracy, equality, equity, and solidarity. In the tradition of their founders, cooperative members believe in the ethical values of honesty, openness, social responsibility, and caring for others.

BENEFITS OF COOPERATION

Economic Benefits

Cooperatives helps to rationalize distribution patterns, increase purchasing power and promote consumer protections, narrow the housing gap. They contribute to the modernization of small-scale production in agriculture, fisheries, handicrafts and industry. They ensure improved quality and greater volume of production and more efficient marketing of increased output. They stimulate productive capital formation among large number of individuals. In a wider sense, cooperative growth is an effective stimulant for economic growth.

Cooperatives are engaged in securing for their members services of various kinds at low costs. These may include services of various socio-economic activities in the consolidation of holdings, the establishment of irrigation schemes, the contouring of land, the procurement of technical knowledge, the administration of credit, the buying of fertilizers, pesticides, seeds, electricity, and machine services, of consumers, goods and services, the processing and marketing of produce, the provision of insurance, health and medical care or education.

Cooperation is also playing a vital role in checking the monopolistic tendencies.

The following is the list of economic advantages of cooperative organizations:

1. The substitution of the profit incentive in business by that of service to humanity or production for consumption. (In other words, priority is given to the satisfaction of human needs instead of greed of profits).
2. A more equitable distribution of wealth.
3. The breaking up of monopolies and trusts, which operate at expenses of consumer.
4. The increase of workman's purchasing power an real wages by giving him more and better goods for his money.
5. The reduction in cost of distributive system by:
   (i) elimination of unnecessary middlemen.
   (ii) removal of useless duplication of services.
   (iii) eradication of such practices as misleading advertisement and high pressure salesmanship.
   (iv) the elimination of fraudulent practices like adulteration, short weight, etc.

6. The rejection of accounting inaccuracies by encouraging frankness in business.
7. The more accurate correlation of demand and supply as a result of the greater certainty and regularity of consumer market.
8. Stabilization of employment, which will result from the regularity of demand and the absence of speculation.
9. The fair treatment of all labor and general improvement in employer-employee relations.
10. The training of people to spend wisely.

Social and Moral Benefits

Cooperation offers not only economic benefits to members but also confers a number of benefits to the society. This is so because the object of cooperation is to transform the member's condition in such a way that he makes his social life richer and happier.

The ultimate aim of cooperation is to develop men-men imbued with the spirit of self-help and mutual help in order that individually they may rise to a full personal life and collectively to full social life (Dr. Fauquet).

Modern life is full of social tensions: Urban *vs.* rural, consumer *vs.* producers, labor *vs.* capital, there are tensions with regard to religion, caste, language, state, race and occupation. Cooperatives tend to lessen these tensions and show all people how they can work together on common group.

The cooperative movement frees its members not only from usurers and profiteers, but also from themselves and their bad habits. It teaches them the virtues that are not always natural to them, such as, orderliness, foresight punctuality and a strict respect for engagements entered into. A cooperative order returns ownership of the means of production, in an indirect form, to the workers, and the class struggle is resolved.

It is the claims of the cooperators that it can be the principal means of bringing about in a peaceful manner social change of a fundamental nature, ushering in a social order non-exploitative, egalitarian, tolerant that harmonizes the dignity of the individual with the well-being of the community.

The social purposes of cooperation are more diverse than economic purposes. They may be to provide unique education in democracy, responsibility and toleration, to train for political power, to evolve an industrial relationship in which the element of authority is much more evenly distributed than in private business, to preserve a strong friendly or family spirit and a sense of pride and power which is impersonal, to encourage a general advance rather than the advance of particular individuals, to secure rations, constructive and unifying approaches to social and economic problems.

Cooperation teaches that man is his brother's keeper and that he can best lighten his own burden by lightening the burden of others, that he can achieve his own happiness only by including within the happiness of others. The cooperative movement is an exercise in fellowship, which seeks to end the exploitation of man by man. The movement teaches man and woman to rise above their own interests and to think in terms of general good.

Summary

- There are different forms of business organizations: sole proprietorship, partnership, corporation, cooperatives. They have advantages and disadvantages based on their nature of business operations and services.

Self-learning Activity

Try to answer the following questions on your own:

1. What are the types of partnership?
2. List out disadvantages of Corporation?
3. Describe cooperative form of enterprise?

6

Fundamental Steps to Entrepreneurial Venture

Meaning of Project

In the precise sense, a project presupposes commitment to tasks to be performed with well defined objectives, schedules and budget.

It can be defined as *a scientifically evolved work plan devised to achieve a specific objective within a specified period of time.*

PROJECT IDENTIFICATION AND CLASSIFICATION

PROJECT IDENTIFICATION

Meaning

Project identification is concerned with the collection, compilation and analysis of economic data for the eventual purpose of locating possible opportunities for investment and with the development of the characteristics of such opportunities.

Opportunities, according of Drucker (1955), are of three kinds: additive, complementary and break-through.

- Additive opportunities are those opportunities which enable the decision-maker to better utilize the existing resources without in any way involving a change in the character of business.
- Complementary opportunities involve the introduction of new ideas and as such do lead to a certain amount of change in the existing structure.
- Break-through opportunities, on the other hand, involve fundamental changes in both the structure and character of business.

Factors to be considered for Project Identification

Input, Output and Social Costs and Benefits

Project identification can not be complete without identifying the characteristics of a project. Every project has three basic dimensions — inputs, outputs and social costs and benefits.

The *input characteristics* define what the project will consume in terms of raw materials, energy, manpower, finance and organizational set up. The nature and magnitude of these inputs must be determined in order to make the input characteristics explicit.

The *output characteristics* of a project define what the project will generate in the form of goods and services, employment, revenue etc. The quantity and quality of all these outputs should be clearly specified.

In addition to inputs and outputs, *every project has an impact on the society*. It inevitably affects the current equilibriums of the demand and supply in the economy. It is necessary to evaluate carefully the sacrifice which the society will be required to make and the benefits that will accrue to the society from a given project.

Internal constraints

Internal constraints arise on account of the limitations of the management system which will eventually be responsible for the implementation of a project. The internal constraints for the entrepreneurs while venturing the projects comprise inputs, resources and outputs. These are narrated as under:

- Entrepreneurs, while implementing the projects, rely more on outside consultants for preparation of feasibility reports in the formulation of their projects. The limitation on the part of entrepreneurs to provide inbuilt project services in the form of preparing feasibility reports is an important internal constraint in the early implementation of the project.
- For early implementation of projects within the budgeted cost and time schedule, all the entrepreneurs cannot develop independent project management systems, organization structure, network analysis and other elements. In such a situation, the entrepreneur's inherent internal constraints are developing well equipped project management strategies and tools which implementing them.
- Project goals and objectives lay down the main purpose for which an organization exists. Practically, project management team is not much involved with the determination of project objectives. Certainly, this will be another internal constraint for the project team to achieve the unrealistic objective which is decided by the top management personnel of the business.

- The availability of the necessary internal project elements and resources are physical and non-physical resources. The physical resources include finance, personnel, inventories and facilities. The non-physical resources are patents, secret processes, unique experiences and skills. Both physical and non-physical resources are the important constraints for the entrepreneurs to make available at a time the project implementation is in progress.

External Constraints

The external constraints are also another important constraint for the entrepreneurs who venture into project implementation. The important external constraints are the project environments comprising things, people and situations outside a project constitute the environment of the project. The other tangible environment factors are namely social taboos, government policies and the state of capital market. These are described as under:

- The external environment factors like nature, size, location and the extent of project are the important limiting factors for the entrepreneurs when the project does not conform to the socio-economic objectives of the country.
- Government policies and regulations are another major hurdle for the entrepreneurs while implementing the projects. They are mainly in the form of delay in giving approval to the entrepreneurs in the medium of industrial licensing, foreign collaboration approval, CCI clearance, environmental clearance, foreign exchange permit, capital goods approval and import goods clearance.
- Financial institutions, banks are the important financial source for the entrepreneurs while financing their projects. The financial institution's and commercial bank's cumbersome procedures and documentation system are important external constraints for the entrepreneurs in the form of delay in financing the projects.

Project Objectives

Project objective is an important element in the project planning cycle. Project objectives are concerned with defining in a precise manner what the project is expected to be achieved and to provide a measure of performance for the project as a whole. The essential requirements for project objectives are:

- Specific, not general
- Not overly complex
- Measurable, tangible and verifiable
- Realistic and attainable

- Established within resource bounds
- Consistent with resource available or anticipated
- Consistent with organizational plans, policies and procedures.

Project objectives are divided into two categories, namely, 'retentive' objectives and 'acquisitive' objectives.

Retentive objectives are concerned with the retention and preservation of resources like money, time, energy, equipment, and skills.

Acquisitive objectives, on the other hand, involve acquisition of resources or attaining status that the organization or its managers do not have.

Project objectives are also economical and social in nature. The economical objectives of the project are in the form of profit-oriented. The social project objectives are service-oriented.

Desk Research and Techno-Economic Survey

Desk research and techno-economic survey are two important techniques of project identification. Desk research implies the collection and use of information from published sources like journals, magazines, reports, etc. Techno-economic survey is an investigation conducted by a team of experts for identifying the industrial development potential of an area.

Data and product identification may be obtained from the following sources:

- Industrial potential surveys
- Lead bank survey reports
- New process/product development in research laboratories
- Literature on industries within the country and abroad
- Import/Export statistics
- Profitability studies of selected industries
- Studies on price and shortage of certain commodities

Project Life Cycle

Like human beings, projects also have a life cycle. Project life cycle consists of three main stages.

The pre-investment Phase

This is the first phase in the life of a project. It is primarily concerned with objective formulation, demand forecasting, selection of optimal strategy, evaluation of input characteristics, projections of the financial profile, and if necessary cost-benefit analysis and ultimately the pre-investment appraisal. The project idea is developed into an investment proposition during this phase.

The Construction Phase

This phase begins after the investment decision is taken. Resources are invested during this phase in building the basic assets of the project, which can in due course be utilized to achieve the project objectives. The assets may in the nature of land and buildings, plant and machinery, ancillary accommodation, communication services, control systems and marketing organization. In projects not involving the use of plant and machinery, the construction phase may merely consist of developing necessary manpower resources. Thus, the construction phase consists mainly of developing the infrastructure for the project. It is one time effort.

The Normalization Phase

This phase starts after the trial run of the project framework developed during the construction phase. It involves routine procedures which are performed in a cyclic order. The primary objective of this phase is to produce the goods and services for which the project was established. For this purpose, a provision has to be made for raw materials and other consumables. These can be determined by analyzing the process cycle identifying the sequence of process operations. Projects which do not involve production of goods do not require raw materials but only supplies or supporting goods needed to sustain the project process. Thus, the assets created during the construction phase are utilized during the normalization phase.

PROJECT CLASSIFICATION

The project classifications are explained below.

Quantifiable and Non-quantifiable projects

Quantifiable projects are those in which a plausible quantitative assessment of benefits can be made. Non-quantifiable projects are those where such an assessment is not possible. Projects concerned with industrial development, power generation, and mineral development are forming part of quantifiable projects. The non-quantifiable projects category comprises health, education and defense.

Sectoral Projects

A project may fall in the following sectors:

- Agriculture and Allied Sector
- Irrigation and Power Sector
- Industry and Mining Sector
- Transport and Communication Sector
- Social Services Sector
- Miscellaneous Sector

The sector classification of projects is quite useful for resource allocation at macro levels.

Techno-Economic Projects

Techno-economic projects classification includes factors intensity-oriented classification, causation-oriented classification and magnitude-oriented classification:

(*a*) *Factor intensity-oriented classification:* The factor intensity is used as base for classification of projects such as capital-intensive or labour-intensive which depends upon the large scale investments in plant and machinery or human resources.

(*b*) *Causation-oriented classification:* The causation-oriented projects are determined based on its causes namely demand-based or raw material based projects. The non-availability of certain goods or services and consequent demand for such goods or services or the availability of certain raw materials, skills or other inputs is the dominant reason for starting the project.

(*c*) *Magnitude-oriented classification:* The size of investments forms the basis for magnitude oriented projects. Projects may thus be classified based on the investment such as large scale, medium scale and small scale projects.

United Nations and its specialized agencies use the International Standard Industrial Classification (ISIC) of all economic activities in collection and compilation of economic data. Economic activities are under this classification grouped into ten divisions, which are sub-divided into ninety sub-divisions. The divisions are:

- Division 0 — Agriculture, Forestry, Hunting and Fishing
- Division 1 — Mining and Quarrying
- Division 2 & 3 — Manufacturing
- Division 4 — Construction
- Division 5 — Electricity, Gas, Water and Sanitary Services
- Division 6 — Commerce
- Division 7 — Transport, Storage and Communication
- Division 8 — Services
- Division 9 — Activities not adequately described

Financial Institutions Classification

Financial Institutions classify the projects according to their age and experience and the purpose for which the project is being taken up.

They are as follows:

- New Projects
- Expansion Projects
- Modernization Projects
- Diversification Projects

The projects listed above are generally profit-oriented and the services-oriented projects are classified as under:

- Welfare Projects
- Service Projects
- Research and Development Projects
- Educational Projects.

Strategic Decision-Making Process for Entrepreneurial Venture

The strategic decision-making process for undertaking entrepreneurial venture is comprised of the following fundamental steps:

Step 1: Develop a Basic Business Idea

This step calls for identifying the broadest needs and wants of customers that will be a base for the development of product lines and product ranges. The basics of this step is that it is based on the prevailing needs and wants of customers and it consists of the following three sub-steps:

1. Creating business ideas
2. Study and process the ideas
3. Select the best idea

Creating Business Idea

It is mainly concerned with generating product ideas that would be profitable if capitalized. It is like identifying opportunities based on the wants and needs of consumers or else it is searching for markets that arise for new products and services. The ideas are generated from various sources and put for preliminary evaluation and testing.

Idea Generation Methods

Methods to generate new ideas include:

1. *Focus groups:* A group of individuals discuss and provide information in a structured format to arrive at new business ideas. Here a group that is made up of individuals is created as a structured part of the overall organizational hierarchy to obtain new ideas.
2. *Brainstorming:* It is a group method for obtaining new ideas and business solutions. This method is extensively used for generating ideas for new product packing and distribution. The groups are organized for sitting

together and stimulate greater creativity by exchange of mutual experiences and participating in the discussions. Different group of stakeholders will be organized and think hard to generate ideas. What makes this method different from the former is, it may include informal groups that are not part of the organizational structure.

3. *Check list:* The new ideas for the business are developed based on discussions on list of related issues. A specific area of discussions is listed by entrepreneur and a list of questions, suggestions and statements are developed for in-depth discussions and arrive at a business idea. For instance if a burning issue in a given time interval turns out to be environmental protection, entrepreneurs may look towards producing a new product that is an eco-friendly. An issue that is meant for discussion can take many forms.

4. ***Problem inventory analysis***: It is a method of obtaining new ideas and solutions for business by focusing on the problems. In this case the individual are used similar to focus groups for generating new business ideas. The group discusses category of products. The group is given the problems that are commonly felt by consumers, dealers, transporters and general public and based on the identified problems, product ideas that provide solutions are hallucinated.

Study and Process the Idea

Once the business ideas are lacerated, study, screening, and testing of these ideas are done based on the entrepreneur's own experience or with the help of experts in the field.

While evaluating the points to be considered are:

1. ***Technical feasibility*** that is the possibility of production with the available skill and technology.

2. ***Commercial viability*** of the idea based on cost and profitability. It evaluates the tradeoff between cost and income to judge the attractiveness of a business idea.

Selecting the Best Idea

After the technical feasibility and commercial viability of a given business idea has been proved, not every business idea represents the best opportunity. Therefore, the prospective entrepreneur performs selection based on the following criterions:

1. Product where the entrepreneur has firsthand manufacturing experience.

2. Product where the entrepreneur has the marketing work experience with the particular product.

3. Product which is perceived as highly profitable.
4. Product where government has banned imports
5. Product where the export demand is high and with good margins.
6. The raw material requirement of an existing nearby big unit.
7. Products on which government declares subsidies incentives, other industrial/financial benefits.
8. Products where there is demand growth.
9. Products that are easy to distribute

Step 2: Analysis of Internal and External Environment (SWOT Analysis)

Entrepreneurial environments are critical to the creation of favorable atmosphere to the development of entrepreneurs. Entrepreneurship environment refers to the various facets within which enterprises have to operate in. These entrepreneurial environments are most rationally divided into two major parts: internal and external environment. Analysis of internal and external environment follows after the selection of the best business idea. The major objective of this step is to identify the threats and opportunities faced by the prospective entrepreneur in the light of the strengths and weaknesses that are apparent, hence the name SWOT analysis. The two major parts of this step are:

- Scanning the External Environment
- Assessing the Internal Environment

Scanning the External Environment

By and large, entrepreneurship is influenced by environments created by the external forces. These external forces are demarcated as macro and micro environmental forces.

Macro Environment

Macro environment is the type of environment that is not specific to a given entrepreneur or company. It has universal application to all the entrepreneurs in a given country irrespective of the type of entrepreneurs. Macro environmental force more or less include the following environments:

(*a*) ***Economic environment:*** related to factors of production and distribution like economic stage, economic system, economic policies, economic indices (per capita income), infrastructural factors, living standards, etc.

(*b*) ***Socio-cultural environment:*** related to social attitude and cultural factors. Demographic factors, social concern and attitude, education level, aspirations and values, consumer motives etc.

(c) ***Political-legal environment:*** related to government regulation and consumer protection, like political system, consumer protection, taxation laws, quality leadership, etc.

(d) ***Technological environment:*** It relates to the knowledge applied and equipments used, like source of technology, communication and infrastructure facilities, and patent protection.

Micro Environment

Micro environmental forces on the other side are forces that are specific to companies or entrepreneurs. It includes forces like customers, suppliers, competitors, intermediaries, etc.

Sources of Environmental Scanning

- Formal Sources: Research studies, consultants
- Secondary Sources: Publications, magazines, books
- Internal Sources: MIS records, co-employees
- External Sources: Marketing intermediaries, customers, suppliers etc.
- Spy

Assessing the Internal Environment

This is the second part of SWOT analysis. It identifies the weaknesses and strengths that are internal in nature. In sensible terms it is assessing the expertise, resources, abilities, skills, costs, organizational structure and culture, manufacturing techniques etc.

Step 3: Developing Feasibility Study (DECIDE GO/NO GO)

After weaknesses and strengths have been identified in terms of the prevailing opportunities and threats, feasibility study can be undertaken.

If the basic business idea appears to be a feasible business opportunity, the process should be continued.

Feasibility study should focus on the following:

- ***Marketing feasibility:*** Total demand size, growth rate of market.
- ***Technical feasibility:*** Technical know how of production, cost of acquisition.
- ***Physical resource feasibility:*** Availability of raw materials and suppliers.
- ***Financial feasibility:*** Availability of adequate capital, and cost of funds.
- ***Time feasibility:*** Duration required to operationalize the business and make expected profit.

If feasibility fails, no go is the option.

If feasibility test results positive, go is the option.

Step 4: Generating Business Plan

After testing the feasibility of business idea, a business plan is prepared. A business plan transforms the idea in to how it will be applied and projects the likely results to be attained. It leads the transformation of idea into reality. It is used to convince the shareholders and creditors for raising capital.

To be successful, the business plan must begin with the real foundation of any business — the customers. Too often, entrepreneurs fall victim to marketing myopia, concentrating solely on their product or service and waiting for the world to beat a pate to their doors to buy it. Linking the purposeful action of strategic planning to an entrepreneur's little ideas can produce results that will shape the future.

Specifically, a business plan performs the following activities:

(*a*) Develops the proposed mission, objectives, strategies and policies.

(*b*) Defines the proposed enterprise in terms of its product or service, market characteristics, the entrepreneurial team, the likely BOD.

(*c*) Specify the market plan, manufacturing plan, financial plan.

(*d*) Develop performance projections (monthwise for at least 3 years).

Let's capitalize on strategies. In business planning, the strategies to be followed in order to overtake the competitors, are outlined by entrepreneurs. In this spirit, entrepreneurs may adopt one of the following competitive strategies. There are three types of competitive strategies.

(*a*) Cost leadership: Being cost efficient

(*b*) Differentiation: Making your product different, i.e. superior products

(*c*) Focus: Being sensitive to customers than your competitors

Step 5: Developing Action Plans

No strategic plan is complete until it is put in to action. To make the plan workable, the business owner should divide the plan into projects, carefully defining each one of the following:

1. ***Purpose:*** What is the project designed to accomplish?
2. ***Scope:*** Which areas of the company will be involved in the project?
3. ***Contribution:*** How does the project relate to other projects and to the overall strategic plan?
4. ***Resource requirements:*** What human and financial resources are needed to complete the project successfully?
5. ***Timing:*** Which schedules and deadlines will ensure project completion?

Under this particular step, how strategies are going to be undertaken is specified. The questions like — Who does it? Why it is done? When it is done? How it is going to done? are answered. For instance in answering the how and who questions, an entrepreneur tries to focus on the ways of obtaining finances, licenses, raw materials, equipments, recruiting staff, distribution network, construction of plant etc.

Step 6: Implementation and Evaluation

Now it is the time of reality. When action plans are materialized, business plans are considered to be implemented. Evaluation follows after implementation. Evaluation is mainly concerning towards making sure the achievement of mission, objectives etc

Deciding on Development Approach

After an entrepreneur establishes him/herself, he/she looks for how to develop further. In general, there are three approaches for the expansion of business activity.

Approach 1: Start up Venture (New set-up)

It is a new venture established from the scratch as per the dreams and plan of entrepreneur.

Advantage

1. The business is created as per entrepreneurs planning and being a new venture; there is no compromise on entrepreneurial dreams or plans.
2. Owner (entrepreneur) doesn't inherit the ill will of previous organization.
3. If a business idea is unique, this is the only viable option.

Disadvantage

1. High cost of equipment and organization.
2. Lack of source of genuine advice since there is no past records.
3. It may saturate the existing market.
4. Lack of recognition.

Approach 2: Buying an existing business (Buyout firms)

It is the second approach of launching a new venture when the entrepreneurs feel that they can quickly change direction of existing firm as per his own plans and dreams in a fairly substantial way. The following steps are recommended as a checklist before buying an existing firm.

Do the product/service fit to the entrepreneur's interest/need?

Yes

Is it an appropriate business for sale (Profitability/Legality)? Accountants may be consulted to prove profitability, while lawyers may be consulted in terms of legality.

Yes

Is Business condition good? (Financial health)

Yes

Purchase price reasonable

Yes. Buy the firm

Advantages

1. A successful firm can provide immediate returns.
2. Existing firm comes with an advantage of good location, working staff, established supply of raw materials, distribution network installed machineries and inventories etc.
3. Advice can be sought from previous owners on the strength and weaknesses of the firm.
4. Low cost of organization when it is specially compared to starting a new venture.

Disadvantages

1. Bad reputation of previous owner may be faced if the previous entrepreneur is not well established or don't possess a good will.
2. Poor staff, obsolete machineries and layout can trouble entrepreneur.
3. Buyout costs are usually high.

Approach 3: Purchasing a license (Franchising/Licensing)

It is the third major approach to develop a business. A new venture is not something obtained in this approach. The key terms of this development approach include:

Franchise: It is the right and license to sell a product or service and possibly the entire business system developed by another company in return of a royalty and conformity to a standard operating procedure. It is an intellectual property which is sold in return of royalty.

Franchisor: It is usually the manufacturer or sole distributor of a trademarked product or service who has a considerable experience in that business, eg., owners of Kodak, Pepsi, etc.

Franchisee: It is an individual entrepreneur who purchases the franchise in return for royalty and conformance to standard operation and who in the process gets the opportunity to enter an established entrepreneur.

Types of Franchising

1. ***Trade name franchising:*** Franchisee gets only the right to use trade name of franchiser.
2. ***Product distribution franchising:*** Right to use name as well as selected products of franchiser.
3. ***Pure/Comprehending franchising:*** Right to use entire business of the franchiser.

Advantages for Franchiser

1. Expanding the existing business network at low investment or limited capital.
2. Company grow with minimum risk without expanding the HR and other facilities.
3. Regular income from royalty (5%).

Disadvantages to the Franchiser

- Absolute control cannot be exercised.
- Physical separation.

Advantages for Franchisee

1. Gets advantage already established brand name.
2. Easy to establish business using well developed system
3. Initial financial assistance.
4. Opportunity to marketing training and counseling
5. Greater chance of success

Disadvantages to the Franchisee

- Sharing profits in terms of royalty is mandatory.
- Strict adherence to standard operating procedures or limited freedom.
- Restriction on buying other's product.

Self-learning Activity

Try to answer the following questions on your own:

1. Describe project identification?
2. Explain about scanning the environment?
3. Give an account of buying an existing business as a development approach?

Summary

- Project identification is concerned with the collection, compilation and analysis of economic data for the eventual purpose of locating possible opportunities for investment and with the development of the characteristics of such opportunities.
- Project classifications are: quantifiable, non-quantifiable projects, sectoral projects, techno-economic projects, and so on.
- There are fundamental steps involved in entrepreneurial venture starting from developing business idea to implementation and evaluation.
- Start up venture, buying an existing business, and purchasing a license are different of approaches development.

Business Plan

Business Plan Preparation: Scope and Elements

Business plan is a written summary of the entrepreneur's proposed venture, its operational and financial details, its marketing opportunities and strategy, and its manager's skills and abilities.

The plan describes the direction the company is going to, what its goals are, where it wants to be, and how it's going to get there. The plan serves two essential functions:

1. It guides the company's operation by charting its future course and devising a strategy for following it.
2. It attracts lenders and investors. The best way to secure the necessary capital is to prepare a sound business plan.

Purpose of Business Plan

Well conceived business plan can thus serve:

(i) When

- *At star-up stage:* After conception of idea and feasibility study, detailed planning stage follows so as to develop operation guidelines.
- *Buyout stage:* Risk is benefit undertaken.
- *On going review stage:* Review start up, buyout performance, matching against relatives changes due to environment.

(ii) WHO

- *Managers:* Developing strategies, establish standards and attracting capitals.

- *Owners:* Evacuating enterprise's elements and enhance of success.
- *Lenders:* Determining principles, risk involves in business.

(iii) WHY (Purpose)

- *Managers:* Clarifying ideas and finding strength, weariness, opportunity and threats.
  - Building a team of committed people
  - Assist in raising capital
- *Owners:* Assessing feasibility and viability of business.
  - Setting objective and budgets.
  - Calculating capital investments.
- *Lenders:* Evaluate risk vs. benefits.
  - Appraise quality of managements

Scope of Business Plan

Business plan includes information on the following aspects:

(a) ***Economic aspects:*** Economic justification like market size, market growth, market share.

(b) ***Technical aspects:*** Details on technology needed, equipment and match their sources.

(c) ***Financial aspects:*** Total investment, cost of capital, ROI, source of capital, enterprise contribution.

(d) ***Production aspects:*** Product, its design, standard of quality, usage, production aspect like production process, schedule, technology.

(e) ***Managerial aspects:*** Qualification and experience, commitment and planning.

Elements of Business Plan

(a) ***Executive summary:*** It should be concise and should summarize all of the relevant points of proposed deal. It is designed to capture the reader's attention.

(b) ***Company history:*** A brief history of the operation, highlighting the significant financial and operational events in the company's life. This section should concentrate on the accomplishment of past objectives and should convey the firm's image.

(c) ***Business profile:*** This section should begin with a statement of the company's general business goals and a narrower definition of its immediate objectives. Together they should spell out what the business plans to accomplish, how, when and who will do it.

(d) ***Business strategy:*** This segment of business plan should outline the methods the company can use to meet the requirements for success cited earlier Game-plan to compete with competitors like cost leadership, innovation, strong sales force.

(e) ***Description of the firm's product:*** describe company's overall product line, giving an overview of how the goods/services are used. Besides, a statement of the goods' position in the product life cycle may also be helpful. This section should include also a summary of any patents, trademarks, or copy-rights protecting the product from infringement by competitors. Finally, it should describe the production, process, strategic raw materials required and sources of supply used.

(f) ***Marketing strategy:*** The plan must discuss the company's target market and its characteristics. It must show how the entrepreneur plans to turn the idea into a product that customers will want to buy. Proving that a profitable market exists takes two steps:

(i) Showing market place interest.

(ii) *Documenting market claims:* Target market, market size and trends, pricing, advertising and distribution.

(g) ***Competitors analysis:*** Demonstrate that the entrepreneur's company has an advantage over its competitors. What distinguishes ones product from others already on the market, and how will these differences produce a competitive edge?

(h) ***Officers' owners' resumes:*** The resumes of business offices, key directors, and any person with at last 20 per cent ownership in the company.

(i) ***Plan of operation:*** Organizational chart identifying the business's key positions and the personnel occupying them; the steps taken to encourage important officers to remain with the company; and form of ownership and description of any leases contracts other relevant agreements.

(j) ***Financial data:*** A detailed outline of the loan or investment package. The owner should supply copies of the firm's major financial statements from the past three years audited by certified public accountant; monthly projected financial statement for the operation for the next two to three years, which includes income statement, balance sheet, cash budget, and schedule of planned capital expenditures.

(k) ***Loan proposal:*** The purpose of the Loan, the amount requested, and the plans for payment.

Common Mistakes Committed during Business Plan Preparation

Raymond Loen offers the following list of the ten most common mistakes that business owners make in using their plans and the remedies for them.

1. ***Single-purpose use:*** Entrepreneurs typically prepare a plan to raise money and seldom give thought to actually using it.
   - *Remedy:* Stress implementation. The plan must include specific objectives for managers and plan to accomplish them.
2. ***One-person commitment:*** If one person writes the entire plan managers are unlikely to be fully committed to it.
   - *Remedy:* Involve all members of management.
3. ***Benign neglect:*** Once completed, the business plan sits on the shelf and collects dust. Out of sight, out of mind.
   - *Remedy:* Make following up the plan easy, schedule regular meetings to discuss the plan and the progress made in accomplishing the goals and objectives established.
4. ***Unworkable document:*** Managers create a plan that is so huge and complex that it discourages every one from actually using it.
   - *Remedy:* Give the plan life by supplying one-page action summaries for each department.
5. ***Unbalanced application:*** Sometimes managers give a disproportionate amount of attention to one portion of the plan.
   - *Remedy:* Get balanced participation from managers and employees in all areas of the company, and also focus 90 per cent of management's attention within the next year.
6. ***Disillusionment:*** Managers become disillusioned when the scenario laid out in the plan fail to develop.
   - *Remedy:* Develop contingency plan—both positive and negative.
7. ***Too-action oriented:*** Action oriented managers tend to forget about the plan once it is completed. They want get back to the real world of business.
   - *Remedy:* Use these mangers' action orientation to encourage them to develop plans for their areas of responsibility.
8. ***No Performance standard:*** Too often, managers fail to establish measurable standards in the plan.
   - *Remedy:* Encourage managers to establish specific, measurable objectives in their respective areas.
9. ***Poor progress control:*** Implementing the plan is without control because progress reports are lost in the jumble of everyday business.
   - *Remedy:* Hold regular meetings to discuss progress on the plan and nothing else.

10. *Early consumption:* The plan becomes outdated because no one bothers to update it.
    - *Remedy:* Update the plan every six months.

Five "Cs" that Bankers look in Business Plan.

Most bankers consider a loan acceptable if it conforms to the five Cs of credit: Capital, Capacity, Collateral, Character, and Conditions.

(*a*) ***Capital:*** A small business must have a stable capital base before a bank will grant it a loan.

(*b*) ***Capacity:*** A synonym for capacity is cash flow. Venture should have ability to meet its regular financial obligation and repay bank loan.

(*c*) ***Collateral:*** Includes any assets the owner pledges to the bank as security for repayment of the loan.

(*d*) ***Character:*** The evaluation of character frequently is based on intangible factors like honesty, competence, determination, intelligence, and ability.

(*e*) ***Conditions:*** Bankers consider factors relating to the business operation such as potential growth in the market, competition, location, form of ownership, and loan purpose.

Business Plan Template

I. Description of the Organisation

Under the title description of the organisation, we have to discuss the nature of the business, location of the business, the competitors, competencies,, etc.

Nature of the Business

1. The type of products and services to be dealt with (milk, milk products, vegetables, fruits, processed foods, etc.)
2. Organisational description of the organisation (how to organize, when to organize, composition of the members, etc.)

Location of the Business

1. Name the proposed headquarters for the organisation.
2. Examine the transport, communication facilities available to the members.
3. The number of households in the proposed area of operation.
4. Approximate households to be absorbed as members and their background, and economic potential.
5. The sustainability of the membership—target to increase the membership every year.

6. The number of dairy animals owned and the expected supply of milk to the organisation.
7. The type of vegetables/fruits grown and the expected supply.

The competitors

1. Examine the type of competition that may come once the organisation is started.
2. Form strategies to face the competition.
3. Examine the role and stake of the prospective members and directors to face the competition.
4. How far the price mechanism can be used as an instrument to resist the competition.

Competencies

1. Geographic location—Ideal location for the vast majority of the members in terms of transport, communication, accessibility, all season mobility, etc.
2. Superior customer satisfaction—to attend to the needs of the consumers and the grievances of the consumers.
3. Form a mechanism to attend the daily problems and grievances of the customers.
4. Try to enlist as much institutional customers as possible.
5. Dedicated personnel—Recruiting the talents locally available.

II. Organisational Analysis

The organizational analysis consists of selection/election of competent and dedicated committee members/board of directors, manager, and staff.

Committee Members

1. Even during the preliminary stage, locate educated, dedicated and competent committee members.
2. Short training programme can be arranged for them as well as for the prospective members about the business plan.
3. The committee members must be educated about the competitive nature of the business, using of price and dividend mechanism to enlist the permanent loyalty of the members.
4. To work for the viability and sustainability of the organisation by means of enrolling more and more members on a time frame basis.
5. To conduct the committee meeting and general assembly meetings periodically and to introduce transparency in the operations of the organisation.

6. Exposure visits to the committee members can be arranged at frequent intervals.

Manager and Staff

1. To go for a qualified manager, if available in and around the particular location.
2. From the beginning he must be paid reasonable salary with adequate perquisites (fringe benefits).
3. Select adequate staff to work for the services of the members and for the faster growth of the organisation.
4. Selfless service must be expected from the employees.
5. Training programme for the manager and the staff must be made a continuous process.
6. Exposure visits to the staff can be arranged at frequent intervals.

III. Marketing and Sales Analysis

Overall marketing strategy

1. Marketing penetrating strategy
2. Growth strategy (monthwise and yearwise)

Procurement strategy

1. Procurement timings every day
2. Fixation of procurement responsibility to each staff
3. Purchasing/procurement target
4. Storage facility
5. Preservation facility
6. Steps to avoid wastage, pilferage during procurement stage and storage stage.

Pricing strategy

1. Study the market price for the intended produces.
2. Try to fix a price slightly above the market price.
3. If possible, from the beginning create a price fluctuation fund, from out of the net profit, to offset the down fall in market price.

Sales strategy

1. Identify institutional customers (institutional customers are bulk purchasers and payment will not be a problem).
2. Timeliness and speed of sales are very important.

3. The sales force (employees) must be motivated to take care of the quality, timeliness, cleanliness, etc., of providing supplies.

Transport and communication services

1. To start with higher private transport services.
2. The transport system must cover nearest cities, and institutional and individual customers.
3. Alternative arrangements to be made if regular transport service is disrupted.
4. Any transport dislocation should be communicated to the customers immediately.
5. The sales staff must be provided with communication facilities.
6. The head office and manager must be provided with round the clock communication facilities (mobile phone).

IV. Financial Analysis

The organisation needs two types of capital viz., block capital (long term capital) and working capital. Block capital is needed to construct office buildings, purchase equipment, etc. Working capital is needed to meet the day-to-day expenses and monthly establishment.

Members stake

1. To start with members may contribute very little amount as share capital. But minimum shares to be taken and value of each share can be fixed.
2. From out of the business dealings, members can be asked to contribute compulsory savings.
3. Voluntary savings can also be opened to the members.

Voluntary agencies

1. Voluntary agencies like the SHDI can be approached to contribute towards the funds by way of revolving fund, etc.
2. Voluntary agencies can be approached to provide equipment and furniture.

Government

1. Government can be approached to provide block capital (repayable long-term loan, as being practiced in many developing countries).
2. Government can provide subsidies for the purchase of equipment.
3. Government can provide tax exemptions and duty exemptions while import of equipment.

Commercial banks

1. Commercial banks can be approached for raising block capital and working capital.

V. Cost and Profitability Analysis

Break-even analysis

The proposed organisation must be able to earn a profit at the end of third year. Strategies must be worked out.

Cost analysis

Cost must be worked out in terms of fixed cost and variable cost. Flexibility must be allowed in the case of variable cost to attain profitability at the end of third year. To keep the cost minimum, the organisation can go for rented building, hired vehicles, etc., during the beginning years.

Profit analysis

The proposed organisation should give a reasonable dividend and not a high dividend. A ceiling of 25% can be fixed.

Reserves and retained earnings

Every year from the net profit reserves must be created. A percentage of retained earnings (e.g. 25%) must be created to plough back the profit money to the business.

Summary

- Business plan is a written summary of the entrepreneur's proposed venture, its operational and financial details, its marketing opportunities and strategy, and its manager's skills and abilities.

Self-learning Activity

Try to answer the following questions on your own.

1. What are the components of Business Plan?
2. What are the Five C's in Business Plan?

8

Managing the Enterprise

Marketing Management

Meaning

The decade of this millennium is one of great promise and great uncertainty. Already sea change have been taking place in global economy—the rising power of Far East in the global markets: development of ECM; the mass privatization of state-run enterprises worldwide; the giant advances in technology and so on. Companies today are learning that it is hard to build a reputation and easy to lose it. In the end, the companies that best satisfy their customers will be the winners. Today, smart companies are not merely looking for sales; they are investing in long-term mutually satisfying customer relationship based on delivery, quality, service and value. Authentic marketing is not the art of selling what you make but knowing what to make!

Marketing is the business function that identifies unfulfilled needs and wants, defines and measures their magnitude, determine which target market the organization can best serve decides on appropriate products, services and programmes to serve these markets and calls upon everyone in the organization to "think and serve the customer".

According to Philip Kotler, "Marketing is a social and managerial process by which individual and groups obtain what they need and want through creating, offering and exchanging products of value with others".

Marketing management takes place when at least one party to a potential exchange thinks about the means of achieving desired responses from other parties.

"Marketing management is the process of planning and executing the conception, pricing, promotion, and distribution of ideas, goods and services to create exchange that satisfies individual and organizational goals".

Importance of Marketing

Marketing is extremely important to the consumers, producers and other intermediaries in the economy of the country. Marketing completes the basic mission of the economic system. Broadly, the importance of marketing can be summarized in to two categories, namely:

1. Discovering what goods and services consumers need and want.
2. Providing these items for the customers in the places where they are, at the times they want, and at prices that they are able and willing to pay.

In other words, marketing creates certain *form utility, place utility, time utility and possession utility or marketing utilities.*

Core Concepts of Marketing

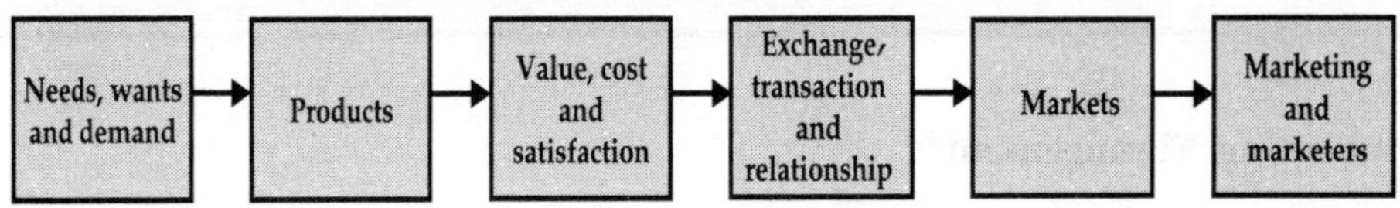

Need: A human need is a state of felt deprivation of some basic satisfaction. People require food, clothing, shelter, safety, belongingness, esteem, etc. These needs are not created by the society or the marketer but exist in the very texture of human biology and the human conditions.

Wants: Wants are desires for specific satisfiers of needs. It differs from society to society. An Ethiopian needs food and may want "injera", "wat" and a "tej" for satisfying it, while it may differ for a European who may be wanting "Burger", "Pizza", etc.

Demands: Demands are wants for specific products that are backed by ability to and willingness to buy them. Wants become demands when they are supported by purchasing power. Many people want a Mercedes; only few are able to buy. Companies must therefore measure not only how many would actually be willing and able to buy it.

Products: People satisfy their needs and wants with products. A product is anything that can be offered to satisfy a need or want. Physical products are really vehicles that deliver services to us. Services can also be supplied by other vehicles, such as persons, places, activities, organizations and ideas.

The marketer's job is to sell the benefits or services built into physical products rather than just describe their physical features.

Value: Customer value is the difference between the benefits that the customer gains from owning and using a product and the costs of obtaining the product.

Cost: The investment incurred in the acquisition of the product or the services.

Satisfaction: The extent to which a product's performance falls short of the customer's expectations, the buyer is dissatisfied. If performance exceeds expectations, the buyer is delighted. If performance matches exceptions, the buyer is satisfied.

Exchange: Exchange is the act of obtaining a desired product from someone by offering something in return. Exchange must be seen as a process rather than as an event. Two parties are engaged in exchange if they are negotiating and moving toward an agreement. When an agreement is reached, we say that a transaction takes place.

Transaction: A transaction consists of a trade of values between two parties. Transactions are basic units of exchange.

Relationship Marketing: A marketing effort sought to build up long term, trusting "win-win" relationship with customers, distributors, dealers and suppliers. The operating principle here is, build good relationships, and profitable transactions will follow.

Markets: The concept of exchange leads to the concept of a market. A market consists of all the potential and actual customers sharing a particular need or want who might willing and able to engage in exchange to satisfy that need or want. Thus the size of the market depends on the number of people who exhibit the need or want, have resources that interest others, and are willing and able to offer these resources in exchange for what they want.

Marketing: Marketing means working with the markets to actualize potential exchange for purpose of satisfying human needs and wants.

Marketer: A marketer is someone seeking a resource from someone else and willing offer something of value in exchange.

Classification of Markets

Markets may be classified in various ways based on different characteristics:

Classification of markets on the basis of free intercourse

Markets have been classified as perfect and imperfect markets on the basis of free intercourse. A market is said to be perfect market when all potential buyers and sellers are promptly aware of the prices at which transactions take place and all the offers made by other sellers and buyers and where any buyer can purchase from any seller. Under such conditions, the price of commodity would be the same all over the market. A market is in perfect when some buyers and sellers or both are not aware of the offers being made by others.

Markets on the basis of time classification

(i) *Very short period market:* Time is insufficient to make any adjustment between the demand and supply. This is applicable to highly perishable articles like vegetables, milk and fruits.

(ii) *Short period market:* Time is given to adjust the supply to meet the demand. The time given is not enough and influence of demand is greater than that of supply.

(iii) *Long period markets:* Sufficient time is given for the changes in supply to adjust them to the change in demand. Under these circumstances supply influences demand.

Classification on the basis of the position of sellers

(i) *Primary markets:* In this market all farm products are sold to wholesaler in the village itself by the primary producers. This market deals in sales of fruits, vegetables etc.

(ii) *Secondary Market:* Here wholesalers supply their goods to the retailers for selling them to consumers.

(iii) *Terminal Markets:* The goods are finally disposed of directly to consumers.

Classification on the basis of the characteristics of the consumer

Markets are broadly classified as consumer or industrial markets. Consumer markets consist of purchasers and/or individual household members who intend to consume or benefit from the purchased products and who do not buy products to make profits.

Industrial markets, also called business-to-business markets, are grouped broadly into producer, reseller, governmental, and institutional categories. These markets purchase specific kinds of products for use in making other products, for day to day operations.

Marketing Philosophies

We have defined marketing management as the conscious effort to achieve desired exchange outcomes with target markets. But what philosophy should guide marketing efforts? What relative weight should be given to the interest of the organization, the customers, and society? Very often these interest conflict.

There are five competing concepts under which organizations can choose to conduct their marketing activities—the production concept, the product concept, the selling/sales concept, the marketing concept, and the societal marketing concept.

The Production Concept

The production concept is one of the oldest concepts in business.

- The production concept holds that consumers will favor those products that are widely available and low in cost. Managers of production-oriented organisations concentrate on achieving high production efficiency and wide distribution.

The assumption that consumers are primarily interested in product availability and low price holds in at least two situations. The first is where the demand for a product exceeds the supply; the second situation is where the product's cost is high and has to be decreased to expand the market.

The Product Concept

- The product concept holds that consumers will favor those products that offer the most quality, performance, or innovative features. Managers in product-oriented organizations focus their energy on making superior products and improving them over time.

The managers assume that the buyers admire well made products and can appraise the product quality and performance. The product concept leads to "marketing myopia" an undue concentration on the product rather than the need.

The Selling Concept/Sales Concept

- The selling concept holds that consumers, if left alone, will ordinarily not buy enough of the organization's products. The organization must therefore undertake an aggressive selling and promotion effort.

The selling concept is practiced most aggressively with unsought goods, those goods that the buyers normally do not think of buying. Most companies practice selling concept when they have overcapacity. Their aim is to sell what they make rather than make what they can sell. The selling concept is also practiced in the non profit area by fund - raisers, college admissions officers, and political parties.

The Marketing Concept

- The marketing concept holds that the key to achieving organizational goals consists of being more effective than competitors in integrating marketing activities toward determining and satisfying the needs and wants of target markets.

The marketing concept rests on four pillars namely a market focus, customer orientation, coordinated marketing and profitability.

(*a*) *Market focus:* No company can operate in every market and satisfy every need. Nor can it even do a good job within one market. Company do best when they define their target markets and prepare a marketing programme for each target market.

(*b*) *Customer orientation:* Even after defining market carefully, company-orientated marketing requires defining customer need from customer's point of view and not from its own point of view.

(*c*) *Coordinated Marketing:* It means that on one hand, various marketing functions (sales, advertising) must be coordinated among themselves while on other hand; marketing must be well coordinated with departments of company.

(*d*) *Profitability:* The purpose of marketing concept is to help organization achieve its goals where the key is not to aim for profits alone but to achieve them as byproduct of doing the job well.

The Societal Marketing Concept

- The societal marketing concept holds that the organization's task is to determine the needs, wants and interests of target markets and to deliver the desired satisfaction more effectively efficiently than competitors in a way that preserves or enhances the customer's and society's well being.

The societal marketing concept calls upon the marketer to balance three considerations in setting their marketing policies namely consumer want satisfaction, public interest and company's profits.

Market Segmentation

A company that decides to operate in a broad market recognizes that it normally cannot serve all customers in that market. The customers are too numerous and diverse in their buying requirements. Instead of competing every where, the company needs to identify the market segments that it serves most effectively.

To choose its markets and serve them well, many companies are embracing target marketing. In target marketing sellers distinguish the major market segments, target one or more of these segments and develop products and marketing programmes tailored to each segment. Instead of scattering their marketing effort, they can focus on the buyers whom they have the greatest chance of satisfying.

The marketers requires to take the following major steps in figure 8.1.

- *Market Segmentation:* Identify and develop profiles of distinct groups of buyers who might require separate products and/or marketing mixes.

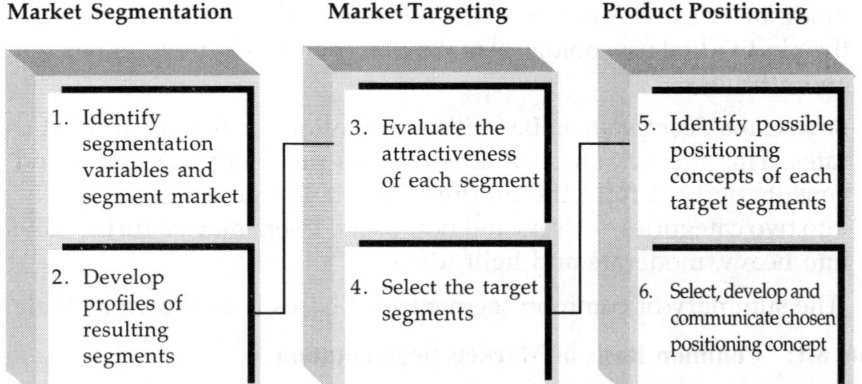

Fig. 8.1: **Major Steps Required in Marketing by Marketers**

Market segmentation is dividing a market into distinct groups of buyers with different needs, characteristics, or behaviour who might require separate products of marketing mixes.

Basis for Segmenting Consumers Market

There are four commonly used bases for segmenting consumers markets. These are:

(*a*) *Geographic Segmentation:* Geographic segmentation is the dividing of an overall market into homogeneous groups on the basis of population location. This is the earliest form that served a base for segmenting markets. It considers current population location and residence (urban or rural) and future expected shifts. Geographic segmentation is used in order to know regional variation in customer taste and also determine and supply goods appropriate to climate changes.

(*b*) *Demographic Segmentation:* Demographic segmentation is dividing an over all market into homogeneous group based upon population characteristics such as age, sex and income level. It is now the most common approach used for market segmentation. This method uses such variables as sex, age, income, occupation, education, household size and stage in the family life cycle. These variables are often used because:

1. They are easy to identify
2. They are associated with the sale of many products and services
3. They are typically referred to describing the audiences of advertising media.

(*c*) *Psychographics:* Psychographic segmentation utilizes behavioural profiles developed from analyses of the activities, opinions, interest and life styles of consumers. The lifestyles of potential consumers may prove important in order to determine their preferences; lifestyle refers to the mode of lives. Consumer's lifestyles are regarded as a composite of their individual psychological make-ups, their needs, motives perceptions and attitudes.

(*d*) *Behavioural Segmentation:* Benefit segmentation focuses on product usage rates. This focuses on such attributes as product usage rates and the benefits derived from the product. Potential segments may be divided into two categories— Users and non-users. Users may be further divided into heavy, moderate and light users.

The summary of common segmentation bases is as shown in Table 8.1.

Table 8.1: Common Basis of Markets Segmentation

Demographic	Psychographic	Geographic	Behavioural
Age	Personality	Region	Volume usage
Gender	Attributes	Urban, Suburban, Rural	Enduse
Ethnicity	Motives	Market density	User Expectations
Income	Lifestyle	Climate	Brand loyalty
Education		Terrain	Price sensitivity
Occupation		City size	Benefits derived
Family size		Country size	Occasion
Family life cycle		State size	User status
Religion			Buyer readiness stage
Social class			

In psychological segmentation, buyers are divided into different groups on the basis of VALS (Value and Lifestyle).

- *Market targeting*

  For market targeting sellers first evaluate the profile of and profit potential of each segment. The seller decides how many segments to cover based upon the size and growth of the segment, its structural attractiveness and company's objectives and resources.

- *Product positioning*

  Positioning is an act of designing company's offer and image so that target market understands and appreciates what company stands for in relation to its competitors.

Marketing Mix

Marketing mix is the set of controllable tactical marketing tools that the firm blends to produce the response it wants in the target market. The marketing mix consists of everything the firm can do to influence the demand for its product. The marketing mix is the blending of the four P's strategic elements of marketing decision-making that satisfies chosen consumer segments.

According to McCarthy, the four P's are— product, price, place and promotion.

- Product means the goods and service combination the company offers to the target market.
- Price is the amounts of money customers have to pay to obtain the product.
- Place includes company activities that make the product available to target consumers.
- Promotion means activities that communicate the merits of the product and persuade larger consumers to buy it.

Product

Product is the first and most important element of marketing mix. A product is anything that can be offered to a market for attention, acquisition, use or consumption that might satisfy a want or need. Product strategy calls for making coordinated decisions on product mixes, brand packaging and labeling.

A product mix is the set of all product lines and items that a particular seller offers for sale to the buyers. It includes breadth, length, depth and consistency.

A brand is a name, symbol or some combination used to identify the products of one firm and to differentiate them from competitive offerings.

A trademark is a brand that has been given legal protection. It is granted totally to the brand's owner.

Product Classifications

Products can be classified in three groups according to their durability or tangibility.

(a) *Non-durable goods:* Non-durable goods are tangible goods that normally are consumed in one or few users, e.g., beer, soap, salt, etc.

(b) *Durable goods:* Durable goods are those tangible goods that usually survive many users, e.g., Refrigerator, TV, clothing, etc.

(c) *Services:* Services are activities, benefits or satisfactions that are offered for sale, eg., haircut, repairing, etc.

Consumer Products

Consumer products are those bought by final consumers for personal consumption. Marketers usually classify these goods further based on how consumers go about buying them. Consumer products include convenience products, shopping products, special products and unsought products. These products differ in the ways consumer buy them and therefore in how they are marketed.

- Convenience products are consumer products that the consumer usually buys frequently, immediately, and with a minimum of comparison and buying effort.
- Shopping products are less-frequently purchases consumer products that customers compare carefully on suitability, quality, price, and style. When buying shopping products and services, consumers spend much time and effort, in gathering information and making comparisons. Examples include furniture, clothing, hotel services etc.
- Special products are consumer products with unique characteristics or brand identification for which a significant group of buyers is willing to make a special purchase effort.
- Unsought products are consumer products that the consumer either does not know about but does not normally think of buying, most major new innovations are unsought until the consumer becomes aware of them through advertising.

Product Life Cycles Strategies (PLC)

What is product? A product is a bundle of physical, service and symbolic attributes designed to produce consumer want satisfaction. An important feature of many products is the product warranty. Warranty is the guarantee to the buyer that the manufacturer will replace the product or refund its purchase price if it proves defectives during a specified period of time.

Product Life Cycle

Product, like individuals, passes through a series of stages. Successful products progress through four stages, namely, introduction, growth, maturity and decline as shown in figure 8.2.

Stage I: Introduction

The firm's objective in the early stage of the product life cycle is to stimulate demand for the new product. Since product is not familiar to the public, promotional campaign stresses information about its features. The basic features are as listed below:

- Customers are hesitant in buying the product.
- Productivity is low since demand is low.
- Sales volume is low.
- High amount of money is placed in advertisement.
- Expenses are high.
- Therefore it is the least profitable stage.

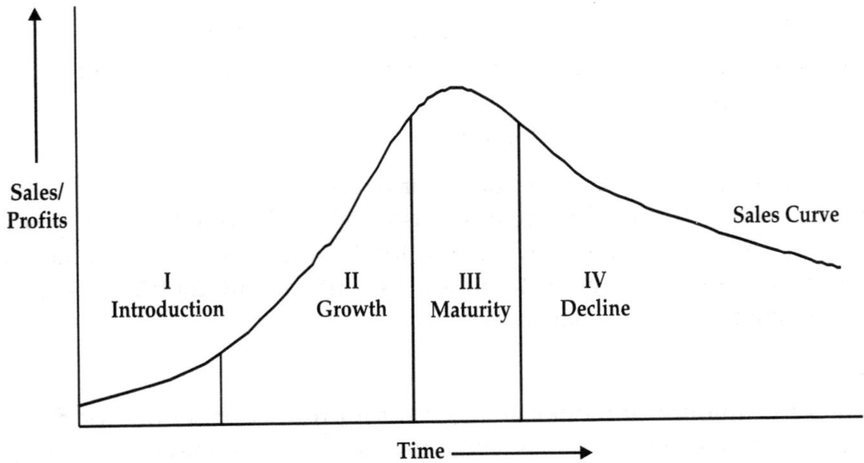

Fig. 8.2: **Product Life Cycle**

Stage II: Growth

Sales volume raises rapidly during the growth stages as new customers make initial purchases. The basic characteristics of the growth stage are listed below:

- This stage has the highest growth rate.
- Customers are now familiar with the merits and demerits of the product.
- Accordingly, sales volume increases very rapidly.
- A proportional rise in profits occurs.
- In this stages, competitors enter the market bringing about imitation of the product.
- Promotional campaign is still very high.

Stage III: Maturity

Sales continue to grow during the early part of the maturity stage. This stage can be summarized as:

- Large number of competitors have entered market.
- Available products exceed customer demand.
- Sales increase levels out into a plateau reaching its highest peak.
- Reduction in prices may occur in this stage.

Stage IV: Decline

In the final stage, shifting consumer preferences brings about decline in sales. Important trends that follow are:

- Sales show downward trends.
- Profits decline, in some cases actually becoming negative.
- It necessitates product differentiation, that is having different uses for the same product.
- Or a totally new product may have to be introduced.

Product life cycle predicts that profits assume and go through certain pattern. The length of the life cycle is considerably different from one product to another. A new fashion may have a total lifespan of one calendar year, with an introductory stage of two months. But the automobile has been in maturity stage for more than twenty years.

Price

It is the amount of money charged for a product or service, or the sum of the values that consumers exchange for the benefits of having or using the product or service.

It is the only element in marketing mix that produces revenues, the other elements produce costs.

Prices are determined by the cost and supply conditions and the demand and competitive conditions. The cost and supply conditions dictate the minimum price that producer can charge while demand and competitive conditions determine the maximum price he can charge.

Types of Costs in Marketing

There are broadly two types of costs in marketing namely:

- Production costs (i.e. fixed costs and variable costs)
- Selling and delivery costs.

Factors considered when setting prices:

A company's pricing decisions are affected both by internal company factors and external environmental factors. (*Fig. 8.3*)

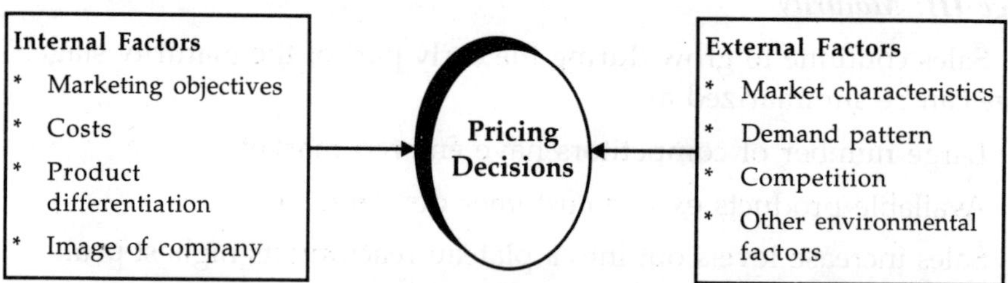

Fig. 8.3: **Factors Affecting Company's Pricing Decisions**

Steps in Pricing

Step I: Defining Pricing Objectives: Pricing objectives (as market penetration, market share, market skimming, fighting competition, optimum capacity utilization, profit maximization, etc.) are to be determined at the onset of price determination.

Step II: Analyzing Market Characteristics: There are several market characteristics like demand pattern, consumer income level, trade characteristics, competitive environment, etc. about which information have to be collected to establish prices of the product.

Step III: Calculating Costs: The main elements that should be covered in a calculation of costs are:

1. Direct production costs
2. Production overheads
3. Marketing and distribution costs

Step IV: Establishing target price and ascertaining feasibility: The next step is to establish a target price based on the analysis of the market characteristics and to ascertain whether it will be possible to sell at that price. There after any one of the pricing methods is adopted which best meets the company's objectives.

Pricing Methods

1. ***Cost-plus pricing:*** Cost-based pricing, also known as cost plus pricing, and includes a certain percentage of profit margins on the sum total of the full cost of production, marketing costs and an allocation of overheads.

   Price = [Fixed cost + Variable Cost + Overheads + Marketing Costs] + Specified Percentage of Total Costs
2. ***Market oriented pricing:*** This is a very flexible policy in the sense that it allows the prices to be changed in accordance with the changes in the market conditions. The product may be priced higher when demand conditions are very good and the prices may be lowered when the market is sluggish provided it helps in increasing sales.
3. ***Following competitors:*** Many firms follow the dominant competitors, particularly the price leader, in setting the price. The various alternatives can be setting price at the same level; below that of the competitor; higher than that of the competitor.
4. ***Negotiated prices:*** Deciding the price by negotiation between the seller and the buyer is very common in government and institutional purchases.
5. ***Break-even price:*** The firm tries to determine the price at which it will break even or make the target profit it is seeking. Break-even point is a point in a graph or mathematical model where cost equals revenue.

   Break-even Price = [Fixed Costs + Variable Costs]/Quantity

   Break- even Price for pre-determined profits = [FC + VC + Required profits]/Quantity

6. *Creative pricing:* Creative pricing means taking advantage of the flexibility between the lower limit of break even pricing and the upper limit of the competitor's price for similar product.

Distribution (Place)

Place i.e., placing the product refers to distribution of products, covering both channel of distribution (which includes direct and indirect transfer of title to a product) and physical distribution (which includes management of movement of raw materials, parts and supplies into and through firm and management of movement of finished products to consumers).

There are a number of channels for the distribution of goods. The one adopted depends upon numerous factors. The common channels of distribution are stated below:

Channels to Consumer Products

1. *Producer to Consumer:* This channel, often called the direct channel, includes no marketing intermediaries.
2. *Producer to retailer to consumer:* A retailer is a middleman that buys from producers or other middlemen and sells to consumers. This channel is most often used for products that are bulky and perishable.
3. *Producer to wholesaler to retailer to consumer:* This channel is known as the traditional channel because many consumer goods pass through the wholesalers to retailers.
4. Producer to agent to wholesaler to retailer to consumer. Agents are functional middlemen that do not take title to products and that are compensated by commissions paid by producers.

This channel is used for highly seasonal products and by producers that do not have their own sales force.

Channels for industrial products:

Producers of industrial products generally tend to use short channels. We will obtain the two that are most commonly used.

1. *Producer to industrial user:* In this direct channel, the manufacturer's own sales force sells directly to industrial user. Heavy machinery, airplanes and major equipment are usually distributed in this way.
2. *Producer to agent middlemen to industrial user:* Manufacturers use this channel to distribute such items as operating supplier, accessory equipment. Small tools and standardized parts. The agent and independent intermediary between the producer and the user. Generally, agents represent sellers.

Promotion

Marketing communication or promotion means the transmission of a message to the buyers/consumers/channel of distribution in which the supplying company aims to tell each one of these receivers why they should buy or handle the product. The company must blend the major promotion tools advertising, personal selling, sales promotion, and public relations.

1. *Advertising*

   Advertising refers to any paid form of non-personal presentation and promotion of ideas, goods or services by an identified sponsor.

   - The many forms of advertising contribute uniquely to the overall promotion mix.
   - Advertising can reach masses of geographically dispersed buyers at a low cost per exposure.
   - It enables the seller to repeat a message many times, and it lets the buyers receive and compare the messages of various competitors.
   - Advertising also has some *shortcomings*. Although it reaches many people quickly, advertising is impersonal and cannot be as persuasive as company sales people. In addition, advertising can be very costly.

2. *Personal Selling*

   It is a personal presentation by the firm's sales forces for the purpose of making sales and building customer relationships.

   - Personal selling is the most effective tool at certain stages of the buying process, particularly in building up buyer's preferences, convictions, and actions.
   - Compared to advertising, personal selling has several unique qualities.
     - It involves personal interaction.
     - It allows all kinds of relationships.
     - The buyer usually feels a greater need to listen and respond.
   - These unique qualities come at a cost. A sale force requires a longer-term commitment than does advertising — advertising can be turned on and off, but sales forces size is harder to change. Personal selling is also the company's most expensive promotion tool.

3. *Sales promotion*

   - It consists of a diverse collection of incentive tools, mostly short term, designed to stimulate quicker and/or greater purchase of particular products/services by consumers or the trade.
   - Where advertising offers a reason to buy, sales promotion offers an incentive to buy.

- Sales promotion includes tools for consumer promotion (samples, coupons, premiums, warranties, prices off etc.
- Sales promotion effects are usually short lines, however, and are not effective in building long-run brand preference.

4. *Public Relations*

   Public relations offer several unique qualities. It is very believable news stories, features, and events seem more real and believable to readers than advertisement do. Public relation departments perform the following:

   – *Press relations:* Presenting news and information about organization in the most positive light.

   – *Product publicity:* Sponsoring various efforts to publicize specific products.

   – *Corporate communication:* Promoting understanding of the organization with internal and external.

   – *Lobbying:* Dealing with legislators and government officials to promote or defeat legislation and regulation.

   – *Counseling:* Advising management about public issues and company positions and image.

Steps in Developing Marketing Communication

Step I: Identifying target audience: Even for same product, the target audience may be different in different markets because the decision-making roles of different categories of people are not the same in all the markets.

Step II: Determining communication objectives: The communication objectives may also be different in some cases. For example, when the product is in the introduction stage in a market, the emphasis is on consumer education and creation of primary demand while in other stages of PLC, the communication objectives could be fighting the competition, increasing market share, product differentiation, etc.

Step III: Determining message: This involves the decisions regarding the message content, message structure, message format, message source.

Step IV: Budget decisions: The size of total promotional expenditure and apportioning of this amount to the different elements of promotional mix are very important. The common methods used are namely; affordable method, percentage of sales method, objective and task method and competitive parity method.

Step V: Communication mix decision: Differing in marketing environment may necessitate variations in the communication mix because a channel or medium that is very effective in one market may not be so effective in other market.

Promotional Strategy

Promotion includes all the activities the company undertakes to communicate and promote its products to the target market.

Promotion Mix Strategies

Marketers can choose from two basic promotion mix strategies— push promotion or pull promotion.

(*a*) *Push Strategy*

This strategy involves "Pushing" the product through distribution channels to final consumers. The producer directs its marketing activities (Primarily personal selling and trade promotion) toward channel members to induce them to carry the product and to promote it to final consumers.

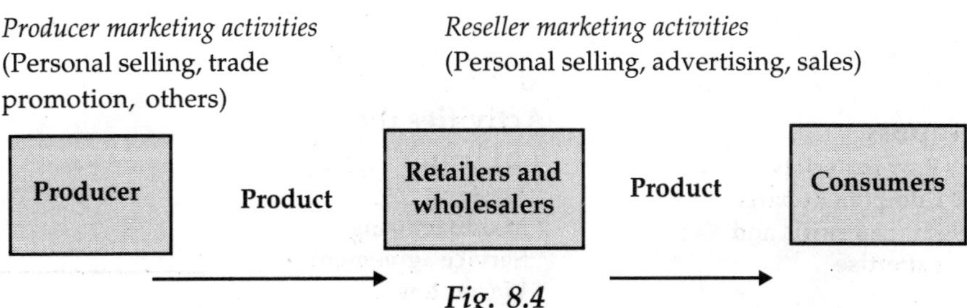

Fig. 8.4

(*b*) *Pull Strategy*

The producer directs its marketing activities (Primarily advertising and consumer promotion) toward final consumers to induce them to buy the product. If the pull strategy is effective, consumers will then demand the product from channel members, who will in turn demand it from producers (Fig. 8.5).

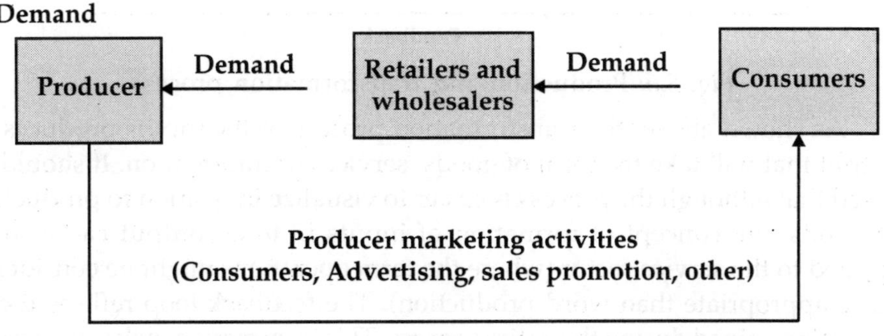

Fig. 8.5

Production and Operations Management

Meaning

Production is the transformation of resources into goods and services that have value to the customers. In businesses, this transformation takes the form of production processes, which have following components:

1. *Inputs:* Inputs are the four factors of production as land, labour, capital and entrepreneurship.
2. *Activities that add value:* These activities include engineering, design, manufacturing, and similar activities that add value for the customers.
3. *Outputs:* These are in the form of finished goods, services, idea.

There is also an additional component in the form of option of being repeated.

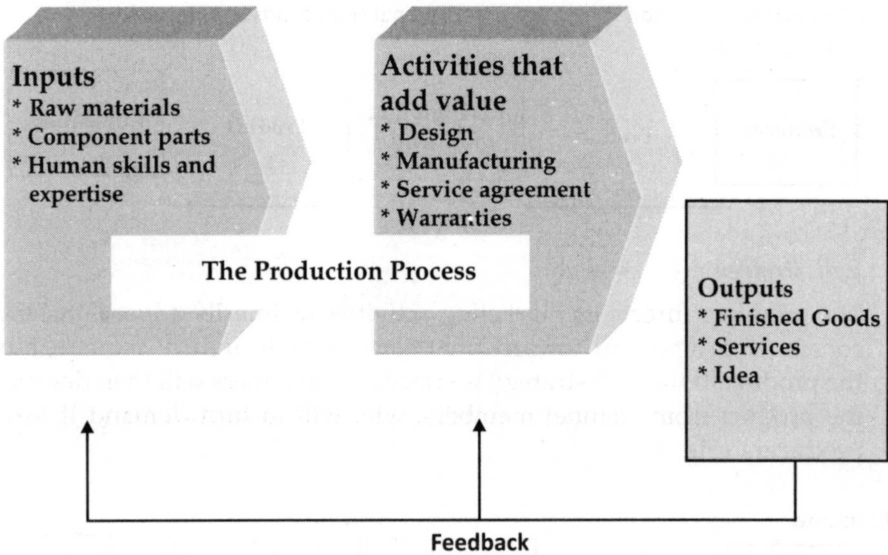

Fig. 8.6: **Production and transformation process**

As shown above, the transformation process of the inputs produces an output that will take the form of goods, services or information. It should be noted that although the process is easier to visualize in relation to production of goods, the concept of formation of inputs in to an output can also be applied to the service sector (where the term operations might be considered more appropriate than word production). The feedback loop reflects the in formation gained during the entire process. This information makes it possible to decide whether changes are required.

Definition

Productions and Operations Management is the coordination of an organization's resources to produce finished goods or services.

More conservatively called as production management, now operations has been incorporated into that term to emphasize that production processes also apply to services.

The objective of production and operations management in a business firm is to maximize the value created. Briefly the difference between the value of inputs and the value of output represent the value created through production activities, i.e. profit and customer satisfaction.

Table 8.2: Examples of Inputs and Outputs Values

	Inputs	Processing	Output	Feedback
Hospital	Doctors, Nurses, Medical Supplies, Healthcare-equipments	Healthcare treatment	Treated patients	Hospital costs, No. of treated patients, Quality of care
Farm	Land, Labour, Farmer, Tractor, Seeds	Ploughing, Harvesting, Fattening	Grain, Beef, Milk, Fruits	Prices received, Turnover, Crop condition

Criteria for Plant Location/Site Selection

With rare exceptions, production facilities are expensive and permanent and cannot be easily moved. As a result, site selection is an important decision that can increase or decrease the costs and affect the future profits of a business. In general, production sites are chosen on the basis of five main criteria:

1. ***Labour Issues:*** Companies that produce services or goods are dependent on the location of skilled labour. A company may want to go where the most productive or technically skilled workers can easily be found. Besides, companies also choose to avoid those areas for labour related reasons such as high union activity and the higher wage and benefits packages sometimes associated with union labour.
2. ***Government receptiveness:*** Government receptiveness influences site selection because many towns, states and foreign countries offer tax breaks or favorable regulatory environments to attract business.
3. ***Condition of infrastructure:*** Infrastructure, from road and railways to electricity and water systems, can be a critical factor in site selection. Examples are locations of automobile industry.
4. ***Proximity to suppliers:*** Production facilities must be convenient to suppliers. To avoid costly transportation expenses, facilities are built around the sources that are used as necessary inputs in the production processes. Examples are those like cotton textile industries.

5. *Convenience for customers:* Many services must be produced where they are consumed, so some businesses place multiple production facilities within easy reach of their customer markets. Examples are those of consumer non durable and fast food industry.

Basic Kinds of Production System

Conversion System or methods of production can broadly be categorized as:

1. *Intermittent Production System*

   These systems produce a variety of products either one at a time or finite number of different products in batches. Therefore they can be classified as:

   (a) *Job Production:* A job is a one-off product; if it is repeated there will be considerable interval between the similar jobs. Job production is a method of production found mainly in the civil engineering and construction industries.

   (b) *Batch Production:* Batch production involves a group of products of the same design passing through the production process together. It is mainly found in production of a batch of cases of wine of same type, construction of estate of twenty houses of same design, manufacture of rolls of wall paper, etc.

   Intermittent manufacturing is conversion with production characteristics of low product volume, special purpose machine equipment, labour intensive operations, etc

2. *Continuous/Flow/Process/Mass Production System*

   Continuous conversion operations are featured by large volume deliveries of materials, highly automated equipment, highly specialized workforce, products of standard design and construction.

   Basic comparisons between the two production systems

   (a) Continuous processing system usually yields a lower unit cost of products due to economies of scale, specialization of labour, and the likes while in comparison the unit cost is higher in intermittent production system due to the unique nature of production.

   (b) Storage costs per unit are usually lower in continuous processing system because of low inventories.

   (c) In Continuous processing system, fixed path material handling equipments are used while in intermittent production system variable path material handling equipments are used.

   (d) Time required for production is usually shorter in continuous processing system.

(*e*) Continuous processing system requires larger investments because it uses special purpose machine, fixed path material handling equipment and larger scope.

(*f*) In Continuous processing system marketing efforts are directed towards developing distribution channel for high volume while for intermittent production system all efforts are directed towards satisfaction of individual taste of the customers.

Plant Layout

1. ***The process layout:*** Methods of arranging equipment so that production tasks are carried out in discrete locations containing specialized equipment and personnel. A process layout is arranged according to the specialized equipment, workers and materials involved in the various phases of the production process.
2. ***Product layout:*** Resources such as equipment, personnel, materials and supporting resources are arranged according to the functions being performed to produce a certain product. Factories such as chemical, cement, sugar, and textile factories are full under the product layout systems.
3. ***Assembly-line layout:*** Methods of arranging equipment in which production is in a flow of work processing along with a line of work stations. Systems such as automobile and personal computer manufacturing follow assembly-line layout.
4. ***Fixed position layout:*** Methods of arranging equipment in which the product is stationary, equipment and personnel are brought to it. Examples are airplane assembly, road, building, and bridge construction.

Production Planning and Control

In the planning stage, it is necessary to analyze the business plans and long range production plans of the company and then create a working plan that specifies how these will be carried out. Production control involves determining whether current performance meets the standards set out in the plans. Production planning takes place in three steps. Then control processes give managers or employees the feedback necessary to track and control performances and if necessary, to revise plans in order to meet goals.

Basic Steps of Production Planning and Control

Production planning and control takes place in four basic steps as follows:

Step I: Analyzing overall business plan: Before making specific plans, the production manager analyses the organization's overall business plan to ensure that the business will have an adequate supply of products to reach this goal which may be increasing sales or profits, launching a new product, entering a foreign market, collaboration with another company and the likes. This helps in determining what needs to be produced, how, when and where.

Step II: Create a Long Range Production plan: Creation of long range production plan includes decisions concerning capacity needs and how additional capacity should be added. Increasing output means increasing capacity which a production manager can do by increasing the efficiency of current production processes, increasing the size or number of production processes or subcontracting with other companies to use their production processes.

Step III: Develop Working Plans: Working plans for running the production process specifies who does what, when and where. Here, working plans are drawn up for the production process and production facilities. Working plan generally takes place in two forms— a master production plan and a facilities plan. The master production schedule lists products, the facilities where they will be made and when they will be made. The facilities plan specifies the location and layout of facilities that will be needed. Detailed schedules state what employees and suppliers will need to do to meet the master schedule, the parts that will be needed and the number of workers who will be needed.

Step IV: Production Control: It includes the development of control and the tracking and correction of performance. There are five steps in production control:

1. *Production planning:* Estimating material and resources that will be needed and stating where and when they will be used.
2. *Routing:* Deciding what value-adding activities should take place, where, and when. It is the task of specifying the sequence of operations and the path through the facility that work will take. The way production is routed depends on the type of the product and the layout of the plant.
3. *Scheduling:* Preparing a detailed timetable for labour, materials, and production activities. It is the process of ensuring that materials are at the right place at the right time. In any production process, the production manager must incorporate a time element in to the routing plan, setting up a time for each operation to begin and to end. Some of the most widely used scheduling tools are Gantt Charts, Critical Path Method (CPM) and Programme Evaluation and Review Technique (PERT).
4. *Dispatching:* Sending people, materials, and equipments to where they are needed. It is the issuing of work orders and the distribution

of papers to department-supervisors. These orders specify the work to be done and the schedule for its completion. The production manager would dispatch orders to the appropriate departments, which are responsible for delivery of the needed materials and machines before the schedule starting time.

5. *Follow-up:* Activities by managers or employees to compare actual work performed with plans and schedules for that work. Once the schedule has been set up and the orders dispatched, a production manager cannot just sit back and assume that the work will automatically get done correctly and on time. Accident, mechanical-breakdown or suppliers' failures can delay production. Thus the production manager must have a system for handling delays and preventing a minor disruption from growing in to chaos.

The production manager must also develop a system of production control that will help to make sure the company's products meet quality standards, through physical inspection, testing and quality control.

Quality control is the process of ensuring that goods and services are produced in accordance with the design specifications. The major objective of quality control is to see that the organization lives up to the standard it has set for itself on quality.

Financial Management

Finance—a Company's Lifeblood. Financial Management can be defined as an effective acquisition and use of money.

Process of Financial Management

Developing a financial plan for a company is done with two objectives in mind— achieving positive cash flow and effectively investing excess cash flow to make the company grow. The process consists of five basic steps (Fig. 8.7):

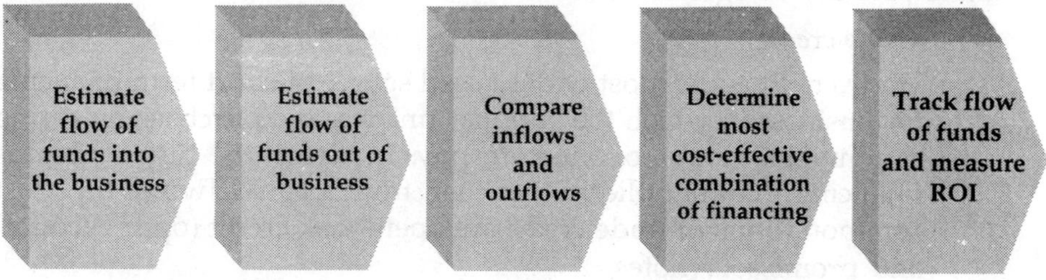

Fig. 8.7: **The Process of Financial Management**

Step 1: Estimating month-by-month flow of funds into the business from all the sources, including gains on external investments.

Step 2: Estimating month-by-month flow of funds out of the business, including both operating expenses and capital investments.

Step 3: Compare inflows and outflows. If cash flow is negative, determine how to make it positive, either by reducing the outflows or increasing the inflows. If cash flow is positive, determine how to invest excess funds most productively.

Step 4: Choose which capital investments should be made for continued growth. Determine the most cost effective combination of inside and outside sources of financing.

Step 5: Establish a system for tracking flow of funds and measuring the return on investment.

Sources and Uses of Funds

From where can a firm obtain the money it needs? The most obvious source would be revenues, or suppliers who may extend credit, or loans from financial institutions, or through stocks and bonds. Generally speaking, the goal of a company is to obtain money at the least cost and risk, whereas the goal of lenders and investors is to receive the highest possible returns on their investments at the least risk. Therefore, a company's cost of capital, the price it pays to raise the money, depends on the risk associated with the company (the quality of venture and time), the prevailing level of interest rates and management's selection of funding vehicles (internal *vs.* external; short *vs.* long term funding; debt *vs.* equity).

Initial capital consists of ownership equity (owner capital) and debt capital (credit capital) obtained from internal and external sources respectively.

1. *Individual investor as sources of funds*

   This includes sources as personal savings, funds from friends, relatives and local investors and the sale of capital stock as major sources of funds.

2. *Short-term financing*

   Short-term debt is any debt that will be repaid within one year. The three primary categories of short term debt are:

   (*a*) ***Trade credit***

   Trade credit is the most widely used source of short term financing for business in which the supplier finances the purchase by giving the buyer 30 days or more to pay. In effect, the buyer obtains financing from supplier rather than from a bank. Two of the most common forms of trade credit are open-book credit (open account) and promissory notes.

   - *Open-book credit:* It is an informal credit agreement that a buyer makes purchases and pays for them later. It is "open" because the buyer is not required to sign a written repayment agreement in advance.

- *Promissory notes:* It is a signed "promissory to pay". The note indicates in writing the amount of money owed by the buyer and the repayment date. It is drawn by the buyer in advance of the purchase.

(*b*) ***Loans***

As important as trade credit may be to a business, a time may come when other sources of short term funding are required. The real business of most banks is lending money to commercial borrowers. The interest on a short term loan may be either fixed (constant-rate) or floating (variable-rate).

- *Secured Loans*: Secured loans are those that are backed by something of value, known as collateral, which may be seized by the lender if the borrower fail to repay the loan. The three main types of collateral are accounts receivable, inventories, and other property. When a business loan is secured with accounts receivable, its customers' outstanding balances on open book accounts are used as collateral. A less attractive alternative, known as factoring, for most business is to sell accounts receivable to a finance company instead of using them for collateral. Another form called as chattel mortgage, is an agreement where the movable property purchased through the loan belongs to the borrower, although the lender has a legal right to the property if payments are not made as specified in the loan agreement.

Unsecured Loans: An unsecured loan is one that requires no collateral. Instead the lender relies on the general credit record and the earning power of the borrower. To increase their returns on such loans and to obtain some protection in case of default, most lenders insist that the borrower maintain some minimum amount of the money in the bank, known as compensating balance, while the loan is outstanding. Although the borrower pays interest on full amount of the loan, a substantial portion of it remains as deposit in the bank. Another important type of unsecured loan that eliminates the negotiation with the bank each time the business needs to borrow, is called the line of credit. However the line of credit does not guarantee that loan will be available. If a firm's commitment is required, a revolving line of credit is agreed upon which guarantees that the bank will honor the line of credit up to the stated amount, for an extra fee.

(*c*) ***Commercial paper***

A short-term financing option that has become increasingly popular is to borrow from other business and investors. The company borrowing money issues commercial paper, which represents a promise to pay back a stated amount of money within the stated number of days (legally, 1 to 270 days). The business or investor generally buys commercial paper at a price lower than the face value; then at the end of the period, the buyer receives the face value, the difference of which is the equivalent of the interest on the loan.

3. *Long-term financing*

One of the basic principles of finance is that long-lived assets are purchased with long-term funds. To finance long-term projects such as major construction, acquisition of other companies, research and development, most companies rely on a combination of internal and external funding resources (Fig. 8.8). The four main sources of external funding are loans, leases, bonds and equity.

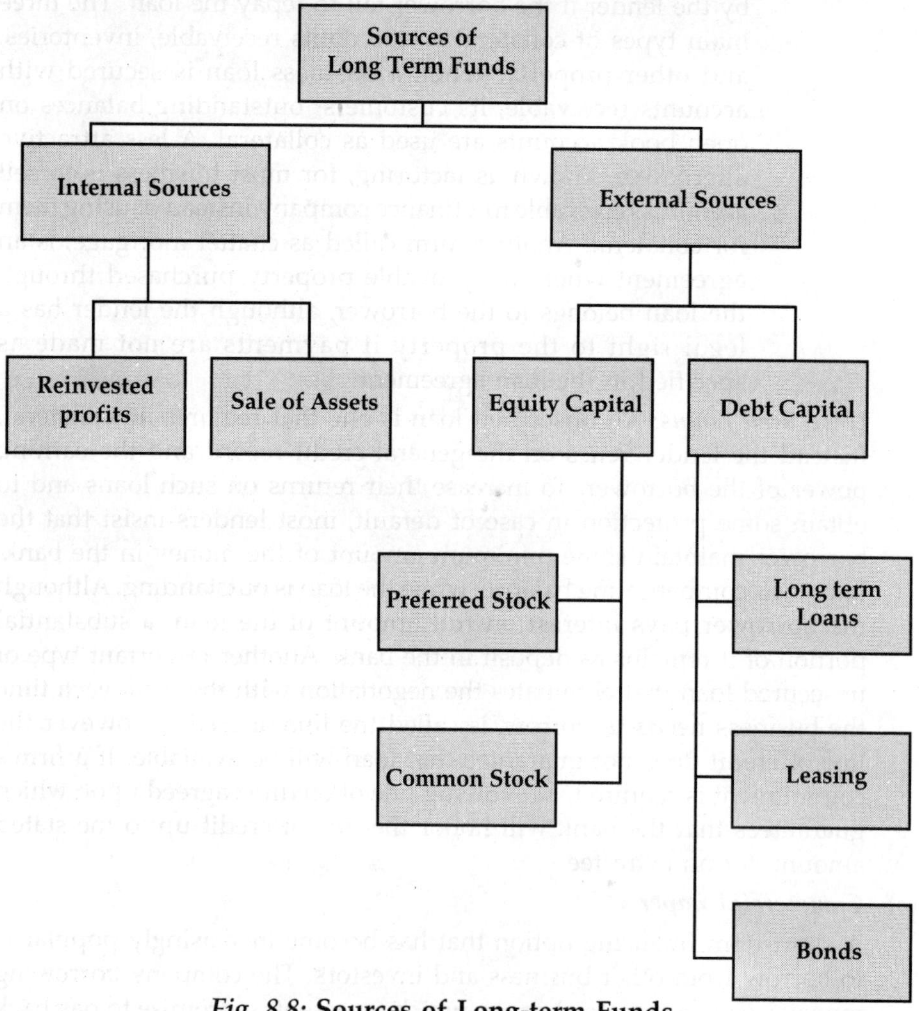

Fig. 8.8: **Sources of Long-term Funds**

1. Debt Capital

(*a*) *Long-term loans:* Long-term loans are repaid over a period of one year or more and can be either secured or unsecured. Most common type of secured loan is a mortgage, in which a piece of property is used as collateral.

(*b*) *Lease:* A firm may enter in to a lease agreement rather than borrowing from a commercial lender to buy a piece of equipment or property. In a lease agreement, the owner of an item allows another party to use it in exchange for regular payments.

(*c*) *Bonds:* When a company needs to borrow a large sum of money, it may not be able to get the entire amount from a single source. Under such circumstances, it may borrow from many individual investors by issuing bonds. A bond is a certificate of indebtedness that is sold to raise funds, and the company is obliged to repay the sum plus interest to the bondholder. Each bond has a denomination, amount of loan represented by one bond. Bonds typically have maturity dates of 10 years or more. Like loans, bonds may be either secured bond (backed by specific property of one kind or another) or unsecured bond also called debentures (backed not by collateral but by the general good name of the issuing company).

2. Equity Capital

Unlike debts, which must be repaid, equity represents a "piece of action". When a company raises capital by increasing equity, it expands the ownership of the business. Stocks can be sold to many individual investors on the open market. A company may issue two types of stocks:

(*a*) *Preferred stock:* Preferred stock gives its holders certain privileges that holders of common stock do not have. They are preferred as to dividends. They are preferred as to assets. It has some of the features of a bond and some of a common stock. Like a bond, preferred stock carries a fixed income payment or dividend. But the dividend represents a distribution of corporate profits, not payment of interest on debt. Like ownership of common stock, ownership of preferred stock represents ownership of the issuing company (corporation). Preferred stock doesn't have a maturity date. In the event of liquidation of the firm, the claims of preferred stock come before those of common stockholders but after those of the bondholders.

(*b*) *Common stock:* Common stockholders are owners of corporation. By purchasing a share of stock, an investor is buying a "share" of the ownership pie. The total number of shares held by all investors represents the total ownership of the corporation. Common stock is less predictable but potentially more valuable.

3. Retained Earnings

Retained earnings are the amount of money left at year end after all expenses, interest payments, taxes and dividends have been paid. They are just about the only source of capital for smaller companies.

4. Sale of Assets

A company may also decide to sell its unutilized or non-performing assets to maintain its liquidity or reinvest that amount in some productive areas that could fetch it higher returns or help it repay its outstanding or market debts.

Personnel (Human Resource) Management

Managing Human Resource in today's Business Environment

As national economies are getting integrated with the global economy, the businesses are forced to develop strategies that help them compete by cutting costs and permitting flexibility, so that they can respond to customers' changing needs. But necessary as these strategies are, they can bump headfirst into another important organizational need—finding, hiring, training and motivating employees who can function as empowered members of teams, pursuing organizational goals at a level of high productivity. Add to this the dynamics of an increasingly diverse workforce and managing human resource becomes a constant challenge.

Human Resource is the sum of activities required to attract, select, develop and retain people with knowledge and skills needed to achieve an organizational objective.

The Changing Workforce

Here are some of the predicted changes and some current findings for the next decade:

1. ***Many more women will work outside the home:*** It is predicted that more and more working-age women will join the workforce. They will also join that segment of jobs that were hereby held exclusively by males.
2. ***Minority and immigrant workers will be a larger portion of workforce:*** The number of immigrants joining the workplace across major service locations throughout the world is going to increase as major economies around the world are integrating the global economy.
3. ***Percentage of workers in the contingent workforce will increase:*** Part-time, temporary and self-employed workers will be found in increasing share as more and more people opt for being entrepreneur and companies too focus on cost cutting.

4. *Labour shortages will occur:* The rate of growth in labour force will fall sharply, as per year lesser numbers of people join the workforce and more start up their own enterprises.
5. *Jobs will require developed skills:* As increased number of jobs will be service, technical or managerial positions, employers will increasingly demand more skilled and trained employees.

Human Resource Process/Functions

1. *Human resource planning:* It is a process of determining future manpower requirements and the means for meeting these requirements in order to carry out integrated plans of the organization.
2. *Job analysis:* It is a systematic collection; evaluation and organization of information about a job i.e., job duties, qualifications required, working environment, and evaluation of worth of a job.
3. *Recruitment:* It is a process of finding and attracting capable applicants for employment. It can be done either through the internal or external procedure.
4. *Selection:* It is the process by which an enterprise chooses from a pool of applicants those persons who best meet the organizational criteria for positions available in given environmental conditions.
5. *Training and Development:* Training is a process of increasing the knowledge and skills of an employee for doing a particular job. It is usually applied on current job applications of non-managerial staff. Development is a programme designed to improve existing capacities of a manager to meet future organizational requirements. Various on-the-job as well as off-the-job methods are available for imparting training and development to the employees.
6. *Performance appraisal:* It is a formal system of periodical review and evaluation of an individual job performance. There are various formal and informal methods for performance appraisal.
7. *Compensation:* It refers to every type of reward that an individual receives in return of his labour. It can be either in financial terms or non-financial terms.
8. *Movement of personnel:* It refers to the displacement of the personnel within the organization. It is done through promotion, transfer or initiating disciplinary action.

Summary

- The entrepreneurs should know and practice different areas of management as business functions. Through marketing, finance, operations, and human resource business functions they manage their enterprises.

Self-learning Activity

Try to answer the following questions on your own:

1. Explain market segmentation?
2. Discuss the financial management process?
3. Give an account of HRM's significance in managing enterprises?

9

Factors that Influence Entrepreneurship Development Programme

Need for/Benefits of Entrepreneurship

Entrepreneurship has social and economic benefits to the individual and to the nation. The following are the benefits of Entrepreneurship Development Programme (EDP).

1. ***Economic growth:*** EDP encourages fast economic growth and new employment opportunities are created. EDP also encourages the growth of multi-national organizations and large-scale industries.
2. ***Productivity:*** Productivity denotes the ability to produce more goods and services with less labour and other inputs. Higher productivity is guaranteed by EDP, through improved production techniques. Research and development and investment in new plant are ensuring productivity.
3. ***New technologies, products, and services:*** Through innovative techniques, products and services entrepreneurs bring new knowledge and techniques of production.
4. ***Market change:*** Market change and expansion of markets take place by the entrepreneurs. They act as agents of change in a market economy. The international markets also provide entrepreneurial opportunity.

Factors that Influence EDP

The factors that influence entrepreneurship development can be classified as internal factors and external factors.

I. Internal Factors

Internal factors are relating to the personality of an individual and they are psychological in nature and motivate an individual to become an entrepreneur. Family plays an important role as an internal factor for entrepreneurship. The internal factors are categorized as follows:

Demographic Factors	Personal Characteristics	Social Factors
• Age • Gender • Birth order • Education • Ethnic background • Nationality	• Technical expertise • Managerial expertise • Entrepreneurial expertise • Leadership skills • Personal values	• Parental role models • Cultural role models • Family support • Community
Personality Traits	**Cultural Factors**	**Environmental Factors**
• Achievement motive • Focus of control • Risk taking • Tolernce of ambiguity • Need for independence	• Individualism/Collectivism • Uncertainty avoidance • Materialism • Dynamism	• Lack of employment • Little opportunity for advancement • Economic resources • Economic resources • Political climate

II. External Factors

External factors lay outside the environment and they influence internal factors. They also motivate and encourage a person to take decisions to become an entrepreneur.

1. *Political environment*

   The political environment within a country influences government policies, which in turn influences entrepreneurship. Political stability, stable governments, stable policies, encouraging taxation policies, foreign investment opportunities, etc. come under political environment.

2. *Social and cultural environment*

   This factor is an extended version of family environment. The encouragement of certain societies and communities towards entrepreneurship could be a factor in certain countries for entrepreneurship. Some cultures encourage entrepreneurship, some encourages government jobs, and some encourages private sector jobs.

3. *Economic environment*

   The economic environment denotes the ancestral property or property earned by an individual, current income status, standard of living, financial status he enjoys, etc. These factors influence the size of business and capacity to take risk. At the macro level, factors like market structure, competition, availability of capital, raw material, etc., have influence on entrepreneurship.

4. *Legal environment*

   Business has to operate basically in a legal environment. There are various laws that prevail in a country relating to license, permit, tax, labour laws, etc., which encourage or discourage entrepreneurship.

5. *Technological environment*

   A new entrepreneur must have sound knowledge on latest technology and new product development. The best example is computer-based industries.

Business Success and Failure of Entrepreneurship

Business Success – Factors

In running a business or small-scale industry, there are number of social, economic, political and environmental factors that may lead to the business success. Here below, find some of the important factors for business success.

1. ***Hard work:*** Hard work of the entrepreneur during the initial stages of the enterprise as well as hard work in due course will lead to the success of the business. An entrepreneur should give continuity in his hard work.
2. ***Time/Speed:*** In undertaking a business, an entrepreneur must do the stages of work in time. For example, conducting feasibility studies, project preparation, and project appraisal must be done in time. Speed is also essential for the success of a business. Punctuality and timeliness are also relative factors of time and speed.
3. ***Self-reliance:*** Self-reliance denotes the dependability of the entrepreneur in taking risks on his own. He cannot depend on others to take risk.
4. ***Communication:*** An entrepreneur has to communicate with the customers, marketers, financiers, and other people involved in his business frequently.
5. ***Motivator:*** A successful entrepreneur motivates others around him and gets himself motivated. He has to motivate his workers as well as his distributors and customers to make his venture success.
6. ***Initiative:*** In organizing the business as well as running the business, he himself undertakes the initiative. He will not depend on others to take initiative, but he may consult others for improving his business.
7. ***Discipline:*** A successful entrepreneur is disciplined one in organizing the business, running the business, spending the resources, and keeping punctuality. His whole concentration is to make the business success.
8. ***Willpower:*** Willpower is the determination one should have to complete a work successfully. Willpower goes with hard work and facing so many challenges in running a business.

Leadership

A leader is one who is taking initiative to organize a business and run the business successfully. He performs himself as an example to others and spearheads the business for success. Some of the leadership qualities in business are as follows:

1. Selfless nature
2. Dedication
3. Example for others
4. Clean and uncorrupt nature
5. Creating followers
6. Achievement motivation
7. Impress people around him

Need for Leadership in Business

The following are the factors, which explain the need for leadership in business:

(*a*) ***To run a business successfully:*** To run a business successfully, an entrepreneur must act as a leader. He must plan the programs properly and must take steps to implement the program stage by stage.

(*b*) ***To face competition:*** In any business or industry, stiff competition is there. The success of an entrepreneur lies in facing the competition and come out successfully. For this purpose, leadership quality is necessary.

(*c*) ***Sustainability:*** Sustainability denotes the running of business successfully from the beginning to the end. There should not be any leniency in the middle in running the business.

(*d*) ***Expansion:*** A business leader after the initial success would like to expand his business. Through this process, many famous industrial houses have come up in various countries.

(*e*) ***Team building:*** Leadership is necessary to provide team spirit in the particular organization. Team spirit is necessary especially among the employees who are working in the organization.

(*f*) ***To face external environment:*** External environments like social, economic, and political situations affect the success of a business organization. To face them, leadership is necessary.

Critical Elements of Entrepreneurship

Entrepreneurship has lot of characteristics, which have been explained in the introduction chapters. Here, we can discuss the critical elements apart from the characteristics of an entrepreneur, which are needed for an enterprise.

1. ***Risk taking:*** This is the basic element needed for an individual to undertake an enterprise. There are various types of risks that may come across in a business like organizational risk, financial risk, marketing risk, environmental risk, etc.
2. ***Negotiating skill:*** To make the enterprise a success, an entrepreneur must have negotiating skill. He must come in to contact with officials, customers, distributors, financiers, partners, etc. He should have the bargaining skill to achieve his objectives successfully. His manners and activities should please the above group.
3. ***Time management skill:*** To start a business and to run the business, time management is one of the critical elements needed. All activities must be completed punctually as per the time schedule planned.
4. ***Motivating and leading:*** An entrepreneur should motivate his colleagues and workers and take the lead in running the business successfully.

Barriers to Entrepreneurship

While undertaking a business, the following difficulties may have to be encountered by the entrepreneurs.

1. ***Government regulations:*** An entrepreneur has to follow government regulations and such regulations may be changing very often.
2. ***Competition:*** This is the most important challenge an entrepreneur has to face.
3. ***Unsteady market:*** Many times, the market situations may fluctuate and may put lot of difficulties for an entrepreneur.
4. ***Change in consumer behaviour:*** Due to change in fashion and taste, the consumers may change their consumer behaviour, which may affect the marketing of the product of an entrepreneur. So, he has to watch closely the consumer behaviour.

Factors for Failure

The following are the factors, which may lead to the failure of enterprises.

1. ***Delay:*** Delay in starting the venture and delay in getting infrastructure facilities like license, power, water, etc., may lead to the failure.
2. ***Coordination:*** Coordination between various financial agencies, distributors, etc., is needed to make a venture successful. Lack of coordination may lead to failure.
3. ***Suppliers:*** Raw material suppliers must supply the materials in time and with prescribed quality to the organization. Their failure may lead to total failure.

4. ***Following the rules and regulations:*** An entrepreneur has to follow the government rules and regulations relating to tax payment, labour laws, etc. Any failure to follow the rules may lead to action by the government and failure of the business.
5. ***Labour turnover:*** Labour turnover denotes shifting of the job by a worker from one industry to other industry frequently. This may affect the working condition of a firm.
6. ***Raw material:*** Raw materials must be available cheaply and nearer to the production center. Otherwise, this may lead to failure.
7. ***Cost escalation:*** The cost of erecting machineries, the cost of labour, etc are high, which may lead to the failure of the firm.
8. ***Training:*** Lack of training for the workers and the manager may lead to the failure of the enterprise.
9. ***Technology updating:*** If a firm is not updating its technology, production may come down, quality may be affected, and ultimately lead to the failure.
10. ***Competition:*** Any industry will have competition. If a firm is not surviving in the competition, it may lead to the failure.

Summary

- There are internal and external factors which influence EDP. They resulted to success and failure means that there are some factors lead to success and some failure.
- There are also certain critical elements of entrepreneurship.

Self-learning Activity

Try to answer the following questions on your own:

1. What are the factors for success of EDP?
2. What are the critical elements of entrepreneurship?

10

Small Scale and Rural Industries

Meaning of Small Scale and Rural Industries

A Small Scale Industry or a small business is defined by USA's Small Business Association as "is one that does not dominate its industry".

1. A small scale industry is one which is organized with low capital;
2. It is labour-intensive in nature;
3. A small beginning is made to start with;
4. Entire risk is taken by the promoter.

Classification of Small Scale Industries

1. Manufacturing industries
2. Feeder industries – Casting, welding etc.
3. Service industries – Repair, etc.
4. Mining or quarrying
5. Ancillary or spare parts

Rural or Village or Cottage Industries

1. Located in rural areas
2. Using locally available raw material
3. Traditional technology applied
4. Dependence on local market
5. Entire family members are involved

Objectives of Small Scale Industries

1. Provide employment opportunities to the local population.
2. Promoting the production of large variety of goods – labour intensive methods.

3. Encouraging the adoption of modern techniques without causing technological unemployment.
4. Facilitating the mobilization of capital and skill which are remained unused.
5. Integrating small sector with large scale industries.
6. Encouraging and supporting local talents using local resources.
7. Avoiding the problems of unplanned industrialization.
8. Equitable distribution of national income and balanced growth of industries and avoiding regional imbalances.
9. Creating a cadre of small entrepreneurs, professionals and self-employed experts.
10. Dispersal of industries throughout the country.

Advantages of Small Scale and Rural Industries

1. They are mainly located in rural areas.
2. They are the main sources of employment opportunities in countries where the density of population is high.
3. They remove the drawbacks of large-scale industries like monopoly, abnormal profit, concentration of wealth and economic power.
4. They avoid the concentration of industries in a particular area.
5. New but simple techniques of production can be adopted with less capital.
6. They foster individual skill and initiative, and promote self-employment particularly among educated youth.
7. They pave the way for decentralized industrial growth.
8. Small industries result in higher national income, higher purchasing power in rural areas and high standard of living.
9. They reduce the rural urban gap.
10. Reduction in urban pollution.
11. Encouragement of even development of industries and encouragement of traditional industries.

Summary

- Small scale and village industries are playing crucial role in economic development of a country. They contribute much to the nation's GDP.

Self-learning Activity

Try to answer the following questions on your own:

1. What are the objectives of small scale and village industries?
2. List out the advantages of small scale and village industries?

11

Agencies for Entrepreneurship Development Programme

Role of Government and Non-Government Agencies in Entrepreneurship Development Programme (EDP)

In the entrepreneurial development government as well as non-government agencies are engaged in their promotion. There are three types of roles that are played by government and non-government agencies. Such roles are as follows:

1. ***Promotional Role***

   In this role both government and non-governmental agencies try to promote entrepreneurship by awareness building, encouragement, motivation, and guidance. The entrepreneurial spirit is encouraged by publicity and promotional efforts. Various EDP measures fall under this category. The objective of the role of these agencies is to attract people to start new ventures on their own. Identification of potential entrepreneurs through research and scientific methods has to be done. The efforts for the promotion of entrepreneurship are of three types:

   (*a*) *Awareness creation programme:* Through such programmes efforts are taken by agencies to create awareness among prospective entrepreneurs about various schemes, financial arrangements, marketing channels, etc.

   (*b*) *Programme on creation of new entrepreneurs:* Under this promotional role, training arrangements are made for the prospective entrepreneurs.

   (*c*) *Programme for current entrepreneurs:* Under this programme, the existing entrepreneurs are given managerial training and related programmes on marketing, new technology, etc.

The above programmes can be grouped again under three categories:

(*a*) *Target group oriented:* Under this category, promotional role is given to specific groups like youth, women, rural, technical entrepreneurs.

(*b*) *Products specific:* Under this category product base promotional role are given to entrepreneurs. Example, food products, engineering units, mechanical units, etc.

(*c*) *Location specific:* Promotional role is given to entrepreneurs on regionwise or particular industrial areawise.

2. ***Supportive Role***

Various agencies lend support in establishing and managing enterprises. Supportive role helps in promotional, maintenance, and development of entrepreneurship. Supportive role includes setting up of industries in exclusive areas like industrial estates and giving infrastructural facilities (road, water, power, etc). Financial support in the form concessional rate of interest, tax holidays, etc., are also given. Institutions providing supportive role are established at regional levels and national level.

3. ***Regulatory Role***

After the promotion and supportive role, the need for regulation and control emerges. Through various laws, government tries to regulate and control entrepreneurs. The regulatory institutions give clearance for the construction of factories, supply of power, tax relief, concessions, etc. All regulatory institutions have their policies and programmes to provide necessary support to entrepreneurs. The rules and regulations relating to the regulatory role should be simple and positive for the promotion of entrepreneurship.

The promotional and development activities for entrepreneurs are undertaken under two categories, namely entrepreneurship development programmes and entrepreneurial training.

Phases of EDP

An EDP involves three phases:

1. ***Initial Phase (Pre-Training Phase)***

Through publicity and training programmes awareness is created about the entrepreneurial opportunities.

2. ***Development Phase (Training Phase)***

Under training two types of training are given to the entrepreneurs, the first one is general training, which imparts need for entrepreneurship, factors affecting entrepreneurship, benefits of entrepreneurship, etc.,

Under the second type of training, motivation training is given to the entrepreneurs. Factors that motivate people to become entrepreneurs are taught to the prospective entrepreneurs.

3. *Support Phase (Post-Training Phase)*

   Under this category, counseling, encouragement, infrastructural, financial support are provided for establishing and running a new enterprise.

An EDP can be promoted in different phases. It is not necessary that all EDPs have to go through all phases. Some EDPs can be developed to take care of only one phase. First, the pre-training phase, where the programme is to be advertised, trainees have to be selected and arrangement of venue, infrastructure, framing of syllabus, etc., is to be organized. In the second phase training is given, which is the training phase. After the programme is over, feedback should be collected and it is the post-phase training or follow-up phase.

EDPs should develop programmes on the latest issues and train the entrepreneurs to face challenges, for example in the case of WTO. It paves the way for the free exchange of goods and services across countries, resulting in free imports, which would have a direct impact on the small-scale industries. As quantitative restrictions on as many as 800 items are to be lifted as per the agreement of WTO, training on such programmes can be organized.

Some of the criticisms relating to EDP are as follows:

1. Poor quality of training
2. Lack of commitment from the organizers
3. Lack of focus
4. Lack of follow-up
5. Lack of support
6. Emphasis on quantity but not on quality

MASLOW'S NEED HIERARCHY THEORY

In order to understand what motivates people to become entrepreneurs, Maslow's Theory would be helpful. His theory is based on human needs. He classified human needs into five different categories in order of priority from lower to higher needs (*Diagram 11.1*). He called them hierarchy of needs. The reason why they are called so is because certain needs have to be fulfilled before human beings seek the next higher level need. If one is hungry, he will first demand food, before seeking prestige or status. Thus, when the lower needs are satisfied a new and higher need emerges and the process continues.

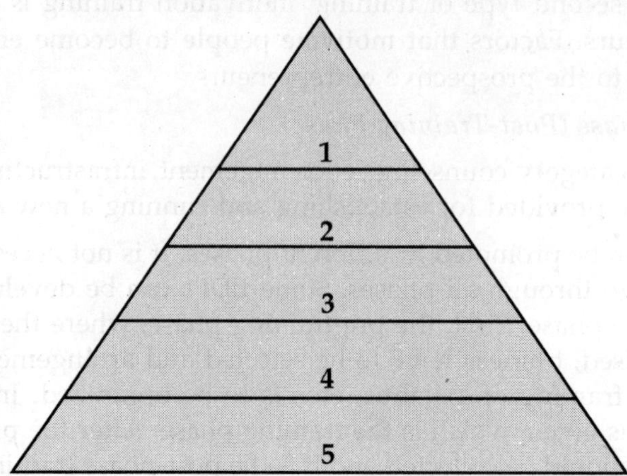

Diagram 11.1

1. *Physiological Needs:* Needs like food, clothing, shelter, air, and other necessities of life.
2. *Safety and Security Needs:* Such as economic security and protection from physical dangers.
3. *Social Needs:* Refer to a sense of belonging, recognition, acceptance, interaction, etc.
4. *Esteem Needs:* Which are in terms of self-esteem, self-respect, self-confidence, achievement, reputation, etc.
5. *Self-Actualization Need:* Which aims at self-fulfillment. Once this need is satisfied, human needs cease to be a motivating factor.

For entrepreneurs mainly the social, esteem and self-actualization needs motivate them to work more and more. Different types of motivating factors could be:

(*a*) ambition, compelling or facilitating;

(*b*) economic or non-economic;

(*c*) intrinsic or extrinsic.

Some of the factors, which prompt one to become entrepreneurs, are enterprising attitude, training and education, previous experience which are intrinsic factors and extrinsic factors like shortages, government assistance, taking over the running units, made available at a cheap price, etc.

Summary

- In the entrepreneurial development government as well as non-government agencies are engaged in their promotion. There are three types of roles that are played by government and non-government agencies: promotional, supportive and regulatory roles.

- Initial, development and support phases are involved in EDP.

Self-learning Activity

Try to answer the following questions on your own:

1. What are the roles played by agencies?
2. Give an account of different phases of EDP?

12

Schemes and Incentives for Women and Unemployed Youth

Problems of Women Entrepreneurs

Women entrepreneurs may be defined as 'woman or a group of women who initiate, organize, and run a business enterprise'. According to another definition, a woman-run enterprise is defined as 'an enterprise owned and controlled by a woman having a minimum financial interest of 51 per cent of the capital and giving at least 51 per cent of the employment generated in the enterprise to women'. The following are the major problems of women entrepreneurs.

1. ***Lack of education***

   Compared to men, the rate of literacy among women is low. In the competitive world, women also lag behind men in getting technical and professional education, which are needed to manage an enterprise. Having little education and less experience, it is not possible to run an enterprise in today's context.

2. ***Male dominated society***

   Our society is still dominated by men. In very many societies women are not allowed to take jobs or organize their own enterprises. Such seclusion makes women not to venture in organizing business or small scale industries.

3. ***Limited mobility***

   Due to primary household responsibilities towards her family, her time gets divided between two worlds. She has restricted timings for work due to which, she is not in a position to travel frequently and be away for longer periods. Thus, her mobility is restricted, which will have its impact on business.

4. ***Problem of finance***
   To raise finance from banking organizations and other sources, property is necessary. In many societies, property is in the name of male members and this restricts them to raise funds. They have to manage funds through other ways of raising money from friends and relatives. Under restricted financial conditions, an enterprise cannot be run on a successful line.

5. ***Low risk bearing ability***
   Women by nature are unable to take risks which are very high in organizing and running business organizations. The protected nature of bringing the girl child from the childhood also makes her inability to take risks.

6. ***Social recognition***
   In many conservative societies, women are not given due recognition to undertake business enterprises. They are looked down as small and weak. Even in advanced societies, women take lot of time to get recognition for their achievements in their enterprises.

7. ***Management and control***
   In managing business organizations as well as controlling such organizations, she has to depend on the men folk or her husband or family members. Even in Europe, it has been pointed out only three per cent of the CEOs consist of women.

8. ***Continuity in enterprises***
   An enterprise can be successful if it is taken care from its inception to the final successful stage. Continuity is needed. But women due to their family and related commitments are not in a position to give continuity. This can be endorsed by the failure of enterprises started by women.

Scope/Steps to Encourage Women and Unemployed Youth

Encouragement of Women

The following steps are advocated to encourage women to undertake enterprises:

1. ***Access to capital, infrastructure, and markets***
   Government and related organizations like banking institutions must come forward to provide liberal capital to organize enterprises by women. Infrastructure facilities in the form of industrial estates exclusively for women can be established. Marketing facilities for the products of women entrepreneurs can also be arranged by governments.

2. ***Development of managerial and production capacities***
   Training and development activities can be developed especially for women entrepreneurs and such training could be given to selected target groups. Training should be made a continuous process for such women entrepreneurs.

3. ***Identifying investment opportunities***

   Government and NGOs must come forward to identify investment opportunities and production venture suited to women. In all regions of the country selected areas can be located and such investment opportunities can be initiated and it can be extended to other areas in future.

4. ***Promotional measures***

   Promotional measures like sponsoring, delegating, participation in trade fairs, exhibitions, arranging buyer-seller meets and specialized conferences, etc., can help the promotion of women entrepreneurs.

5. ***Seminars and workshops***

   Organizing seminars, workshops, and training programs for giving wider exposure to women entrepreneurs will be useful to develop their entrepreneurial capabilities.

6. ***Tie up arrangement***

   Women enterprises can be tied to medium and large scale industries for marketing their products and to make a permanent development for their enterprises.

Unemployed Youth

The following are the measures considered to develop unemployed youth in organizing their enterprises.

1. ***Identification of enterprises***

   The government and the promotional agencies must identify suitable areas for developing the enterprises for unemployed youth. Areas like computer, engineering, technology, etc can be identified and can be addressed to the youth.

2. ***Banking institutions***

   The banking institutions must come forward to finance the unemployed youth liberally. Only banking institutions can initiate the enterprise revolution among the unemployed youth.

3. ***Training***

   At the national level various types of technical and managerial institutions must be promoted by government to promote the entrepreneurial interest of unemployed youth. Various types of training on a continuous basis must be given to them.

4. ***Marketing***

   The products and services, which are the outcome of the unemployed youth and their enterprises, must be helped in the form of marketing. Marketing is an important area for the success of the ventures promoted by unemployed youth.

5. *Seminars and conferences*

   Seminars and conferences relating to self-employment and new ventures must be arranged by the government, chamber of commerce, industrial associations, etc.

Schemes for Women and Unemployed Youth

Government's latest strategy followed for the development of industries, including small-scale industries in Ethiopia is known as Agriculture Development Led Industrialization (ADLI). This implies to increase agricultural productivity and industrialization based on the utilization of domestic raw materials with labor-intensive technology. Thus, the economic development strategy visualized export-led growth, which feeds into an independent agricultural and industrial development. By and large, the strategy of ADLI in Ethiopia focused primarily on agricultural development. This is to be attained through improved productivity in small holdings and expansion of large scale farms particularly in the low lands. The contribution of agriculture to economic development is conceived into two ways, on one side agricultural output and on the other side it will expand the market for domestic manufacturers.

Economically women in Ethiopia are given important role in the implementation of five year development programs, which is based on ADLI. The question of access to their basic economic rights has been addressed by the new constitution of Federal Democratic Government of Ethiopia, guaranteeing the equal rights with men. Land re-distribution programmes were undertaken in some regions where women were treated equally with men.

According to the 1995-96 Central Statistical Authority survey, there were about 2731 small-scale manufacturing industries and 8,92,719 cottage or handicraft industries registered in Ethiopia. The gross value of production of small scale manufacturing industries and cottage/handicraft industries in 1995-96 was 187.8 million birr and more 2 billion respectively. The number of persons engaged in these sub-sectors was 8,929 and 1.3 million respectively.

To encourage small scale industries and to encourage women entrepreneurs, the federal government carried out economic policy reform measures and formulated sound development strategies. In every region a Micro and Small Scale Development Agency was established to promote small scale industries. In Oromiya region the agency was established in the year 1998. It started its operations from January 2001. This agency has opened its branches in the zones of the region. In the post-1974 period, an agency called Handicrafts and Small Scale Industries Development Agency (HASIDA) was set-up to promote small-scale industries. But the agency has not been materialized.

I. *Specific women projects*

The specific women projects were also undertaken to improve the employment opportunities and entrepreneurship of women. In specific women's projects, women are the main target group and the main participants are also women. An example of women's project is Chacha project of the Amhara Women's Development Association of Region 3. The main objectives of the project are as follows:

1. To create income and food access to deprived households.
2. To organize educational discussion forums to create awareness against harmful traditional practices and negative attitudes.
3. To improve women's technical know how, skills, and self-employment.

The project has two components—a credit service and training workshops. In the workshops the participants deal with issues like women's rights, family planning, and advantages of organizations. Some of the advantages of this project are as follows:

1. There is more flexibility to respond specifically to women's needs.
2. Women can make decisions and assume leadership roles.
3. Women can undertake activities and initiatives, which may lead a community to change their attitudes on women and their capacities.
4. In the long run the project may be a catalyst for change, contributing to the development of strong women's institutions.

II. *Project with women's component*

A women's component in a project is characterized by the organization of separate activities for women within a general project. A team of people and budget are assigned to these activities. A good illustration is the Ethiopian Environmental NGO located in Selalle. The project covers agro-forestry, agricultural practices, water development, institutional capacity building, rehabilitation of disadvantaged groups such as drop-outs and ex-soldiers. The women's component is women's development. It has training and credit as main activities and an expert is assigned for running the project activities. Some advantages of the project are:

1. Women are assured of access to project resources.
2. Women have equal access as men to the main activities of the project.
3. Women's component will make women visible and draw attention of the decision-making to women's problems.

Problems of Women Entrepreneurs in Ethiopia

The following problems are encountered for women entrepreneurs:

1. Shortage of working and investment capital resulted from gender inequalities

Due to deep rooted social norms and values, women in most of the communities in Ethiopia lack equal rights in passing decisions on properties or resources. This condition puts women in a most difficult situation to raise sufficient money for investment either from their own savings or credit, as they cannot meet collateral requirements of lending institutions.

2. Work burden of women

Women in Ethiopia are entrusted with wide range of responsibilities that include contributing labor to production activities, upkeeping home, rearing children, and others. In this regard, they face shortage of time in carrying out the business activities.

3. Lack of basic business skills and technical knowledge

In Ethiopia, in many parts of the country, women do not have equal access to education and training with men. As there are general shortages of such services, men seize the existing limited opportunities. Therefore, women remain losers and consequent lack of proper skill and knowledge to undertake business activities.

4. Other cultural barriers

Women are not encouraged or motivated to own and run income generating activities that could improve their economic conditions. Although women significantly participate in all economic and production activities, they are not accorded proper recognition for their contribution due to the cultural barriers, which consider women as weak, less reliable, and inefficient.

Problems Relating to Youth

1. *Poor entrepreneurial qualities*

   The educational system that the country pursued in the past years did not prepare the youth technically and psychologically for self-employment. This developed negative attitude towards self-employment.

2. *Lack of basic managerial and technical skills*

   The school system, which the students underwent, did not equip them with adequate technical and managerial skills that would enable them to harness the existing and potential resources for enterprise development.

3. *Shortage of capital and working premises*

   These are also the major pressing problems that hindered the entrance of unemployed youth to the small scale sector.

Summary

- Women entrepreneurs may be defined as 'woman or a group of women who initiate, organize, and run a business enterprise'.
- Youth entrepreneurs are engaged in business activities that they can do better for their livelihood.
- There are problems faced by women and youths in venturing a business. The government through schemes and programmes is trying to curtail the problems and encouraging them to engage in business activities as entrepreneurs.

Self-learning Activity

Try to answer the following questions on your own:

1. What are the problems of women entrepreneurs?
2. What are the problems relating to youth?
3. Give an account of measures to encourage women entrepreneurs?

13

Procedures and Steps Involved in Establishing Small Scale and Village Industries

Before a venture is started, certain preliminary steps must be taken as a logical step. An entrepreneur starts with business idea generation and identification of business opportunities. Then, marketing, financial, and technical feasibilities are undertaken. The last stage is the preparation of project report by the entrepreneur and the project appraisal by the banking institutions and promotional agencies.

Business Idea Generation Techniques and Identification of Business Opportunities

A business idea is a business seed, which expands and grows into a business tree. A business idea can emerge from two sources, namely, technical source and market source.

A. Technical Source (within the company)

Technical source emerges within the company. Technicians, managers, supervisors, and workers think over new products and new ideas. New ideas are generated as follows:

1. By the scientist working in the Research and Development department of the organization.
2. By the engineers working in the production department.
3. By the field staff who may get new ideas while solving problems. These new ideas are relating to:
   (*a*) New methods to be adopted for production
   (*b*) New product design
   (*c*) New machinery, etc.

B. Market Source (outside the company)

There are various methods of generating ideas from market sources. They are:

1. ***Focus groups***

   In this method, group of consumers are interviewed. A moderator leads the group through an in-depth discussion. A group consisting of 8 to 14 members is stimulated for developing a new product.

2. ***Brain storming***

   In this method also a group of consumers are selected. Brain storming tends to generate lot of ideas. In this method, the group is encouraged to combine various ideas and improvement of these ideas leads to new ideas.

3. ***Problem inventory analysis***

   This method uses individuals rather than a group to generate new product ideas. Instead of generating new ideas themselves, participants are provided with a list of problems for a product category. They are then asked to identify and discuss products in this category.

4. ***Checklist method***

   In this method a new idea is developed through a list of related issues or suggestions. An entrepreneur can use a list of questions to guide the direction of developing entirely new ideas. The checklist may take any form at any length.

5. ***Free association***

   This technique is used in developing entirely a new idea. First, a word or phrase related to a problem is written, and then it is developed, thereby creating a chain of ideas with a new product.

6. ***Value analysis***

   This technique develops methods for maximizing value to the entrepreneur. In value analysis procedure, regularly scheduled times are established to develop, evaluate, and refine ideas.

Identification of Business Opportunities

After the generation of various business ideas, the next step would be to screen them for identifying the business opportunities. An entrepreneur should have an ability to spot a business opportunity among the various business ideas. An opportunity has the qualities of being attractive, durable, and timely and is anchored in a product or service, which creates or adds value for its buyer or end-user.

Various sources of business identification opportunity

There are three sources through which we can identify a business opportunity.

1. *Systematic innovation*

   According to Peter Drucker, systematic innovation means monitoring the seven sources innovative opportunities. The first four sources of innovative opportunities lie within the enterprise. The other three sources refer to changes outside the company.

Internal sources of innovating opportunities

(*a*) ***Unexpected success and unexpected failure:*** No other area offers rich opportunities for successful innovation than an unexpected success. Unexpected successes are totally neglected. On the other hand, unexpected failures cannot be rejected and rarely go unnoticed.

(*b*) ***Incongruity (Inconsistency):*** This is a symptom of an opportunity to innovate. It creates an instability in which minor efforts can move large masses and bring about a re-structuring of the economic or social conditions.

(*c*) ***Process need:*** It is task-focused rather than situation-focused. It perfects a process that already exists and sometimes it makes possible a process by supplying the missing link.

(*d*) ***Industry and market structure:*** A change in the industry's structure and market structure offers exceptional opportunities.

External sources of innovating opportunities

(*a*) ***Demography:*** Change in population provides innovative opportunities.

(*b*) ***A change in perception:*** A critical problem in perception-based innovation is timing. Timing is the essence of exploiting change in perception.

(*c*) ***New knowledge:*** They are based on the convergence of different kinds of knowledge. Knowledge-based innovation requires careful analysis of all the new factors, whether knowledge itself, or social, economic, or perceptual factors.

2. *Trade Fairs and Exhibitions*

   They are conducted at local level, regional level, national level, and international level. They provide greater opportunities for identifying business opportunities.

3. *Positioning*

   Positioning is the position of the product or brand in the minds of the consumers. With the help of marketing research, it is possible to quantify and see the perceptual map, which shows the gap in the market. Positioning can be undertaken by means of promotional and advertising measures.

Marketing, Financial, and Technical Feasibilities

A feasibility study is the evaluation of a business idea. A feasibility study can be undertaken by the entrepreneur himself or through professional bodies.

Marketing Feasibility

The success of any product depends on the capturing of the market. A market should be captured by facing competition. When new products are introduced, to make it a success, marketing efforts are very much needed. The stages in new product development are as follows:

1. Idea generation
2. Screening
3. Concept development and evaluation
4. Business analysis
5. Product development and evaluation
6. Development and evaluation of marketing mix
7. Test marketing
8. Commercialization of the product

The marketing feasibility also includes the market structure, the competitors, market share estimation, market growth, and price feasibility.

Financial Feasibility

After ascertaining the marketing feasibility, financial feasibility is ascertained. Here, the income and expenses are estimated on the basis of cost and price. Marketing feasibility tests the business idea for marketing, whereas, in financial feasibility, the financial soundness of the idea is tested. Finance is the most important pre-requisite to establish a business.

Methods of evaluating financial feasibility:

1. Cost of production and marketing
2. Break-even analysis
3. Assessment of fixed and working capital requirements
4. Capitalization
5. Sources of finance
6. Cost of capital

Technical Feasibility

Technical feasibility is also known as techno-economic feasibility. In a technical feasibility study we can ascertain whether a business idea is feasible, whether it can be transformed into a product, and whether a business opportunity really exists. *The technical study evaluates the choice of technology, production process and the location of the business.* The technical analysis has the following items:

1. Technology analysis (labour-intensive or capital-intensive)
2. Raw material analysis
3. Make or buy decision
4. Plant size and location
5. Market-oriented location or material-oriented location
6. Cost benefit analysis

Apart from these three analysis (marketing, finance, and technical feasibilities), there are other related feasibilities like managerial feasibility, legal feasibility, and location feasibility.

Project Report and Project Appraisal

Project Report

Project identification is done first. Then on the basis of feasibility studies selection is made. The preparation of the project report is the next stage. Project report is the presentation of detailed business plan in writing. The project reports are used primarily for raising the capital. It is a blueprint of a business plan. The objective of the business plan is to attract investors and lenders. A project report contains the following items.

1. Introduction
2. Details of the promoters
3. Details about the proposed structure and operations of the business
4. Proposed project location
5. Project cost
6. Foreign exchange required
7. Sources of project funding
8. Technology and manufacturing process
9. Raw material, power, and water
10. Human resources
11. Market

12. Environment impact
13. Financial projection of the project

Project Appraisal

Assessing the viability or feasibility of a project by the lending institution is called project appraisal. The difference between feasibility and appraisal is that, the feasibility is done by the entrepreneur, while appraisal is done by the investors and lending institutions.

There are different methods followed by lending institutions to evaluate a project proposal. Marketing, economic, financial, management, and other feasibilities are studied by lenders. Various methods of profitability appraisal are used, they are pay back period method, return on investment method, discounted cash flow method, internal rate of return, net present value method, and profitability index method.

Summary

- Before a venture is started, certain preliminary steps must be taken as a logical step.
- An entrepreneur starts with business idea generation and identification of business opportunities. Then, marketing, financial, and technical feasibilities are undertaken.
- The last stage is the preparation of project report by the entrepreneur and the project appraisal by the banking institutions and promotional agencies.

Self-learning Activity

Try to answer the following questions on your own:

1. What are the methods of business idea generation?
2. Describe marketing feasibility?
3. Explain project appraisal?

14

Prominent Small Scale and Village Industries

The Genesis of Ethiopian Industry

Ethiopia has a very long history of handicrafts production, but modern industry is quite of recent origin. Number of important developments took place during Menilik era and these were having great impact on the country's subsequent industrialization. To begin with Djibouti-Addis Ababa railway was a critical factor for the country's industrial development. Another important development of this period was founding of Addis Ababa as the capital city, where scope for industries was created. Thirdly, during Menilik era foundations for modern education, communication, and centralized government were laid down, which were having a bearing on economic structure. But during his period industrialization was limited to mining and medium sized coffee and fruit plantations. During the Italian occupation (1936-1941) a road network of 6,000 km was laid down.

Emperor Hailesilasie's attempts for industrialization started with a Ten Year Industrial Development Program of 1945 and the Notice for the Encouragement of Foreign Investment of 1950. During this period industrialization was buoyant with coffee exports, which greatly expanded domestic purchasing power and enhanced foreign exchange earnings. During this period, the state policy was to promote mixed economy based on public and private initiative. During the Derg period, all the major industries were nationalized. A Ten Year Perspective Plan (1984/85 - 1993/94) outlined the basic objectives of industrial sector satisfying domestic demand for basic commodities, strengthening handicrafts and small scale industries, strengthening linkages with agricultural and construction sectors, laying the basis for heavy industry, savings and earning foreign exchange, generating employment, and contributing to balanced regional development. Only activities relating to small scale and cottage industries were left to the private sector. A Proclamation issued on 20 December 1975 put Birr 500,000 as a ceiling on capital to be invested in private industry. But investment levels in manufacturing declined after the revolution. During this period an agency called Handicrafts and Small Scale Industries Development Agency (HASIDA) was set-up to encourage small scale industries but it had not made any beginning at all.

With the change of government during 1991, the policy of the government towards industrialization was Agriculture Development Led Industrialization (ADLI). The new government has also encouraged privatization and liberal foreign investment toward industrialization. For the development of small scale and cottage industries in every region a special agency called Micro and Small Scale Development Agency (MSDA) was promoted.

MSDA

Small scale enterprises, next to agriculture are the second major sector providing employment opportunities in Ethiopia. The establishment of MSDA was part of the government's endeavor to promote small scale and micro industries. In the Oromiya region the agency was officially established in 1998 but the operation started only during January 2001.

Organizational Structure of MSDA

The supreme organ of the agency is the board of management that constituted seven members assigned by the regional state from among the regional state organs and relevant private sectors. The major duties of the board are: initiate and deliberate upon policy matters that would facilitate the growth and development of MSEs (Micro and Small Scale Enterprises); provide general directive and coordinates all activities relating to the promotion of MSEs in the region; and approve short-term and long-term promotional plan of the regional MSE. The general manager appointed by the regional government handles the day-to-day activities of the agency. To ensure collective leadership, a management committee chaired by the general manager is in place. The management committee is composed of department and service heads of the agency.

Funds

The major source of fund is the budget annually allocated by the regional government. In addition, funds will be mobilized from donor agencies and NGOs.

The major achievement of the agency was the arrangement of short term training programs with the technical and financial assistances obtained from UNIDO, GTZ, and other institutions. Short-term training programs were conducted under SIYB (Start Improve Your Business), Women

Entrepreneurship Development, Industrial Extension Services, Consultancy Service Techniques, Business Development Delivery Technique, Project Formulation, Motoring, and Evaluation Methods.

Besides building its human and material capacities, the agency has carried out some relevant field assessments and studies relating to the development of small edible oil plants in the region, coffee hauling plants, outsourcing opportunities in major towns of the region, need assessment survey on TVET trainees at Hawas Technical School Adama, and finally an assessment to identify the problems facing the small industries in the region.

Problems Relating to Micro and Small Industries

The following are the problems identified by Central Statistical Agency (CSA) relating to small industries in the Oromiya region.

1. *Poor entrepreneurship*

   In Ethiopia the entrepreneurial culture was negatively discouraged by the feudal system that prevailed over centuries. The socialistic regime replaced the feudal system and did not give opportunities for the emergence of entrepreneurial talents in small scale and micro sector. Further, the educational system the country pursued did not technically and psychologically prepare the students for EDP. In general, low level of entrepreneurial culture, low level of literacy, and poor training facilities were the factors that hindered the EDP.

2. *Lack of access to capital and credit*

   One of the major problems faced by micro and small enterprises is the shortage of both investment capital and working capital. The following characteristics of the above industries restricted their access to credit.

   (*a*) The small enterprises are heterogeneous and it became difficult for the financial institutions to issue general guidelines regarding loan appraisal, processing and supervision.

   (*b*) Most small enterprises or entrepreneurs lack experience in dealing with financial institutions. They are unaware of terms and conditions for repayment of loans.

   (*c*) They do not have a recognizable credit history like large industries.

   (*d*) They do not have the technical capacities to prepare business plans suitable for lending institutions.

   (*e*) Lack of security for loans.

   (*f*) Lack of managerial experience.

3. *Inadequate infrastructure*

   Infrastructure in the areas of communication, transport, electric power, water, banking institutions, social infrastructure (education, health, training, etc.), were the major inadequacies.

4. ***Lack of training and advisory services***

   Among the inputs necessary for small-scale industries is human resource, which consists of technical, supervisory, managerial, and administrative. Lack of training was the major problem and the non-availability of the support institutions that provide managerial and technical training was also the major problem. Consultancy services do not exist and wherever they do exist the charges were very high and not affordable to small entrepreneurs.

5. ***Inaccessibility to working and business premises***

   Currently in Ethiopia, land acquisition is based on lease system. The problem of getting access to business premises is the crucial infrastructural problem, which discourages new entrepreneurs.

6. ***Poor access to appropriate technology and guidance***

   They are in difficult position in selection and procuring better plant, equipment, and spare parts. The absence of specialized institutions to provide training, guidance, etc. and on the other hand poor access to credit and foreign exchange has contributed to the problem.

7. ***Problem in the supply of raw material and marketing of outputs***

   Needed raw materials sometimes have to be imported and are very costly. They are not within the reach of the new entrepreneurs. The marketing outlet for such products is also very difficult and export avenues were completely blocked.

8. ***Inaccessibility to information***

   Relevant and reliable information on the areas of types, quality, price, and sources of inputs, potential markets, procurement procedures, credit institutions and their terms and conditions, new technology and related training, information relating to the rules and regulations of government, support measures, etc. were not available to the entrepreneurs.

Summary

- For the development of micro and small industries, the government has gone for several measures by establishing development agencies of different kinds. The major concentration is given to such industrial ventures.

Self-learning Activity

Try to answer the following questions on your own:

1. What are the problems of micro and small industries?
2. Give an account of MSDA?

15

Cooperative Entrepreneurship

Economic development originates and fosters in relation to the strength and health of the local entrepreneurship and depends on the rate of its generation and equally to the intensity of its sense of social responsibility, its innovation quotient and its index of management capabilities. Entrepreneurial density, innovative propensity and management capability in the society in a particular period determine the character and future of economic development.

Entrepreneurs are rarely mentioned in connection with cooperative development, which reflects the state of entrepreneurship in conventional economic thinking, where entrepreneurs are more often than not a missing category.

Meaning

Cooperative entrepreneurship denotes the application of entrepreneurship talents and outcome to the cooperative institutions. Unlike the independent, individual entrepreneurs, cooperative entrepreneurs vary in nature and component.

Cooperative Entrepreneurship — Framework

Cooperative entrepreneurship refers to a role or a set of roles whose influences are conditioned by characteristics of group members. The personalities of the entrepreneurs are influenced by the situation. But the true entrepreneurship though individual-oriented has got a collective group foundation in cooperatives. Cooperative entrepreneurs collectively engage in the enterprise activity for the economic interest of themselves.

Cooperative entrepreneurship should function collectively and should have courage to stand up when something wrong is done and should be capable of owning a mistake openly. Such cooperative entrepreneurs will not only succeed but will also make the cooperatives a succeed story in the world.

Definition of Cooperative Entrepreneurship

Cooperative Entrepreneur is one who undertakes and assumes the responsibility to discover innovate cooperative opportunity, on the basis of collective effort, which has the cooperative effect for the socio-economic development of the member entrepreneurs simultaneously with the cooperative values". (M. Karthikeyan, 2004)

Principles of Cooperative Entrepreneurship

1. Principle of innovation
2. Principle of cooperation
3. Principle of active participation
4. Principle of democratic management
5. Principle of communication and information
6. Principle of collective decision-making
7. Principle of honesty and openness (self-confidence)
8. Principle of cooperative development thro' entrepreneurial development
9. Principle of social responsibility
10. Principle of time management

Cooperative Entrepreneurship Ladder

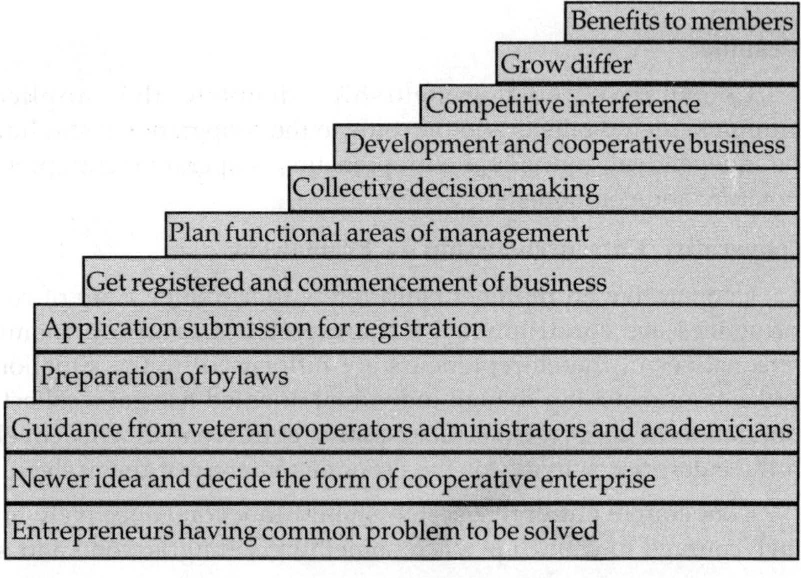

Summary

- Cooperative entrepreneurship denotes the application of entrepreneurship talents and outcome to the cooperative institutions. Unlike the independent, individual entrepreneurs, cooperative entrepreneurs vary in nature and component.
- Cooperative entrepreneurs collectively engage in the enterprise activity for the economic interest of themselves.

Self-learning Activity

Try to answer the following questions on your own:

1. Define Cooperative Entrepreneurship?
2. What are the principles of cooperative entrepreneurship?
3. Give an account of cooperative entrepreneurship ladder?

16

Pattern of Cooperative Entrepreneurship

Classification

The pattern of cooperative entrepreneurship may be classified into the following categories:

1. Cooperative entrepreneurs are part of the class of members (*Member Entrepreneur*).
2. Cooperative entrepreneurs are managers of the cooperative enterprise (*Executive Entrepreneur*).
3. Director Entrepreneurs are elected from among the members as representatives to administer the cooperative enterprise.
4. Cooperative entrepreneurs are part of a governmental or parastatal administration bureaucratic entrepreneurs (*Bureaucratic Entrepreneur*).
5. Cooperative entrepreneurs are members of other non-cooperative orgainsation (such as schools, universities, donor/aid and sponsoring agencies, churches) who provide career possibilities and incentives independent from or in addition to cooperative entrepreneurship (*Catalytic entrepreneur*).

From these five patterns of cooperative entrepreneurship, the first three can be characterized as effort taking, the other two as external, promoting entrepreneurs. In effort taking cooperative entrepreneurship, the vital entrepreneurial decisions are made by person with function within a cooperative society.

In addition cooperatives can be established through the initiative of external agents: functionaries from administrations which very often have been set up especially to organise and assist cooperatives are responsible for the establishment of cooperative organisation: bureaucratic entrepreneur. Usually, but not necessarily, this type of entrepreneurship implies the 'officialisation' of the cooperative movement.

But cooperative can be promoted by outsiders in another way: person who specialize in local institutional development are endowed with responsibilities for getting mutual self help processes started. These catalysts can be paid-professionals of volunteers, employed by the government or non-government organization.

Member Entrepreneurs

This kind of entrepreneurial pattern normally assumes, in order to be successful, a high level of member-heterogeneity, and may result in a quite unequal distribution of the wealth created.

But again, these outcomes of members entrepreneurship should not surprise us, given the difficulties and peculiarities of cooperatives action, the unequal appropriation of cooperative wealth is one of the few realistic avenues open for spontaneous cooperative entrepreneurship and hence for spontaneous cooperative evolution.

The member entrepreneur in cooperation corresponds to the intrapreneurs is a public corporation (public limited company) who own equity (or options for the acquisition of equity) as holders of corporate equity or shares they are (as other non-managerial/entrepreneurial owners/shareholders) residual claimants of the variability in the operation of the firm.

Member entrepreneurs are the basic ingredients for the cooperative entrepreneurship. Individual talents, merits, risk bearing abilities, innovative nature, etc of members are pooled and consolidated for the betterment of the cooperative entrepreneurship. So a member can contribute to the development of the cooperative, as an entrepreneur in the form of contributing share capital, member patronage, participation in democratic associations, providing leadership and acting as the watchdog for the wrongs of his cooperative. Professor K.K. Taimni, ILO COOPNET Director, views that "...individual members take to entrepreneurship, i.e., scan the environment, identify and seize opportunities, assume risks, deploy their own capital and derive benefits. The role of the cooperative is confined here to provide support services, including essential advisory services so that risk-related losses are minimized and links between a member's enterprise and external agents and markets are effectively established".

Executive Entrepreneurs

It is observed that those individuals creating and implementing cooperative opportunities will not necessarily be identical with those who manage the ongoing cooperative. This will be the case especially during the initiating or founding phase of a cooperative venture.

Managers do not necessarily share the objectives of the members owners. They have some choice in the direction, pace, quality, and duration of their efforts, depending, among other factors on the effectiveness of members participation and the cooperative's external environment. Managerial discretion has to be recognized as a fact commercial life also in cooperatives.

(*a*) Manager Entrepreneurs include chief executives of cooperatives with various denominations (general manager, manager, secretary, etc.), deputy managers, line supervisors, and heads of various sections. Manager entrepreneurs implement the policies and programmes assigned by the board. Hence, they must be well-qualified, hard working, must have integrity, and work for the success of the cooperative. They have to look after the day-to-day working of their cooperatives and provide feedback to the board about the problems and challenges of the cooperative. The special competencies required by managers to promote cooperative entrepreneurship are as follows:

1. Knowledge of cooperative principles and practices
2. Knowledge of cooperative laws and bylaws
3. Devotion to the cooperative ideal
4. Sensitivity and responsiveness to members' interests and wishes
5. Community orientation
6. Close watching of the market conditions and the acts of competitors.

Peter Davis, the British cooperator views that "...we desperately need who have the qualities to take responsibility for leading and building the whole community of members and employees into a social and value-based business seeking the fulfillment of the cooperative purpose".

Director Entrepreneurs

The board members are responsible for the administration of a cooperative where they have the board membership. They are the internal administrative entrepreneurs to look after the affairs of the cooperative enterprise. Board members elect the president and vice-president in order to delegate authority and responsiblity. The president is the head of a cooperative enterprise in all respects.

Bureaucrat Entrepreneurs

One prominent and very often also empirically attempted solution to the problems of incentive failure in cooperative has been the take over of entrepreneurial functions by the government: government officials in open of disgusted form try to act as cooperative entrepreneur.

The blue print, up-down or synoptic approach may indeed succeed in establishing cooperatives: by bureaucratic command or force, officials are required to set up cooperative societies. Following the colonial model, the government works at the local level, and often through local leaders.

Hierarchical control, or supervision, become indispensable and hierarchical incentives (power, prestige, rank and status) the main motivators for entrepreneurial action. These are the people who are mostly government officials engaged in the promotion of cooperatives on behalf of their government. In many developing countries cooperatives have been introduced as a state subject by their respective governments. During colonial periods the colonial governments introduced cooperation to eradicate poverty and improving agricultural development. Such countries were not having a level of education to organize and run the cooperatives. So government officials attached to the department of cooperative had to take the responsibility of organizing the cooperatives, giving guidelines and counseling to the cooperative leaders. The success and failure of cooperatives in many countries depended on the nature and outlook of these bureaucrats. In due course, when the voluntary movement (cooperatives) developed, the necessity for the involvement of the bureaucrats was reduced. So at present in developing countries the de-officialization of the cooperative movement is taking place, which denotes reducing the importance of officials to run the cooperatives.

Catalytic Entrepreneurs

Catalytic entrepreneurs are external agents, or members of outside agencies, whose task is to get the process of cooperative institutionalization started and to work with and strengthen local cooperatives. These outside cooperative entrepreneurs (or agencies) can be governmental or non-governmental. What makes the "catalyst" different from the bureaucratic entrepreneur is that

1. he is not working through conventional bureaucratic or technological channels; and
2. the local cooperative institutions he is initiating, promoting and supporting remain autonomous. Self-organising organisations, i.e., do not become an officialised and regulated part of a governmental or parastatal administration.

Catalytic entrepreneurs are specialists in the initialization, promotion and support of cooperative organisations. The designations for such persons are various. The terms "promoter", "change agent", "facilitator", "motivator" have been used.

To sum up, in cooperative theory and policy, is not aware of any approach which has addressed the connection between entrepreneurial behaviour and the degree of economic success and failure of cooperatives. Policy-makers have theoritised, planned and implemented in a virtual vacuum about cooperative entrepreneurship is causally related to the main effects of economic growth (increase in incomes, productivity, employment, living standards), not to include entrepreneurial activity in cooperative policy bias and even policy errors. Preventing the potential of cooperatives for development from being used sufficiently and effectively, when innovative entrepreneurship is a necessary condition for the achievement of economic development in general and an organisation's success in specific, there can be no question that cooperative entrepreneurs will have to be included; without cooperative entrepreneurship, cooperatives cannot succeed, they will not even be established.

Functions of Cooperative Entrepreneurship

The primary function of cooperative entrepreneurship consists of the following:

(*a*) ***Discovering cooperative opportunities***

This denotes the identification of the problems of the members and the capacities of the cooperatives to discharge such problems. In doing so, there are two important tests a cooperative has to undertake, namely, the market test and participation test. The market test can be undertaken by means of studying the market behaviour and to find out ways and means of providing services and supplies effectively and competitively (at a low price) to the members. The second test, namely, participation test denotes the loyalty of the members towards their cooperatives. For the success of the cooperative, the members must express their fuller loyalty by means of actively participating in the management as well as business activities. With regard to business activities, members have to sell their produce only through the cooperatives even during the times of low price and depression period. Likewise, in getting the service of their cooperative, members should show their loyalty by linking their service activities to the cooperative perennially.

(*b*) ***Implement such opportunities effectively and efficiently***

The next stage is the implementation of opportunities explored by the cooperatives to fulfill the needs and desires of the members. Coordination is necessary between members, board, and the executive. They have to keep in mind that they have to face stiff competition from the market economy. To face such economy (private sector) efficiency in service and operations are necessary. Cost of operations must be low and the benefits to be accrued in the form of higher prices and fuller satisfaction must be ensured.

Causes for Cooperative Advantage

The cooperative advantages that will accrue out of cooperative entrepreneurship are as follows:

1. *Monopoly/Market failure*

   Monopoly practices followed by private sector led to the exploitation of the producers and consumers. The market forces of demand and supply have been manipulated to the dictates of the monopolist. The cooperative advantage comes out with balancing the market force and benefiting both the producers and consumers.

2. *Transaction cost*

   The transaction cost of the cooperatives is always less than other forms of enterprises. Cooperatives operate with efficient personnel and they have learnt the market changes and market forces. The operational efficiency and the interdependence of various cooperatives through vertical and horizontal growth led to the reduction of transaction cost, which are transferred to the members.

3. *Interlinked market*

   The cooperative operations are interlinked with each other following the principles of cooperation among cooperatives. Integration between agricultural cooperatives, marketing cooperatives, processing cooperatives, and consumer cooperatives is the best example to express the interlinked market. Such linking of marketing led to the advantage of the producers and consumers and bargaining power of the members has been enhanced.

4. *Uncertainty reduction*

   Cooperative entrepreneurship by the cooperative have reduced the uncertainty in all walks of activities. Uncertainty relating to output of production, price trends, market trends, competition, etc have been avoided to the advantage of the members of cooperatives.

5. *Innovations*

   Cooperatives have introduced innovations in their operations, which redirected the market trend towards them. Recently in UK the cooperative banks have abolished the service charges for current account and gave a rate of interest to that deposit. This made all other commercial banks to extend this benefit to their depositors.

Stages of Cooperative Entrepreneurship

Robert and Weiss (1988) have explained the process of cooperative entrepreneurship into the following four stages.

1. *Opportunity Search*

   This stage consists of identifying the opportunities, no matter what their sources. When cooperatives are doing traditional services for a long time, they have to search for new opportunities for their growth, development, and sustainability.

2. *Opportunity Assessment*

   After searching the opportunity, the practicability of the opportunity is to be assessed. Such opportunity assessment may be useful for the future members of the cooperatives.

3. *Opportunity Development*

   This is to decide which of the opportunities emerging from assessment should be developed further. The high potential opportunities are critically analyzed and final action required is identified.

4. *Opportunity Pursued (Implementation)*

   This is to indicate the implementation process and methods of the opportunities selected and developed.

Preconditions for Cooperative Entrepreneurship

While the training of managers will clearly be a critical element in promoting the entrepreneurial spirit in cooperatives, this is only one element in the creation of a favourable climate for cooperative entrepreneurship. Restrictive legislation and regulations which impinge on cooperatives' ability to function as business organizations may have to be removed. Above all, cooperatives must be autonomous and free from outside control. They must become truly democratic and member-governed. Cooperatives must position themselves in such a way as to be able to nurture and develop a culture of entrepreneurship. They must be ready to try out new programmes and not be constrained by bureaucratic formalities. They must be allowed to dispose of their own financial resources and have discretion over their use. They must not be dependent on government, or on donor agencies. They must be prepared to take calculated risks in the interests of providing more effective and efficient services to their members. The following are the pre-conditions for cooperative entrepreneurship:

1. *Training System*

   The first precondition for the success of cooperative entrepreneurship is to introduce an effective training system for the managers and the employees of cooperatives. Only through training entrepreneurial skills can be developed to the managers. The training components should be aimed at harnessing motivation, developing creativity, innovative thinking, imagination and self-assertiveness. They should increase the individuals' ability to plan strategies and tactics, set goals, solve problems, develop negotiating skills, resolve conflicts, and take calculated risks.

2. *Cooperative Legal System*

   The cooperative legal system should be flexible and should not unnecessarily tax the cooperatives to go through various procedures and formalities. Less interference should be allowed in the democratic function of the cooperative management. Cooperative being business organizations must be allowed freehand to face competition and challenges.

3. *Autonomy and Freedom*

   As per the directions of the principles of cooperation explained by the ICA, cooperatives must be provided autonomy in their operations. There should be less interference from the external agencies like the government and official bodies.

4. *Positioning the Cooperatives to Develop Entrepreneurship*

   Every cooperative position its activities to develop entrepreneurship at the three levels, namely membership level, manager level, and bureaucratic level. The membership level entrepreneurship must be given preference to create leadership and continuous growth of the cooperatives.

5. *New Opportunities*

   As mentioned earlier, cooperatives must find out new opportunities to do more services for their continued growth and sustainability. By means of extending the area of operation, enlisting new members, and adding new services such new opportunities could be created.

6. *Self-Reliance*

   On no account cooperatives should depend on external agencies like government for their financial and other resources. Within the cooperative movement efficient banking and marketing systems should be developed and that system should provide mutual dependence of cooperatives.

7. *Taking Risks*

   Cooperatives, in order to promote entrepreneurship must take calculated risks in the interest of providing more effective and efficient service to the members.

Determinants of Cooperative Entrepreneurial Behaviour

1. *Member Awareness*

   This is a significant aspect to decide the cooperative entrepreneurial behaviour. Awareness of the problems of members, their cooperatives, and vigilance on running their cooperatives are very important to make the cooperative entrepreneurship a success.

2. ***Managerial Abilities***

   The cooperative must also develop the managerial abilities of its employees to work under competitive circumstances and to discharge the services cost-effectively.

3. ***Political Climate***

   The political climate of the country also plays a role in determining the cooperative entrepreneurship behaviour. In spite of drastic political changes in countries like UK, Japan, etc. cooperatives are running successfully. But in developing countries, cooperatives need a favorable political climate to undertake their activities successfully.

4. ***Economic Climate***

   Free play of economic forces and perfect competition situation must prevail to do services to the members. These are the days where fair trade practices have been promoted by the cooperatives, which are to be followed by other market forces.

5. ***Technical Expertise***

   Cooperatives, hereafter must add technical expertise to meet challenges and competition. When they enter into new areas of operation they must go for latest technology and they must train their employees by inculcating new skills.

6. ***Globalization***

   Globalization of the economy among countries have opened great opportunities for the cooperatives. Cooperative products can be mutually imported and exported between countries and the cooperative entrepreneurship can go globally.

An ILO View on Cooperative Entrepreneurship

The deliberations at a seminar sponsored by ILO on cooperative entrepreneurship raised the following important points:

- Given the explosion of cooperative in South Africa it is important to distinguish between fake and genuine cooperatives. The ICA statement of identity and principles as well as the 2005 Act provide a basis to assess cooperatives on the ground. This is important because genuine cooperatives should not be overshadowed by 'fly by night' ones merely chasing financial resources. In many ways the Black Economic Empowerment policy thrust from government has politicised cooperatives in a particular way and has encouraged rent seeking as opposed to bottom up member and worker owner driven cooperatives.
- Cooperative entrepreneurship is not a 'silver bullet' but is a key ingredient in cooperative development. For cooperatives operating in a

market environment enhancing cooperative entrepreneurial skills is crucial. On the other hand, subsistence and social cooperatives might not need to be driven by cooperative entrepreneurship. In both cases cooperative entrepreneurship should not take away from cooperative principles.

- Cooperative entrepreneurship should not be collapsed into SME frameworks and neither should it reduce cooperatives to another business form. Cooperatives are a distinct institutional form with a values-centred institutional model and social character. The hard skills of financial management, marketing, management etc., that are required in cooperatives should be encouraged as part of a wider education and training practice in cooperatives. Most of the successful cooperative movements in the world are grounded in ongoing education and training to build institutional capacity, raise member awareness and ensure skills development. Cooperative entrepreneurship should be part of the culture of cooperative practice and it is an integral part of cooperative ideology.
- Government is busy with various interventions that impact on and close the space for bottom up movement building. In many ways the enabling role of the state, despite the good intentions, easily translates into control. Government is talking about cooperative colleges and various other interventions to build cooperative capacity but all seem to be in a top down framework. Besides government the cooperative movement needs to be challenged to build 'in-house' movement capacity for education and training.
- The economic role and function of cooperatives should not be reduced to poverty reduction. Cooperatives in the global north, in rich countries, play a pivotal role in mainstream economic activity. The multi-class appeal of cooperatives needs to be enhanced to attract different skills and capacities into cooperatives. Professionalizing the training for cooperatives becomes important. For example, securing accredited training in diploma's and degrees on cooperative entrepreneurship, management, financial management and so on is crucial in the South African context.

Human Resource Development in Cooperatives: Towards Cooperative Entrepreneurship

The Changing Environment

In a variety of radically differing political environments cooperatives are being forced to re-examine their basic operating principles in order to survive economically and to continue to serve the needs of their members. In the past, cooperatives in most developing countries were not truly autonomous and member-driven, but instead were dominated, and sometimes controlled, by government. They were, in many cases, instruments of government policies for the achievement of social and economic goals such as rural development, employment promotion, poverty alleviation and so on. Sometimes cooperatives have been utilized for political purposes too.

We are now witnessing a rapidly changing economic, social and political environment characterized by the intertwined processes of democratization, decentralization, globalization and adjustment. The effects of these changes on cooperatives are many and vary from country to country and from one type of cooperative to another. In broad terms however, state-controlled cooperatives which are unable to adapt to the new environment face considerable difficulties. The exposure of state-protected 'cooperative' monopolies to the competition of the market usually dramatically reduces the market share of these cooperatives and may lead to their disintegration. On the other hand, strong, viable, autonomous cooperatives which adapt successfully can play an important role in promoting economic and social development through serving the interests of their members and of their communities. Indeed, the global changes of the past few years may, in the long run, create the conditions for the emergence of a strong, dynamic, autonomous, member-controlled, genuine cooperative movement. However, the transition to a market-oriented economy often involves the collapse of the state-controlled cooperative sector and that the autonomous movement is not always able to fill the vacuum.

The International Cooperative Alliance's Identity Statement adopted at the 1995 Centennial Congress in Manchester, England, gives clear expression to the democratic and voluntary nature of cooperative enterprises and to the values which inspire cooperative members, leaders, managers and employees. The Identity Statement is an important milestone in cooperative history in that it firmly locates cooperatives globally as autonomous associations. Without an identifiable character cooperatives will not be able to survive, certainly not as cooperatives, although they may evolve into other types of business organizations.

Whether one regards the global changes of the last decade or so in a favourable or unfavourable light, cooperators would be wise to adopt a pragmatic approach and examine the ways and means by which cooperatives can survive the transition period and develop management strategies which will enable cooperatives to flourish. The increasingly competitive market environment requires additional approaches and aptitudes, which we can loosely categorize under the heading "Cooperative Entrepreneurship".

Of late, the notion of "Cooperative Entrepreneurship" is increasingly being seen as a key to ensuring cooperative survival under the new, competitive market conditions. What is "Entrepreneurship", what does the term mean in a cooperative context and what are the implications for cooperative human resource development (HRD)? The following discussion may give a clear picture on this issue.

Competencies of Cooperative Entrepreneurship

Competencies can be described which has been provided by a recently published ILO Training Package entitled "Know About Business":

A body of knowledge

Knowledge consists of a set or body of information stored, which may be recalled at an appropriate time. The kinds of knowledge necessary in a business involve having information about the market, the customers, the competitors, business management, sources of funding and more.

A set of skills

Skill is the ability to apply knowledge. The skills needed in business may be of a technical nature such as engineering, computing, farming, etc., or of a managerial nature such as marketing, financial management, organization, planning and leadership.

A cluster of traits

A trait is the aggregate of peculiar qualities or characteristics which constitute personal individuality. A successful entrepreneur takes initiative, is persistent, is concerned for high quality, is oriented to efficiency, solves problems in original ways, takes calculated risks, plans systematically, is assertive and so on.

A balanced combination of these competencies is essential for successful entrepreneurship. What then are the functions performed by the entrepreneur? Peter Kilby suggests the following: Searches for and discovers new information, Translates new information into new markets, techniques and goods, Seeks and discovers economic opportunity, Evaluates economic opportunities, Marshalls the financial resources necessary for the enterprise, Makes time-binding arrangements, Takes ultimate responsibility for management, Provides for and is responsible for the motivational system within the firm, Provides leadership for the work group, Is the ultimate uncertainty or risk bearer.

Entrepreneurship in Cooperatives

Cooperatives have a great deal to gain by examining how an injection of entrepreneurial attitudes and approaches can help them achieve their goals and objectives. Indeed, cooperative managers functioning in a competitive market certainly need to shed bureaucratic modes of operation and adopt entrepreneurial approaches if they are to effectively serve the interests of cooperative members. However, in cooperatives special competencies are required by managers, such as: Knowledge of cooperative principles and practices, Knowledge of cooperative law and by-laws, Devotion to the cooperative ideal, Sensitivity and responsiveness to members' interests and wishes, Community orientation.

Moreover, cooperative values, if mobilized effectively, may provide the cooperative with the competitive edge required to ensure the cooperative's success. Peter Davis, Director of the Unit for Membership Based Organizations of Leicester University, UK, has argued strongly that not only are values essential for determining the "cooperative difference" in the market place, but also that "Value Based Management is the future for management". Davis criticizes cooperatives for "not utilizing their human-centred values dynamically in their communications with their customers and employees". Furthermore, he argues that the cooperative enterprise must be managed as an integrated whole, combining business activities and social purpose, avoiding the view that these "sides" are in some way in conflict. He points to the "ethical banking" approach of the UK Cooperative Bank as an example of a cooperative organization using its values to achieve rapid expansion of the business. Davis writes that the Bank has successfully integrated cooperative values into modern management methods, which he considers to be the key to its prosperity in a very tough competitive environment. He concludes that:

> "...we desperately need managers who have the qualities to take responsibility for leading and building the whole community of members and employees into a social and value based business seeking the fulfilment of the cooperative purpose".

So far we have considered entrepreneurship in the context of cooperative management capabilities and functions. We can also consider the relevance of entrepreneurship to the individual cooperative member. As the ILO COOPNET/COOPREFORM Coordinator for Asia, K.K. Taimni has written:

> "....individual members take to entrepreneurship i.e. scan the environment, identify and seize opportunities, assume risks, deploy their own capital and derive benefits. The role of the cooperative is confined here to provide support services, including essential advisory services, so that risk-related losses are minimized and links between a member's enterprise and external agents and markets are effectively established".

Thus, we are challenged to apply the concept of entrepreneurship to all actors in the cooperative — cooperative members, board members, managers and employees — while maintaining and strengthening the cooperative identity and purpose.

Integrating Entrepreneurial Skills in Cooperative HRD

A critical question to ask, therefore, is to what extent do existing cooperative training institutions and programmes train cooperative members, board members, managers and employees in the competencies required by cooperatives struggling to survive and grow in a competitive market situation? A reorientation of training systems may be necessary if we recognize these competencies as being vital for cooperative sustainability. This reorientation will include the adaptation of curriculum, training materials and methodologies. In addition to more traditional cooperative management training courses on, for example, accounting, business planning, finance, marketing, production, materials, distribution, office administration, data processing, management information systems, personnel management etc., entrepreneurial skills development components should be added. These training components should be aimed at harnessing motivation, developing creativity, innovative thinking, imagination and self-assertiveness. They should increase the individual trainee's ability to plan strategy and tactics, set goals, solve problems, develop negotiating skills, resolve conflicts and take calculated risks.

In some cases existing materials from the non-cooperative sector can be utilized but more often new materials will have to be prepared to take account of the special character of cooperative enterprises. Special training will have to be provided for trainers, many of whom are today not able to facilitate the learning of entrepreneurial skills. Cooperative HRD institutions will have to contribute to the strengthening of management consultancy and auditing systems, which, if effective, can provide significant support to the reorientation of cooperatives to the new environment.

Promotion of Cooperative Development

Entrepreneurship is an essential ingredient of cooperative development. Cooperative development always includes the dual aspect of cooperatives: development of the cooperative enterprise and promotion (motivating and enabling) of member entrepreneurship.

How to promote cooperatives in order that cooperatives can advance their members more effectively? With what kind of services can cooperatives improve the performance of their member entrepreneurs? How can cooperatives stimulate member innovation of their members and promote those that are working out of the economic core and transform these enterprises into ambitious and glamorous firms?

The primary focus of policy-makers, educators, trainers and consultants must be on promoting ambitious and glamorous cooperatives (which probably are rather young) and new cooperatives.

The first thing to do is negative: not to do things which handicap or restrain these class of cooperatives. The second thing to do is to identify new cooperative entrepreneurs and young cooperatives with highly ambitious/innovative entrepreneurs. Thus, policy-makers and government should make a shift to the promotion of cooperative entrepreneurs and through them member promotion.

External assistance should be actively sought by co-operative leaders and managers with the specific goal of increasing entrepreneurial opportunities and management capacity. This assistance usually takes the form of training courses, project or venture finance, or entrepreneurial advice offered by experienced and well trained "catalytic" entrepreneurs from co-operative movements, NGOs or government institutions.

In that way government policy shifts from direct intervention and promoting state goals to indirect assistance and promotion of member goals. Cooperative entrepreneurship has to be promoted instead of promoting the cooperative sector as a whole. Modern cooperative entrepreneurs will have to learn a minimum of theory in order to understand what they are doing and what needs to be done in order to compete successfully and grow by better promoting their members. Thus, a main emphasis is laid upon cooperative education and training, capacity building or human resources development. A special focus should be given to academic entrepreneurs, thus connecting the worlds of science and business.

Summary

- Cooperative entrepreneurship pattern includes member, executive, director, bureaucratic and catalytic entrepreneurs.
- The cooperative advantages will accrue out of cooperative entrepreneurship.
- There are entrepreneurial skills that can be integrated in cooperative HRD.

Self-learning Activity

Try to answer the following questions on your own:

1. What is the pattern of Cooperative Entrepreneurship?
2. What are the causes of cooperative advantages through entrepreneurship?
3. Discuss HRD and cooperative entrepreneurship?

17

Stages in Organizing Cooperatives

Because each situation is unique, there is no specific recipe for forming a cooperative. The steps for starting a cooperative recommended here may be considered as guidelines by cooperative entrepreneurs.

A. Steps to Starting a Cooperative

Like other businesses, every co-operatives starts with the recognition of a need or an opportunity. One or two people willing to put in some time and energy can spark a group interested in starting a co-operatives.

Members of such a group have a mutual need that can be addressed through joint action. They could, for example, lack a market for their products or lack necessary supplies or services. Acting together to address that need, they can achieve something which none of them could achieve alone.

Basic Steps in Starting a Cooperative

1. Hold an organizing meeting; establish steering committee.
2. Conduct a feasibility study.
3. Hold a meeting of potential members to report on the results of the feasibility study.
4. Incorporate the co-op by filing articles of incorporation and bylaws.
5. Prepare a business plan.
6. Secure financing for the co-operatives.
7. Recruit/Admission of members for the co-operatives.
8. Hire co-op management and staff.
9. Hold the co-operative's first membership and board meetings.
10. Start Cooperatives.

1. Hold an organizing meeting and establish a steering committee

(*a*) A core group of interested individuals should hold an informational meeting of potential co-operatives members and others in the community. The primary purpose of the meeting is to explain the identified need and how a co-operatives would address it.

It is important that the group come to general agreement on the nature and importance of the problem and the potential for a cooperative to address it. Such an agreement will become the group's shared vision, so it is worth spending as much time as necessary to achieve it.

(*b*) Provide informational handouts that explain what a co-operative is and how it would work. Also provide information about the steps involved in starting a co-operative so people have a sense of what they may be getting into. Determine the level of interest in exploring a co-operatives among meeting participants.

Many organizing groups have found it helpful to invite speakers from other cooperatives in order to highlight their success stories. This often gives meeting participants a more down to earth vision of what a co-operatives is and how it can work for them.

(*c*) A steering committee should be formed of participants at the meeting which will coordinate activities on behalf of the group. Committee members must be able to provide leadership to the larger group and be willing to put some time and energy into researching the feasibility of the proposed cooperative.

(*d*) Allow plenty of time for questions and discussion. A meeting like this often works best if it is led by an experienced facilitator. In many cases, it is necessary to hold more than one meeting to give all interested parties in the community a chance to participate.

Typical Steering Committee Members

1. PRESIDENT

   Often the "project champion". Facilitation skills a big plus.

2. VICE PRESIDENT

   May chair key subcommittee.

3. TREASURER

   Manages funds. May lead business plan phase. Accounting skills a big plus.

4. SECRETARY

   Coordinates all communications. Computer skills a big plus.

5. NON-OFFICERS

Group Dynamics (Adapted from Henehan)

Various issues must be resolved to proceed:

- Potential members must see that the benefits in adopting a cooperative approach are attainable.
- Individuals must emerge who are willing to assume a leadership role and take the agreed-upon vision to the next steps.
- A level of trust and confidence must evolve within the group.
- The creative tension between visionaries and doers must be harnessed effectively. It cannot be allowed to prevent the group from moving forward.
- Participants must be convinced that the initial risks and costs in adopting the proposed approach are outweighted by the potential benefits to be obtained.
- Roles of members, management and board members should be clear to all.
- Everyone involved should have confidence that the proposed organization is the best alternative available.

Typical Sub-Committee Areas

- Business plan committee;
- By-laws and policies committee;
- Purchasing and construction committee; and
- Personnel committee.

2. Conduct a feasibility study

(*a*) The steering committee can either conduct a feasibility study (using the guidelines provided), or hire a consultant to carry out the study. The purpose of a feasibility study is to examine critical opportunities and obstacles that might make or break the proposed cooperative business. The feasibility study should give the group a good idea of whether the co-op is likely to be successful as a business.

The critical issues that a feasibility study analyzes include the number and interest level of potential members; market issues (can the co-op get better prices, better quality or better services than potential members currently get through other means?); operating costs; start-up costs; and availability of financing.

If insurmountable obstacles are discovered in the feasibility study, the development of the cooperative should be abandoned or shelved before too much time and money has been expended.

(*b*) In some cases, local or state governments or foundations may provide financial or technical assistance with the feasibility study. *The quality of the feasibility study is critical because it will influence all future decisions on the development of the co-op.* Don't hesitate to bring in outside expertise when you need it.

Contributions by potential co-operative members are often used to help cover the cost of a feasibility study. These members will be the primary beneficiaries of the cooperative, so naturally they should assume some responsibility for the financial costs of assessing its feasibility.

3. Report on the results of the feasibility study

(*a*) The steering committee should hold a follow up meeting with potential co-op members to report on the results of the feasibility study. A summary of the feasibility report should be distributed to participants, and the full report made available to anyone who wishes to see it. Allow plenty of time to discuss the report and ensure that potential members understand the results.

(*b*) Be sure to spend time reviewing the financial section of the report. The preliminary financial projections should tell the group how much equity will be required from each member of the co-operative, and whether or not the co-operative is projected to return any patronage refunds (shares of the profits) to members during the first few years of operation. These are key pieces of information that will influence each person's decision about whether to join the co-operative.

This should be a major decision point. If the feasibility study indicates that the co-op is not a viable business, or if sufficient commitment does not exist among the group, the steering committee should not proceed with forming the co-operatives.

4. Incorporate the cooperative and file articles of incorporation and bylaws

(*a*) In most states, a cooperative has to be incorporated under the appropriate state statute in order to conduct business. Most states have statutes specifically governing cooperatives. The articles of incorporation describe the kind and scope of the cooperative's business. Incorporation takes place when a co-op files its articles with the secretary of state. If the steering committee wishes to, it may draft the articles of incorporation and bylaws. Make sure to have a lawyer who is familiar with cooperatives review these documents before they are presented to the membership.

(*b*) The bylaws state how the cooperative will conduct business, and must be approved by the membership. Note that a co-op can start out with very basic bylaws and refine them after the business plan has been developed.

(*c*) As soon as the cooperative is incorporated and thus exists as a legal entity, two members of the steering committee should open a bank account in the co-operative name. This account will be used to deposit equity contributions from new members.

(*d*) *A note about stock:* Articles of incorporation allow the steering committee to decide whether the co-operative will issue stock or not. We recommend that the co-operative do so. In recruiting new members, it can be an important symbolic act to hand over a stock certificate to each individual who joins the co-operative. Many new members feel more comfortable having something in hand to show for their contribution. Some potential members also find a stock cooperative easier to understand than a non-stock structure.

Blank stock certificates are available at most office supply stores. Just fill in the blanks to indicate the number of shares each member buys and the cost per share.

5. Prepare a Business Plan

(*a*) If the feasibility study results are favourable, the steering committee carries out or hires a consultant firm to develop a detailed business plan. The business plan serves two primary purposes: to provide a blueprint for the development and initial operation of the co-operatives and to provide supporting documentation for potential members, financial institutions and other investors.

(*b*) A typical outline of a business plan includes a description of the company, a market analysis, research and development related to the co-operative's product or service, a marketing and sales plan, a description of the organizational structure and key personnel, and financial data.

(*c*) In most cases, a new co-operative will need to borrow capital from a bank or other lending institution in order to get started. The business plan serves a vital function in describing to the bank the co-operative goals and how it plans to accomplish those goals. Most lending institutions will not consider a loan request that is not accompanied by a detailed business plan. In addition, it is a very useful document when recruiting new members to the cooperative.

(*d*) Few steering committees have sufficient skills to develop a thorough business plan. Obtaining technical assistance can make the difference between a business plan that gets a loan and one that does not. Note that many state governments offer grants and loans to assist start-ups with technical assistance and business planning.

A cooperative's business plan should include many of the components of a business plan for any type of firm. However, there are additional considerations for cooperatives which should be addressed in a well thought out plan.

For example, cooperative finance involves a number of unique aspects such as the variety of ways to raise or revolve member equity. Governance structure should be spelled out in the plan to insure that an effective decision-making capacity is designed. Will voting be by member, proportional to patronage, or proportional to investment? Member's rights and responsibilities in relation to the cooperative should also be presented.

Financial projections should be built on several scenarios reflecting the impact of various member actions, such as a given percentage of members not meeting their patronage or investment obligations. What level of losses or prices might members be willing to tolerate? What happens if a share of members over produce or find more attractive alternatives?

6. Secure Financing

(*a*) Cooperative businesses vary greatly in the amount of capital they need to get up and running. The business plan should include the amount and type of financing needed by the co-op and a strategy for obtaining it. The steering committee and its advisors are responsible for implementing this strategy.

(*b*) Virtually all cooperatives require some level of member financing, usually in the form of stock purchases or membership fees. Member financing not only provides equity for the co-op, it also provides a financial base that helps other investors, particularly banks, feel more secure in investing in the co-op. The steering committee should prepare a membership application for new members to fill out and sign. It should identify the member's name, address, and phone number; the number of shares of stock being purchased (or the amount of the membership fee if it is a non-stock cooperative); and a stated agreement that the new member agrees to belong to and abide by the bylaws and contracts of the cooperative.

Each member's initial financial contribution should be collected at the time the membership application is submitted.

(*c*) In addition to member equity, most cooperatives need to borrow money to get started and to maintain their operations. Loans can come from banks and other financial institutions (including several national banks for cooperatives).

7. Recruit/Admission of Members

Laying the groundwork for the cooperatives membership base needs to begin when the steering committee first meets. During their organizational phase, many co-ops hold meetings for potential members, conduct surveys and mail organizing updates to them, and collect initial down payments on membership fees.

All of these activities provide a good indication of the level of interest in, and commitment to, the co-operative. Thus, when the time comes to actually "ante-up" and join, potential members are more primed to act. Even so, the steering committee may need to recruit new members in addition to those who have attended one or more of the organizational meetings. *This should be a major decision point. If the co-op is unable to obtain the necessary debt financing, or if sufficient commitment does not exist among potential members to provide sufficient equity capital, the steering committee should not proceed with developing the co-op at this time.*

8. Hire Cooperative Management

Some new cooperatives identify management personnel early in their organizing process, especially if one or more key individuals are already known to members of the steering committee. However, recruiting staff personnel is listed as a later step in the co-operatives formation process because the co-op is not a definite "go" until the necessary financing has been secured.

One or more of the key individuals can be hired as consultants at an early stage with the mutual intent that they will work for the cooperatives once it is formally established. This approach also has the effect of making investors feel more comfortable about financing the cooperatives because proposed management staff have been identified. For some lenders, competent management is the most important thing they look for in making a loan decision.

9. Hold Cooperative's First Membership and Board Meetings

After financing has been secured and sufficient members have signed up, the first general membership meeting is convened. There are two major pieces of business that must be conducted at this meeting:

- the members adopt the cooperative's bylaws; and
- the members elect a board of directors for the cooperative.

This meeting marks the transition from a steering committee and interim leadership group to a formally elected board and legally approved bylaws.

Allow enough time for members to look over the bylaws and ensure that they are thoroughly understood before the vote takes place. There may be a few amendments suggested; these and the bylaws are approved by majority vote.

In their capacity as owners, members elect the board of directors to function as their representatives in overseeing the administration of the co-op. *It is this mechanism through which a cooperative is member-controlled.* As the members' representatives, the board's primary responsibilities are to develop policies, conduct long-range planning, hire and supervise the co-op manager, and guide the co-op in pursuing its mission and goals.

The new board of directors should hold their first board meeting shortly after the first membership meeting. Among other duties, the board should elect officers, develop job descriptions for management personnel, and initiate the hiring process, if necessary.

10. Start Operations

(*a*) During the initial phase of the cooperative's operations, management should concentrate on implementing the business plan. It is vital that frequent communication between staff, board and members be maintained during this period. Some cooperatives have lost touch with their members after start-up, and have found that to be a recipe for disaster. Management and board need to make sure the co-op is meeting the needs of the members over time. Do this through regular newsletters and member surveys.

(*b*) Another way to maintain good communication between staff, members and board is to conduct educational seminars for them. Remember that continuous education is one of the cooperative principles. It enables members to participate in the cooperative's affairs and make fully informed decisions regarding them.

A strong cooperative is built on a foundation of involved members. Without an active base of members who are willing to work towards the success of the cooperative, the cooperative is bound to fail.

Starting a cooperative can be a lengthy and somewhat arduous process. It can also be very rewarding to see the fruits of your labour turn into economic and social benefits for you and your community.

The steering committee takes responsibility for seeing the organizing process through to the end. Be patient and give yourselves the time to conduct each development stage carefully.

Don't get discouraged if the process appears to get bogged down. Bring in outside technical assistance as needed, and solicit advice from others who have been down the same road.

Additional Information Related to Starting a Cooperative

By-laws, Membership Application, Member Meetings

Bylaws

Bylaws are the rules and regulations that govern the day-to-day working and regular functioning of a cooperative society. They are equal to the Articles of Association followed by a private company. A bylaw can be amended to suit the needs of the cooperative.

Bylaws state how the cooperative will conduct business and must be consistent with both State laws and the articles.

Bylaws usually have membership requirements and lists rights and responsibilities of members; Grounds and procedures for member expulsion; how to call and conduct membership meetings, methods of voting, how directors and officers are elected or removed, and their number, duties, terms of office; time and place of directors meetings; requirement to conduct business; handling of losses; treating non-member business; dissolution of the cooperative; and the process for amending the bylaws.

Also covered is how the board is structured to represent the membership, given geographical distribution and size of the membership and the scope of business and function of the cooperative. Directors may be selected to represent areas based on membership density, to reflect commodities or services to be handled, or some other basis that provides equitable representation. The organizing committee's recommended management structure should include the basis for director representation, voting methods, and board officers, and their terms.

An outline of the major topic areas that the bylaws should cover appears below.

Membership

Identifies the qualifications for eligibility and procedures for joining the cooperative, including requirements for purchase of stock, if any. Describes the procedure by which membership may be ended, either voluntarily or involuntarily.

Meetings of Cooperative Members

Identifies the date for the annual meeting; how and when any special meetings may be held; requirements for notice of upcoming meetings; procedures for voting and requirements for a quorum; order of business at the annual meeting.

Directors and Officers

Specifies the number and qualifications of directors; procedures for electing directors and length of terms; election of officers by the board; frequency of board meetings and requirements for notice of board meetings; any special meetings; compensation of board members and requirements for a quorum.

Duties of Directors

States the director's specific powers and responsibilities, including: guiding the cooperative and articulating its mission, goals, and policies and periodically reviewing those goals. Authorizes directors to employ a manager, define the manager's duties, determine his or her compensation and evaluate his or her job performance. Specifies the director's responsibility to maintain an appropriate accounting system and have the co-op's books audited or reviewed annually. This section also specifies the board's responsibility to indemnify directors, officers and management against liability.

Duties of Officers

Specifies the duties of the president, vice-president, secretary, and treasurer. Also describes the terms of officers and excused absences from board meetings.

Membership Capital Contributions

Specifies the required equity contribution by members and the method by which the co-op will collect the contribution; what type of stock the cooperative has the authority to issue; and any requirements regarding the co-op's stock certificates.

Profits and Losses

Specifies how the co-op's profits, if any, will be distributed based on each member's patronage with the co-op. In addition, any losses experienced by the co-op must be allocated across the membership.

Nonmember Business

Specifies how the cooperative will distribute the benefits, if any, resulting from business with non-members.

Dissolution

Identifies a procedure for dissolving the cooperative, and specifies the distribution of any remaining assets.

Amending the Bylaws

Specifies a straightforward method by which the bylaws may be amended.

Contents of Bye-laws

The bye-laws must contain:

1. The name and the trade name of the cooperative, which may be freely chosen, as long as there is no confusion possible with the name of another cooperative already registered and as long as the public is left in doubt about the limited financial liability of the members
2. The locality of the head office, its postal address and possibly the conditions for a transfer
3. The definition of the objective (including the indication of whether the cooperative is a single or a multi-purpose cooperative)
4. The conditions and procedures for admission, resignation, exclusion and suspension of members as well as eligibility criteria. These must reflect the particular character of the cooperative in question, as also reflected by its being a primary, a secondary or a tertiary cooperative;
5. The value and minimum number of the shares to be subscribed by each member. The GA ensures that the economic means of the least affluent members form the basis for the decision;
6. The procedure and conditions for the subscription and payment of the shares and, possibly, of additional shares. Shares may be paid in cash, kind, labour, service or by leaving the share of the surplus, to which a member is entitled, with the cooperative;
7. The type of financial liability of the members for the debts of the cooperative, the administration of the registers;
8. The conditions and procedures for convening GAs (form of notice, fixing and notifying the agenda, election of the president of the session, preferably not a member of the board of directors, quorum and voting, number of delegates by section or by region if any, etc.);
9. The size of the board of directors and, possibly, of the supervisory committee; the conditions of eligibility to the various offices, the duration of the mandates and their possible remuneration; rights and obligations of officers, mode of decision-taking;
10. The conditions and procedures for convening the board of directors and, if any, the supervisory committee (quorum, voting, etc.);
11. Financing: capital formation, constitution of the legal and of the statutory reserve funds;
12. Surplus distribution and contribution to cover losses;
13. The distribution of the capital in case of resignation, exclusion or liquidation;

14. Definition of the financial year;
15. Auditing;
16. Conditions and procedures for voluntary dissolution;
17. Arbitration procedure;
18. Decision-making;
19. Specification of any other legal matter; and finally
20. The procedure for modifying the bye-laws.

Membership Application

The application, signed by the member and approved by the board of directors, is the legal proof that a patron is a member. A cooperative should have a completed membership application on file from every member. Membership and the amount of business done with members and non-members are important factors for certain activities.

A membership certificate may be issued to each member as evidence of entitlement to all of the rights, benefits, and privileges of the association.

Member Meetings

Further action is usually needed to accept those members who have subscribed for shares or agreed to become members.

If members of the first board of directors have not been named in the bylaws, they should be elected at this meeting or the steering committee can be converted as Board of Directors.

Some suggestions for selecting the first board of directors:

- Use a nominating committee to develop a panel of candidates for the board;
- Select only members as candidates;
- Nominate two candidates for each position; and
- Vote by secret ballot.

Implementing the Business Plan

Officers of the cooperative are elected and directors assigned to individual or committee responsibilities to implement the business plan. Members may be assigned to committees, but at least one board member should be on each committee to enhance communications. Target dates are established for important events such as groundbreaking, construction completion, dedication or open house, and full-capacity operations.

The board needs to act immediately on some specific items:

- Conduct a membership drive;
- Adopt a form of membership application or subscription;
- Acquire capital;
- Initiate steps to hire a manager;
- Authorize officers or employees to handle cooperative funds and issue checks;
- Design and install an accounting system;
- Provide for bookkeeping and auditing services;
- Print bylaws, and other member documents for distribution to all members;
- Bind officers and employees in accordance with bylaws.

Membership Drive

Cooperative normally have open membership. Initially they may have a selective membership policy. Members should feel a responsibility to recommend other believed to be qualified users. That's why it's important for members to understand what their cooperative is, how it operates, its benefits, and its limitations.

People join cooperative primarily for economic benefit-services and increased income. Most people want to be shown the advantages of cooperative membership. If those benefits are not evident, few prospects will join and even if they do, they probably won't regularly patronize the cooperative.

New members may be asked to join by purchasing shares or paying a membership fee and signing and application. The applicant should get a receipt for funds collected. The cooperative must follow-up with membership and related material.

Accurate accounting of money is an extremely sensitive issue. The cooperative should retain an independent accounting firm to assist in recording funds prior to the collection of substantial amounts of money.

Now, we can look into the rights and responsibilities of members, board of directors, chairman, vice-chairman, manager and chief account in the Ethiopian context.

Elections

Elections are conducted routinely as per the bylaws of the cooperative. Every year one-third of the directors will be relieved and elections will be conducted for the post of the directors. Elections can be conducted during the ordinary general assembly meeting as well as during the special general assembly meeting. The members must be given prior intimation by the presiding officer (usually the chairman of the cooperative) relating to the date of election and the nomination by the members. Elections to the posts of president, vice-president, secretary and other office bearers will be conducted among the members of the board of directors.

Members, General Assembly and Board

Members

Cooperative management starts with membership, members formulate the broad, general policies of the cooperative and elect the Board of Directors to supervise the execution of these policies. The manager and his staff put into practice the policies prescribed by the members under the guidance of the Board of Directors. This division of activities places important responsibilities on members, which should not be taken lightly.

The Obligations and Rights of Members

Obligations

Principle

Membership is linked to rights, these being conditioned by the discharge of obligations. The law and subsidiary legislation must ensure that this rule is respected, even in cases where social rules tend to override these rights and obligations.

In no case, must the social mechanisms based on family ties, race, age, religion or any other affiliation to a group affect the independence and the equality of the members.

Personal Obligations

By belonging to a cooperative, members commit themselves to:

- respect the bye-laws as well as all the decisions taken in the general assembly, whether they voted for their adoption or not.
- abstain from any activity detrimental to the objective of their cooperative.
- Membership in several cooperatives having the same objective and territory must not automatically be considered as harming the cooperative(s).
- participate actively in the life of the cooperative. This obligation may not, however, be enforced.

Financial Obligations

Membership in a cooperative implies the following financial obligations:

- Each member must subscribe to and pay for the minimum number of shares fixed by the bye-laws;
- Each member is financially liable for the debts of his or her cooperative. This liability is at least equal to the amount of shares subscribed.

In order to compensate, at least in part, for the financial weakness inherent to most cooperatives, the law or the bye-laws may impose an obligation on the members to make supplementary payments in case the cooperative is unable to pay its debts. This may result in an unlimited financial liability of the members.

The amount of these supplementary payments may be the same for each member, it may be determined as pro rata of the transactions made by each of the members, according to the method used to distribute the surplus, or according to the number of shares held by each member. If not specified in the law, the type of financial liability of the members must be explicitly dealt with in the bye-laws in order to protect the interests of third parties.

Because of the status of legal personality of cooperatives, this financial liability commits the members towards their cooperative only, and not towards the creditors of the cooperative. It extends beyond the termination of membership, during a period to be specified in the law. As a rule, a member must contribute to the discharge of only those debts which show in the balance sheet at the time of the end of his or her membership.

Other Obligations

One might envisage obliging the members to use, to a certain extent at least, the services of their cooperative. Although favouring in the short run the development of the cooperative, such a rule would in time have a negative influence on the competitiveness of the cooperative and it might violate competition law.

Rather than reasoning in terms of legal obligations, one might consider that cooperators have the moral duty to work with their enterprise. Furthermore, it is up to the cooperative itself to offer sufficiently attractive services to its members. In order to guarantee a certain stability in specific cases, the cooperative might have to conclude individual contracts with each of its members.

Furthermore, exceptions are possible particularly in the case where the members decide to make an important investment, the success of which depends on the members using that facility. Members could then temporarily be forbidden to look elsewhere for the rendered services.

Rights

Personal Rights

Each member has the right to:

- use the installations and services of the cooperative;
- participate in the general assembly, propose a motion therein, and vote;
- elect or be elected for an office in the cooperative;
- obtain at all times, from the elected bodies of the cooperative information on the economic situation of the cooperative;
- have the books and registers inspected by the supervisory committee.

Jointly as a group (minimum number to be determined), the members can also:

- convene a general assembly and/or have a question inscribed on the agenda of that GA;
- ask for an additional audit.

Financial Rights

The members have the following financial rights:

They receive a share of the surplus in the form of a bonus, calculated as pro rata of their transactions with their cooperative (patronage bonus), and/ or a limited interest on the paid-up shares.

When terminating their membership, they can ask that the paid-up shares be reimbursed. Losses or devaluations may be deducted from the nominal value of these shares.

In the case of liquidation, members receive a share of the remaining sum, if any, unless the bye-laws stipulate that this must be credited to another cooperative or to a charitable organization.

Members participate in management in a number of ways. The most important are when they:

(*a*) Adopt and amend by-laws;

(*b*) Elect and remove Board of Directors;

(*c*) Approve changes in capitalization and major additions to plants and services;

(*d*) Decide on the appropriation of net surplus;

(*e*) Approve annual activity plan and budget;

(*f*) Make a decision on audit reports;

(*g*) Consider the annual report of the Board of Directors controlling committee and making a decision;

(*h*) Become active in the cooperative affairs by attending meetings, serving on committees, accepting special assignments, and genuinely backing the cooperative;

(*i*) Abide by the decision of the majority;

(*j*) Keep informed about the cooperative by studying annual reports, talking with board of directors and employees;

(*k*) Defend the cooperative and its management when it is unjustly criticized or attacked.

In order for cooperative members to exercise control, they must take action by legally called meetings. The by-laws should specify the procedure to be followed in calling meetings. The highest body in the cooperative is the general meeting. All members of the cooperative should attend meetings.

Summary

- There are ten basic steps involved in starting a cooperative.
- Bylaws of a cooperative give the guidelines to run a cooperative. Conducting the day-to-day affairs and running of a cooperative are clearly explained in the bylaws. Bylaws can be amended according to the needs of the members of the cooperative.
- After bylaws are prepared members are issued member application and members meet to elect the first board of directors.
- The first board has to go through the business plan. A business plan tells the future business activities in terms of figures and targets. A business plan is needed for a financing institution to appraise the credit worthiness of a cooperative.
- A membership drive must be undertaken by the new board to increase the capital structure and the volume of business. A cooperative should see that all the individuals or families in the area of operation of a cooperative are enrolled as members of the new cooperative.
- Members have their own rights and responsibilities which are explained in the bylaws of the cooperative. They have to actively participate in the deliberations of the cooperative to increase the financial resources of the cooperative. They must also actively participate in the elections, to select right persons to the board.

Self-learning Activity

Try to answer the following questions on your own:

1. Discuss the basic steps involved in organizing a cooperative?
2. What are the duties and rights of members of a cooperative?

18

Feasibility and Viability Studies for Cooperative Enterprises

Feasibility Studies

Feasibility studies — also termed project evaluation, pre-construction survey, etc. — are systematic appraisal of the economic and possibly social effects which the realization of a certain project will have, and a survey of the technical problems involved. Co-operatives can be confronted with the need for such an analysis, for example, if a new society or a new branch is to be established, if new activities are to be undertaken, etc. In a wider sense a similar study, though perhaps not so elaborate, should precede any decision which could decisively alter the course of a society.

In smaller matters this analysis can be prepared and assessed by the society's staff or, in the case of societies to be formed, by a pre-cooperative study group of prospective members, but in most cases a qualified economist or engineer, or both, have to be consulted. Within the co-operative sector this type of extension service can usually be contacted through central business organizations, auditing associations or government departments. In some instances feasibility studies are also carried out by international organizations involved in co-operative extension work or by private consulting firms.

In most cases the study is carried out according to a schedule similar to the following:

1. Terms of reference

In this preface it should be established on whose authority the study is being made, and the exact objectives it is to pursue. For the further course of the study it is important that this purpose is clearly stated. It should also include the course the study will follow and the source of information on which it will rely.

2. Introduction

The introduction must present the background information to the project:

(*a*) General aspects which may affect the project, such as the relevant legislation, the structure of local administration, income statistics, etc., and a general description of the area where the project will be carried out, its geographical factors, climate, communication system, people and customs. In the individual case it may also include specialized information, in rural projects, for example, about soil qualities, rainfall, land tenure and utilization, average farm size, methods of farming, etc.

(*b*) The scope for development or the need for new facilities, at present as well as in the future, by showing the faults and disadvantages of the present set-up or situation, or by proving, by way of market analysis, the room for expansion.

(*c*) The suggested target for expansion or the proposed capacity of any new facilities.

(*d*) The possible approach or method to be used and, if necessary, a comparison of several methods, and the planned location of any facilities.

(*e*) The time schedule for the realization of the project considering the recruitment and training period for any new staff, the delivery period for any new machinery and the construction time for any new buildings required as well as the most favorable time to start the project with regard to the market.

(*f*) The size of membership related to the set targets and the possibility of attracting new members.

(*g*) The expected response from present or prospective members, especially whether they realize the necessity of the project and are willing to co-operate, or what steps can be taken to enlist their collaboration.

3. Market Analysis Research

The key questions that should be answered in the Market Analysis section of the feasibility study are presented below:

(*a*) What is the current or projected demand for your proposed products or services? In other words, how many units can you reasonably expect to sell each month?

(*b*) What are the target markets for this product or service? What demographic characteristics do these potential customers have in common? How many of them are there?

(*c*) What is the projected supply in your area of the products or services needed for your project?

(*d*) What competition exists in this market? Can you establish a market niche, which will enable you to compete effectively with the other providing this product or service?

(*e*) Is the location of your proposed business or project likely to affect is success? If so, is the identified site the most appropriate one available?

The market analysis should be conducted first because it is critical to the success of the business. If you cannot substantiate through research that adequate demand for your product or service exists, or if you cannot obtain sufficient quality to meet expected demand, then your project is not feasible. You should not continue to the next step in the feasibility study.

4. Organizational issues

(*a*) What organizational structure is the right one for you?

(*b*) Who will serve on the board of directors?

(*c*) What qualifications are needed to manage this business?

(*d*) Who will manage the business (if possible)?

(*e*) What other staffing needs does the co-op have? How do you expect staffing needs to change over the next 2-3 years?

5. Technical requirements

(*a*) The feasibility of using the existing facilities and the present staff for the new task and the possible changes to be made for their adaptation.

(*b*) Any new facilities and manpower needed and their availability:

(*i*) Land and buildings, their size, design, outlay and equipment.

(*ii*) Lachinery, type, make, capacity.

(*iii*) Transport, type, capacity.

(*iv*) Manpower, required skill and experience, recruitment plan.

Key Questions to answer include:

(*a*) What are the technology needs for the proposed business?

(*b*) What other equipment does your proposed business need?

(*c*) Where will you obtain this technology and equipment?

(*d*) When can you get the necessary equipment?

(*e*) How much will the equipment and technology cost?

6. Capital outlay and finance

(*a*) The total cost of the project assessed according to a detailed list of the costs of any building, machinery or vehicles needed and, if possible, accompanied by tenders of the relevant suppliers.

(*b*) The required rate of finance calculated on the basis of the expected average lifetime of the invested assets.

(*c*) The source of finance available for the purpose of the project.

The following financial aspects are to be considered.

(*a*) *Start-up Costs:* These are the costs incurred in starting up a new business, including 'capital goods' such as land, buildings, equipment, etc. The business may have to borrow money from a lending institution to cover these costs.

(*b*) *Operating Costs:* These are the ongoing costs, such as rent, utilities, and wages that are incurred in the everyday operation of a business. The total should include interest and principle payments on any debt for start-up costs.

(*c*) *Revenue Projections:* How will you price your goods or services? Assess what the estimated monthly revenue will be.

(*d*) *Sources of Financing:* If your proposed business will need to borrow money from a bank or other lending institution, you may need to research potential lending sources.

(*e*) *Profitability Analysis:* This is the 'bottom line' for the proposed business. Given the costs and revenue analysis above, will your business bring in enough revenue to cover operating expenses? Will it break even, lose money or make a profit? Is there anything you can do to improve the bottom line?

7. Analysis of operating costs (includes salary, taxes, interest, etc.)

(*a*) The breakdown of the expected operating cost including the proportional overhead expenses calculated for various levels of output or development.

(*i*) based pm estimated costs

(*ii*) by comparison with a society which has already carried out a similar project taking into account the cost variations caused by differences in size, location, structure of membership and efficiency in management.

(*b*) The comparison of differing methods with respect to operating costs.

8. Analysis of expected benefits

The assessment of added revenue gained from the project or of the expected decrease in cost or improvement in service.

9. Final assessment

(*a*) The comparison of the increased operating cost with the additional revenue expected (break-even graph).

(*b*) The influence of the new project on the overall profitability of the society.

(*c*) The reasons which would make the project feasible despite a decrease in profitability, for instance, the long-term effect on the development of the society.

10. Appendix

The appendix should include all those documents, statistics, tenders, drawings to which the text of the feasibility study refers.

Example: Study of the possibilities of expanding a co-operative marketing society.

(*a*) What is the present economic situation of the society?

- (*i*) Area of operation, membership.
- (*ii*) Activities, turnover.
- (*iii*) Management and staff.
- (*iv*) Balance sheet and other records.

(*b*) Is there scope for an expansion of the established activities?

(*i*) by increasing the membership:

- Are there farmers in the area of operation who are eligible for membership but who are not yet members?
- What is the degree of competition from other marketing institutions in the area?
- What can the society do to attract these farmers despite competition? Can it improve services or give better prices?

(*ii*) by increasing the area of operation:

- Are there co-operative marketing societies already working in adjoining areas? If so, is an amalgamation feasible of possible?
- What other marketing institutions have established themselves in the adjoining areas, and could the society competed with them?
- What effect would the increased average distance between member and society have on the marketing costs?

(*iii*) by increasing the turnover per member:

- Are the present members completely loyal to the society? If not, what can be done to improve this situation? Does the possibility of introducing delivery contracts exist?
- Can the society initiate a scheme by which the members increase their production, e.g. new farming methods?

(*c*) Is an expansion along the current lines desirable? Can the market absorb more produce without a significant fall in price?

(*d*) Is there scope for expansion by taking up new activities?

(i) by marketing other farming products not yet covered?

- What other crop or animal product is produced in the area in sufficient quantity to give a basis for organized marketing?
- For which of these products is there a suitable market?
- What competition would the society have to face in this field?

(ii) by taking up other activities such as credit, supply, or other services:

- For which of these activities is there a sufficient demand among members or prospective members?
- What competition would the society have to face in any of these fields?

(*e*) Would the society be able to cope with an expansion in connection with:

(i) top management?

- Is the present management capable of taking on additional functions? If not, are there suitable facilities for further training? And would the present management be able and willing to undergo such training?
- Is the present management willing to shoulder new responsibilities? If not, would and increase in salary act as an incentive?
- Would it be possible and feasible to replace the present management with more experienced persons?

(ii) staff?

- Is the present staff adequate in quantity and quality to cope with an increase in work and duties?
- Are there staff training facilities?
- Can the society recruit additional experienced staff?

(iii) facilities?

- Are the present facilities of the society adequate for additional functions with regard to space, equipment and transport?
- What new investments would be necessary? And what would be the cost?
- What are the possibilities of securing the necessary finance?
- What sources are available?

(*f*) How would the increased costs compare with the additional revenue? Is the overall profitability of the society maintained, increased, decreased or endangered?

Merits of Feasibility Studies to Cooperatives

1. Whenever a new cooperative is to be organized, the scope for the viability and survival of such cooperative can be predicted.
2. Whenever cooperatives open new branches or offices, the success of such new units could be predicted accurately by cooperatives.
3. In raising deposits and mobilizing resources, feasibility studies can help the cooperatives by suggesting new methods and measures.
4. Sick units and dormant cooperatives can be revived by using feasibility studies.
5. Cooperatives work under competition. What type of competition they face could be ascertained by feasibility studies.
6. The relations of the consumers and the members of cooperatives could be examined by this method. Their problems could also be solved.
7. Reactions and attitudes of Government towards their co-operatives could be predicted by this method of research.
8. Whenever cooperatives introduce new products the success of such new products can be predicted by this method.
9. The market share of bigger cooperatives can be surveyor and steps can be suggested to increase the market share in future, by this research.

Viability Studies

A viability study is an economic analysis of the past and present performance of an enterprise, a department or a special project, of the soundness of its financial structure and economic basis, of its competitiveness, and of the capabilities and efficiency of its management. It is based on the figures obtainable from the accounts of the enterprise and from any supplementary statistics available.

Viability norms and applications may vary from cooperative to cooperative. Such variations may be as follows:

(*a*) *Cooperative Banks:* For cooperative banks, agricultural credit cooperatives and cooperatives which are undertaking banking business the viability norms will be based mainly on the banking services undertaken and customer attraction aspects.

(*b*) *Producers' Cooperatives:* For producers' cooperatives like agricultural producers' cooperatives, manufacturing cooperatives, weavers' cooperatives, etc., the viability norms can be based on production efficiency, operational efficiency, input-output relations, and cost considerations.

(c) *Service Cooperatives:* For service cooperatives like consumer cooperatives, cooperative supermarkets, etc. the viability indicators are customer satisfaction, efficient customer service and price considerations.

(d) *Marketing Cooperatives:* Marketing cooperatives are one of the prominent cooperative organizations. Their viability can be decided on the basis of their operational efficiency, marketing services undertaken; price provided to producers and input services provided.

(e) *Cooperative Training Centers:* For such institutes the viability is decided by factors like number of training programmes conducted, quality of training programmes, efficiency of training instructors and the managerial abilities inculcated by such institutions.

In general, viability norms for all types of cooperatives can be fixed on the following criteria:

1. ***Organizational Aspects***

   The general structure of the society, its organization, activities, volume of business and membership. The society should have adequate membership and it should have enough number of activities to satisfy the needs of the members. Later stage the society can increase its number of activities. Likewise, the volume of transaction is an important aspect. The society should have adequate volume of business to manage the recurring costs of the society. Any society must attain a break-even analysis within three years of its starting.

2. ***The financial structure***

   Any cooperative to be viable should be strong in its financial basis. The ultimate objective goal of a cooperative should be to stand on its own leg and to be self-reliant in its resources. The other financial aspects are as follows:

   (a) *The solvency and stability of the society:* This denotes that a cooperative should be able to raise its own resources and it should keep its credibility in the eyes of the members, depositors, creditors, government and the public.

   (b) *The self-sufficiency in finance:* This is considered to be one of the most important criteria for the viability of a cooperative. As far as possible, a cooperative should mobilize resources by way of owned funds (consisting of share capital and reserves). When this source is not successful, the cooperative can resort to raising of resources by way of accepting deposits from the members and non-members. Borrowings will lead to dependency on other agencies and a cooperative may have to sacrifice its own financial freedom thereby inviting the interference of such creditors.

(c) *The capital intensity, i.e. the relationship of fixed assets to total assets:* This factor denotes that a cooperative, in the long run must be able to build strong assets in order to face any financial and business challenges. This will also facilitate the cooperative to face competition in the open market.

3. ***The Financial Viability***

A cooperative can attain financial viability by mobilizing its own funds. In addition to such self-reliance in resources a cooperative can attain the financial viability through the following measures:

(a) *Administrative Cost:* As far as possible a cooperative must try to check the administrative cost to the total cost of operations. Another way of keeping the administrative cost under control is by way of increasing the operational efficiency, volume of business and services by having the same staff structure.

(b) *Recovery of Loans:* This is one of the significant viability norm for cooperative banking institutions or cooperatives engaged in lending operations. The loans must be recovered in time. Any overdue loan will increase the financial commitment of the cooperative. It will lead to unnecessary locking of capital and the cost will increase by means of paying additional interest for overdue loans. So, an efficient loan recovery measure is a strong indicator for a viable society.

(c) *Length of Operations:* This denotes the loaning and other service operations of a cooperative is short-term or long-term in nature. Depending on the length of operations, a cooperative must raise its resources properly. Short-term resources should not be employed for long-term ventures. Prior planning is necessary in raising the resources and deploying the funds.

(d) *Investment of Funds:* As cooperatives are coming under the purview of the Central Bank of a country (National Bank of Ethiopia), in investing their funds the cooperative has to follow the guidelines given by the Central Bank of the country. Within the purview of such regulations, a cooperative must invest its funds productively and remuneratively in the form of loans, investments and related aspects.

(e) *Growth and Diversification of Activities:* A cooperative, in order to attain viability must grow year after year as well as it must diversify its operations, having the main objective of fulfilling the basic needs of members. Diversification of functions will ensure a cooperative to distribute the financial and business risks equitably.

(*f*) *Sources and Costs of Funds:* As discussed earlier, a cooperative must be self-reliant in its resources. While raising the resources it must see that the cost should be cheaper and the overhead charges should be minimum. For example, while raising deposits, a cooperative can concentrate on current deposits and savings deposits, which are cheaper than on completely relying on fixed deposits.

4. ***The performance of the society***

Finally, the performance of a cooperative in terms of its profitability, productivity and earning power will decide its viability.

(*a*) *Profitability:* An enterprise is basically profitable if the income of the period under consideration meets the current expenditure. For the purpose of comparison this relationship can be expressed as:

Income/Expenditure

Absolute profitability is assured if the result is more than 1.0. Relative profitability is indicated by the figures after the decimal point. In the case of co-operative enterprise the relative profitability will normally remain well below 2.0.

The maximum profitability of enterprise is reached if it can achieve the highest revenue with the lowest costs. As co-operatives are restricted in their revenue by the principle of 'service at cost', a society can reach its maximum profitability by putting the main emphasis on reaching an optimal cost structure.

(*b*) *Productivity:* Productivity is measured by an input-output analysis. As the correlating of the output or results of the society to the individual factors of production, i.e. labor, capital and organization, is extremely difficult, if not impossible, productivity is usually measured as one-factor-productivity (I-III below) or as overall-productivity (IV). The measurement can be based on quantity or value, though it is only feasible to measure the output in quantity if it has a degree of uniformity. Possible relationships are:

$$\frac{\text{Turnover or output}}{\text{W.H. (working hours) or labour costs}}$$

$$\frac{\text{Turnover or output}}{\text{Interest on the average capital* Invested in the business}}$$

$$\frac{\text{Turnover or output}}{\text{Average capital invested in the business}}$$

$$\frac{\text{Turnover or output}}{\text{Cost of management (salaries + expenses)}}$$

$$\frac{\text{Turnover or output}}{\text{Total operation cost}}$$

A co-operative society has reached its maximum productivity if it can realize a maximum of service to the members at minimum cost.

(*c*) *Earning power:* This is an indicator of success comparing profit with invested capital. The earning power of a co-operative society can be established in two ways:

The earning power of the capital owned: (patronage refunds and similar payments + interest paid on share-capital + allocations to the reserve fund + estimated additional benefits to members in the form of price advantages compared to the market) × 100

average capital owned i.e. equity capital, during the period considered

II the overall earning power: (as under I + interest paid on capital borrowed) × 100

average total capital invested in the society during the period considered.

The desirable rate of earning power depends, in the case of the individual society, on the degree of risk involved in its activities, though the invested capital should at least earn the current commercial rate of interest on capital borrowed.

Summary

- Feasibility studies - also termed project evaluation, pre-construction survey, etc. - are systematic appraisal of the economic and possibly social effects which the realization of a certain project will have, and a survey of the technical problems involved. Co-operatives can be confronted with the need for such an analysis.
- A viability study is an economic analysis of the past and present performance of an enterprise, a department or a special project, of the soundness of its financial structure and economic basis, of its competitiveness, and of the capabilities and efficiency of its management.

Self-learning Activity

Try to answer the following questions on your own:

1. What are the components of feasibility study?
2. How does a cooperative attain financial viability?

19

Preparation of Business Plan in Cooperative Enterprises

Business Plan

A business plan is a written document that contains information, an organization that has collected converted into comprehensible and workable plans that can be understood by all parties involved with the business. All aspects concerning the business are addressed by the business plans, including what, why, how, when and where of the business opportunities, as well as all the activities, goals and strategies thereof.

This is a well written statement which outlines the major activities of the business and any future plans for the business. This will act as a guideline when various annual operational budgets are formulated. Business plan mainly is presented to financial institutions when sourcing finance. Before releasing their funds, the financiers would want an assurance from the business that it is a going concern and whatever project they want to venture in will be viable.

Business plan is supposed to involve all line managers and employees of an organization. The use of expert help may be important but the entrepreneur's own input is of vital importance as the plan should contain achievable targets of which the owners and employees are capable of setting.

Business plan should be based on achievable assumptions. As the plan relates to the future there is a need to make a careful assessment of the current and future economic and political conditions which may have a direct impact on the operations of the business. Targets set should be achievable and supported with previous achievements made by the business.

There is no universal way of producing a business plan but here are some of the important sections which are supposed to be found in an ideal business plan.

Uses of and reasons for a business plan

- It gives direction to the business management and activities.
- It helps to identify objectives, problems and also opportunities.
- Performance standards are set.
- Performance is evaluated and monitored.
- It provides a written business tool that can serve as a decision-making tool.
- A backing for obtaining capital or finance.
- Both the entrepreneur and employees use the business plan for guidance.
- It is used for obtaining new business.

BUSINESS PLAN TEMPLATE FOR AGRICULTURAL COOPERATIVE UNIONS

Business Plan Outline for the Proposed Cooperative Unions

Cover Sheet

This contains the basic information about the cooperative business, such as name of the cooperative business. There is a need to have an attractive cover which will captivate the read to read more from the business plan.

An Executive Summary

This contains a summary of the information which is contained in the overall business plan. As reader may not be able to scrutinize every detail of the plan, the executive summary should present an overview of what information the business plan is going to relate. The executive summary need to be brief as it is just an abbreviated version of the business plan.

Table of Contents

The table of contents is an important section which is always undermined. The table of contents assists the readers of the plan to quickly trace where to find a particular section or a specific issue.

Business Background

It contains information about the cooperative enterprise or members of the venture team, together with an indication of the contribution of each person to starting or acquiring business. Would be investors, financiers and the future managers of the business are interested in the details in respect of how the idea for the product or service was developed, why it was decided to start or acquire a business and what process of the business acquisition or start up entailed. The background gives the appraisal or the financier an understanding of the original mission envisaged by the cooperative enterprise and whether there has been any positive or negative deviation from those original objectives of the business. The business background section contains basic information about the proposed business projects which the business require to venture in. The contents are:

- The name of the current owner of the business;
- Location of the business;
- Objectives of the business;
- The reasons for sale of the business;
- The description of any proposed project;
- Registered address of the business;
- Owner's personal details; and
- Business form.

A well written background helps to give the appraiser of the business plan the impression that the bidder knows the operations of the business.

I. Description of the cooperative

1. Profile of the Union

1.1. Name of the Union :

1.2. Location : Region Zone Woreda

1.3. Date of establishment :

1.4. No. of households in the area of operation :

1.5. No. of Member primaries :

1.6. Individual members : Male Female Total

2. The competitors

2.1. Who are your competitors?

(*a*) Private traders

(*b*) Wholesalers

(*c*) Others (specify)

2.2. What are the strategies used to face competition.

(*a*) Purchasing efficiency (inputs)

(*b*) Selling efficiency (output)

(*c*) Marketing services

(*d*) Price mechanism

3. Competencies

3.1. Who are your customers?

(*a*) Individuals

(*b*) Private institutions

(*c*) Government institutions

(*d*) Cooperatives

(*e*) Others (specify)

3.2. What is the mechanism used by you to verify customers satisfaction?

(*a*) Daily complaint by the customers

(*b*) Suggestion box

(*c*) Grievance day (weekly/fortnightly/monthly)

(*d*) Complaint by phone, letter correspondence, etc.

3.3. How many institutional customers you have at present? _________

3.4. What type of institutional customers are they?

(*a*) Wholesalers

(*b*) Private companies

(*c*) Government organizations

(*d*) Cooperatives

(*e*) Others (specify)

3.5. What are the steps taken by you to enlist more institutional customers?

3.6. What are the future businesses you would like to add? (mention business like consumer activities, transport services, etc).

II. Organisational Analysis

1. Committee members

1.1. Name the types of committees of your union.

(*a*)

(*b*)

(*c*)

1.2. How many members are there in each committee?

(*a*) _______ committee: ________ members

(*b*) _______ committee: ________ members

(*c*) _______ committee: ________ members

1.3. Give the educational qualification and experience of committee members.

Sl. No.	Committee member/Name	Level of Education	Experience as committee member	Women participation		Remarks
				Number	%	

1.4. What are the steps taken by you to organize new primaries and to enlist more primaries as members?

1.5. During last three years how many general assembly meetings were held?

Year	Number of meetings	Date of meetings	Number attended	Remarks

1.6. During last three years how many committee meetings were held?

Year	Number of meetings	Date of meetings	Number attended	Remarks

1.7. Give the details of training programme undergone by the committee members.

S. No.	Type of training	Conducted by whom	No. of participants	Duration

1.8. Give the details of your future training programmes for the coming three years.

Year I

1.

2.

Year II

1.

2.

Year III

1.

2.

1.9. Give details on number of exposure visits arranged.

Sl. No.	Visit (place)	Conducted by whom	No. of participants	Duration

1.10. Give the details of your future Exposure visits for the coming three years.

Year I

1.

2.

Year II

1.

2.

Year III

1.

2.

2. Manager and Staff

2.1. Give the details of the staff (manager and other employees)

Sl.No.	Name and Designation	Age	Qualification (Education)	Experience (Years)

2.2. Give the details of future recruitment of staff.

Year/ Sl. No.	Nature of job	Number of staff required	Age	Required Qualification Education)	Experience (Years)
Year I					
Year II					
Year III					

2.3. What is the time frame fixed to recruit new staff? (How many staff to be recruited in each forthcoming year?)

2.4. Training programmes undergone by the staff.

Sl. No.	Type of training	Conducted by whom	No. of participants	Duration

2.5. Give the details of your future training programmes (for employees) for the coming three years.

Year I

1.

2.

Year II

1.

2.

Year III

1.

2.

2.6. Give details of exposure visits.

Sl. No.	Visit (place)	Conducted by whom	No. of participants	Duration

2.7. Give details of your future exposure visits (for employees) for the coming three years.

Year I

1.

2.

Year II

1.

2.

Year III

1.

2.

III. Marketing and Sales Analysis

1. Growth strategy (monthwise and yearwise)

1.1. What was the growth strategy followed by you for the last three years in terms of input and output marketing?

Year	Input marketing		Output marketing	
	Target	Achievement	Target	Achievement
Year I				
Year II				
Year III				

1.2. What is the future growth potential proposed by you for the future three years.

Year	Input marketing		Output marketing	
	Quantity	Value	Quantity	Value
Year I				
Year II				
Year III				

2. Procurement Strategy

2.1. Procurement timings every day.

2.2. Fixation of procurement responsibility to each staff.

2.3. Purchasing/procurement target.

Year	Procurement	
	Target	Achievement
Year I		
Year II		
Year III		

2.4. Purchasing/procurement plan for future three years.

Year	Procurement	
	Quantity	Value
Year I		
Year II		
Year III		

2.5. Storage facility (existing)

Sl. No.	Storage		Capacity (in sq.mts)	Type (modern/traditional)
	Owned	Hired		

2.6. Future plan to construct/hiring/increase the storage capacity (for three years.

Sl.No.	Type of store	Timeframe to complete the process (Year)
1.	Owned	
2.	Hired	
3.	Capacity increase	

2.7. Steps to avoid wastage, pilferage during procurement stage and storage stage (state the steps taken by you in this regard).

3. Pricing Strategy

3.1. Mention the price strategy followed by you for the last three years.

Year	Commodity	Open market price	Cooperative price	Difference
Year I	1			
	2			
	3			
	4			
	5			
Year II	1			
	2			
	3			
	4			
	5			
Year III	1			
	2			
	3			
	4			
	5			

3.2. Mention the price strategy for the future three years.

Year	Commodity	Cooperative price
Year I	1	
	2	
	3	
	4	
	5	
Year II	1	
	2	
	3	
	4	
	5	
Year III	1	
	2	
	3	
	4	
	5	

3.3. Who decides the pricing policy for input purchasing and output sales?

(*a*) Committee members

(*b*) Manager

(*c*) Both committee member and managers

(*d*) Any other, specify.

3.4. What are the future pricing strategies you propose to follow to face competition from private traders?

3.5. Do you have any future plan to create price fluctuation fund or similar arrangements to face price loss during input marketing and output marketing?

4. Sales Strategy

4.1. What are the market arrivals of various commodities? (for current year)

Sl. No.	Commodity	Harvest month arrival month	Market	Remarks
1				
2				
3				
4				
5				
6				

4.2. Market arrivals of various commodities proposed for future three years?

Sl. No.	Commodity	Harvest month	Market arrival month	Remarks
1	2	3	4	5
Year I				
1				
2				
3				
4				
5				
6				

(Contd...)

1	2	3	4	5
Year II				
1				
2				
3				
4				
5				
6				
Year III				
1				
2				
3				
4				
5				
6				

4.3. What is the purchase/procurement made by you for the current year?

Year/ Sl. No.	Commodity	Quantity (in qtnls.)	Value (in Birr)	Remarks
1				
2				
3				
4				
5				
6				

4.4. What is the proposed purchase/procurement for the future three years?

Year/ Sl.No.	Commodity	Quantity (in qtnls.)	Value (in Birr)	Remarks
1	2	3	4	5
Year I				
1				
2				
3				
4				
5				
6				

(Contd…)

1	2	3	4	5
Year II				
1				
2				
3				
4				
5				
6				
Year III				
1				
2				
3				
4				
5				
6				

4.5. What is the incentive (commission) given to the sales force (manager, committee members, salesmen)?

4.6. What is the future plan to give incentive to sales force?

5. Transport and Communication Services

5.1. What is the transport arrangement made by you for input marketing and output marketing?

Year	Type of transport		Transport charges paid (if hired)	Remarks
	Owned	Hired		
Year I				
Year II				
Year III				

5.2. Do you have any future plan to purchase your own vehicle? Yes/No

If yes, give details.

5.3. What is the current communication facilities you have?

(*a*) Phone facility

(*b*) Mobile Phone

(*c*) No phone/mobile facility

5.3. What is the future (Yearwise) communication facilities you would like to add?

1. Phone facility
2. Mobile Phone

IV. Financial Analysis

1. *Members Stake*

1.1. What is the value of a share in the cooperative union?

1.2. What is the minimum shares fixed to become the member of the union?

1.3. Do you have any future plan to increase the share contribution by primary SACCOs to the union? Yes/No

If yes, explain the scheme yearwise.

Year I

Year II

Year III

1.4. What is the amount of compulsory savings prescribed for primary SACCOs?

1.5. Is there any future plan to increase the compulsory savings? Yes/No

If yes, explain the scheme yearwise.

Year I

Year II

Year III

1.6. Capital base

Year	Share capital	Reserve/ Retained earnings	Compulsory deposits	Borrowings from NGO	Borrowings from Govt.	Borrowings from Commercial Banks
Year I						
Year II						
Year III						

1.6.1. Give your future plan of increasing capital base.

Year	Share capital	Reserve/ Retained earnings	Compulsory deposits	Borrowings from NGO	Borrowings from Govt.	Borrowings from Commercial Banks
Year I						
Year II						
Year III						

V. Cost and Profitability Analysis

1. Break-even Analysis

    1.1. In which year the union started functioning?

    1.2. In which year the union started earning profit?

    1.3. Mention the profit/loss for the union since its establishment.

Sl.No.	Year	Profit	Loss	Remarks
1.	First Year			
2.	Second Year			
3.	Third Year			
4.	Fourth Year			
5.	Fifth Year			
6.	Sixth Year			

1.4. Proposed profit for future three years.

Sl. No.	Year	Profit
1.		
2.		
3.		

1.5. Mention the income areas of the union.

Year	Income sources				Total
	Input distribution	Grain marketing	Marketing charges	Others	
Year I					
Year II					
Year III					

1.6. Proposed income areas of the union.

Year	Income sources				Total
	Input distribution	Grain marketing	Marketing charges	Others	
Year I					
Year II					
Year III					

2. Cost Analysis

2.1. Give the details of the following cost/expenditure areas.

Year	Expenditure areas							Total
	Rent	Salary	Hiring (vehicle)	Office exp. (electricity, tax, etc.)	Travel (perdiem)	Marketing cost	Others	
Year I								
Year II								
Year III								

2.2. Give the details of the following cost/expenditure areas for future 3 years.

Year	Expenditure areas							Total
	Rent	Salary	Hiring (vehicle)	Office exp. (electricity, tax, etc.)	Travel (perdiem)	Marketing cost	Others	
Year I								
Year II								
Year III								

3. Profit Analysis

3.1. Pattern of the distribution of profit.

Year	Profit	Dividend	Reserves	Retained earnings	Others
Year I					
Year II					
Year III					

3.2. Pattern of the distribution of profit for future 3 years.

Year	Profit	Dividend	Reserves	Retained earnings	Others
Year I					
Year II					
Year III					

4. Ratio Analysis

1. Use the following and other relevant statements for calculating ratios
   (*a*) Budget and actual statement for three years.
   (*b*) Profit and loss account (Income and expenditure statement) for three years.
   (*c*) Balance sheet for three years.

Summary

- The challenges confronting cooperatives require innovation and a commitment of resources to focused projects. Project management in a broad sense can fit well with and serve cooperatives. Preparation of business plan, attract funding agencies, and sustaining the global competition is a must for cooperatives.

Self-learning Activity

Try to answer the following questions on your own:

1. What are the components of a business plan?
2. *Exercise:* Try to prepare a business plan of a cooperative nearby your institution.

References

Poter, P. and Scully, W. (1987), "Economic Efficiency in Cooperatives", *Journal of Law and Economics*, 30(2): 489-512.

FAO (2006) *Promoting Sustainable Producer Group Enterprises: A review of FAO experience* (1981-2006).

Novkovic, S. (2008), "Defining the Co-operative Difference", *Journal of Socio-Economics*, 37: 2168-2177.

Cook, M. and Plunkett, B. (2006), "Collective entrepreneurship: An Emerging Phenomenon in Producer-Owned Organizations", *Journal of Agricultural and Applied Economics*, 38(2): 421-428.

Valentinov, V. (2007), "Why are Cooperatives Important in Agriculture? An Organizational Economics Perspective", *Journal of Institutional Economics*, 3(1): 55-69.

Bijman, J. and van Dijk, G. (2009), *Corporate Governance in Agricultural Cooperatives: A Perspective from the Netherlands*. Paper presented at the workshop 'Rural Cooperation in the 21st Century: Lessons from the Past, Pathways to the Future', Rehovot, Israel, June 2009.

Bernard, T. and Speilman, V. (2009), "Reaching the Rural Poor through Rural Producer Organizations? A Study of Agricultural Marketing Cooperatives in Ethiopia, *Food Policy*, 34: 60-69.

SAMULI SKURNIK, "The Role of Cooperative Entrepreneurship and Firms in Organising Economic Activities – Past, Present and Future", *The Finnish Journal of Business Economics* 1/2002, p. 103.

Fulton, Murray, "Cooperatives and Member Commitment", *The Finnish Journal of Business Economics*, 4/1999, pp. 418-437.

Macpherson, IAN, *Co-operative Principles for the 21st Century*. International Cooperative Alliance (ICA), 1996. (Available also on the internet http://www.coop.org/ica/info/enprinciples.html).

Boutros Boutros-Ghali, UN Secretary-General, "Report to the General Assembly", 1994.

Parnell, Edgar, *Reinventing the Co-operative Enterprise for the 21st Century*, Plunkett Foundation, Oxford, United Kingdom, 1995. Pellervon vuosikirja, 2001, Osuustoiminta-lehti 5/2001.

Nilsson, Jerker, "Co-operative Organisational Models as Reflections of the Business Environments", *The Finnish Journal of Business Economics*, 4/1999, pp. 449–470.

Jake Carlyle, "A Cooperative Economy – What Might It Look Like?' Paper given at the Hobart Conference: Community, Economy and the Environment: Exploring Tasmania's Future, 15 October 2005.

Dyer, Bruce, *Why Cooperatives: The New Zealand Context*, Proutist Universal, Nelson, 2000, available at www.prout.org.

[National Cooperative Business Association, www.ncba.org.

Karlyle, Jake, "Small-Scale Cooperative Enterprise in Maleny—Creating Prosperous Communities", 2000, available at www.proutworld/features/maleny.html

International Cooperative Alliance, www.ica.org

Message of Mr Papoutsis, Video Opening Plenary Session" ENTREPRENEURSHIP AND COOPERATIVES IN EUROPE, 2000, Bologna, Italy, 30.11.98.

SAMULI SKURNIK, "The Role of Cooperative Entrepreneurship and Firms in Organising Economic Activities – Past, Present and Future, *The Finnish Journal of Business Economics*, 1/2002, p. 122.

Chambers English Dictionary, Chambers, Cambridge, 1988

Nelson, R.E., "Promotion of Small Enterprises", in *Small Enterprise Development: Policies and Programmes*, Eds. Neck, P.A. and Nelson, R.E., ILO, (Geneva , 1987), p. 3.

Nelson, R.E., and Nguiru, R.G., *Training for Entrepreneurship*, pp. 103-106.

McClelland, D.C., *The Achieving Society*, D. Van Nostrand, (New York, 1961).

Manu, G., Nelson, R.E., Thiongo, J., *Know About Business, International Training Centre of the ILO* - Turin, (Italy, 1996).

Kilby, P. (Ed.), *Entrepreneurship and Economic Development*, Collier-MacMillan, Canada, (Toronto, 1971).

Davis, P., "Towards a Value-Based Management for Membership-Based Organisations", *Journal of Cooperative Studies*, Vol. 29, No.1, May 1996.

Taimni, K.K.: "Cooperative Entrepreneurship: Concept, Design and Approaches to Development", unpublished working paper, 1998.

http://publication.pids.gov.ph/details.phtml?pid=3684

http://alishahrivar.blogfa.com/post-156.aspx

Index